Beyond
Endurance

RONALD J. KNAPP

Beyond Endurance

When a Child Dies

SCHOCKEN BOOKS

New York

First published by Schocken Books 1986
10 9 8 7 6 5 4 3 2 1   86 87 88 89
Copyright © 1986 by Ronald J. Knapp

Library of Congress Cataloging in Publication Data
Knapp, Ronald J.
Beyond endurance.
Bibliography: p.
1. Children—Death—Psychological aspects.
2. Bereavement—Psychological aspects. 3. Parent
and child. I. Title.
BF575.G7K6 1986   155.9'37   85–2019

Design by Leslie Phillips
Manufactured in the United States of America
ISBN 0–8052–3994–4

During the seven months of interviewing required to complete the field portion of the study, I shared tender and heartrending moments with many parents—both mothers and fathers. In the process of these talks, I developed strong feelings of affection and respect for the ordeals that these families experienced. I wish to thank all parents who came forth to share their thoughts and experiences with me, and also the children and young men and women who were the central features of these stories.

The sons and daughters who died will never be forgotten by their parents and other loved ones. I would like to present here the names and ages of some of them so that the rest of us, who have never known them, and who have never felt the agony of childhood death, will also never forget. It is really to these deceased sons and daughters, and to the deceased sons and daughters of all parents everywhere, that this book is dedicated.

Michael Keith Arant, 16
William Thomas Ausman, 4
Nicole Marie Beerman, 5
Benjamin Morrison Beidler, 16
Hilary Bowen, 9
Matthew Ralph Bright, 8
Billy Gerald "Jerry" Broom, 28
Ronald L. Bryan, 21
Bryan Edward Carter, 9
Bryan Francis Charboneau, 10
Eric Brian Chrysler, 22
Robert Lindsey Clos, 16
Teresa Marie Cobb, 16
Tim Crane, 14

Robert Egerton Davis, 25
Richard W. Doedtman, Jr., 16
Robert Scott Drum, 19
Michael Joseph Elliot, 12
Julie Paige Ellison, 10
Diane Marie Ewanika, 16
Janet Aubrey Fair, 1
Ryan Douglas Farley, 3
Randall Robert Frame, 6
Jennifer Lynn Garges, 7
Melissa Renee Gillette, 6
Michael Charles Gordon, 24
Susan Gorman, 19
Daniel Gorman, 30

Steven Edward Graulein, 16

Brian Patrick Greeley, 20

Kevin Michael Greeley, 21

Susan Powell Gregg, 25

Carmen Louise Gregg, 19 mo.

Jeffrey Byron Hall, 14

Ronald Dale Hampton, 14

William Elliot Hartnagle, 8

Michael Todd Holland, 17

Charles Kevin Huffstetler, 19

Lisa Gayle Hullinger, 19

Robert William Ibach, 2

Ruthann Sylvia Jensen, 14

Mark Joseph Johns, 7

Corey Jay Johnson, 6

Sarah Jane Kahn, 4

Angela Lynn Kish, 6

Carol Sue Klaber, 16

Mark Gregory Klein, 10

Marcus Bradford Kolesar, 4

Robert Cliff "Bobby" Matthews, 20

Susan Hovis McDaniel, 16

Timothy G. Meisner

David Neel Miller, 2

Kristina Anne Moellenhoff, 4

Rebecca Anne Moore, 24

Todd Alan Morse, 12

Robert Lynn Newberry

Michael Andrew Norman, 5

Vincent van Orsouw, 16

Charles Mark Patterson, 15

Mary Lynn Phillips, 18

Michael Dana Powers, 20

Debra Ann Pressley, 21

Roy Rabun, 12

Michael O. Raven, 24

Rebecca Lynn Reed, 19

Lynda Sue Reep, 6

Thomas Francis Rotz, 3

Andrea Beth Scaia, 15

Lisa Ann Scherer, 15

Mark Harding Scholl, 20

David Jeffrey Scholle, 3 mo.

Michael David Scholle, 2

Paul Mark Schwartz, 16

Lewis Wilson Scott III, 28

Todd Vernon Skalsky, 9

Steven Shawn Smith, 19

Lisa Solarz, 16

Larry Russell "Rusty" Spry, 19

Charmaine Marie Stolla, 17

Ayse Tanberk, 8

Todd Tanberk, 16 mos.

Darrell Clayton Taylor, 20

Jeffrey Bryon Taylor, 20

John Emerson Taylor, 16

Gregory Andrew Thibault, 18

Cheryl Ann Thompson, 19

Sandra Louise Thorn, 3

Scott Treptow, 6

Mathew Charles Vaughn, 12

Andrew Paul Wallace, 17

Howard Ray White III, 16

Richard Dwayne "Sam" Winn, 17

Richard Drewry "Drew" Winstead, 2

Martin "Marty" Lair Wood, 24

Chris Leroy Workman, 14

Michael Joseph Zimmerman, 19

Steven Edward Zimmerman, 16

Contents

Preface

The death of a child is by far one of the most tragic events that can strike the average American family. Barring the death of a spouse after a long marriage, no other type of loss even comes close to extracting the heavy outpouring of emotional anguish that child loss elicits.

Although we live in a protected society in the sense that childhood death is no longer a common occurrence, nevertheless in 1979 there were 66,000 deaths, from all causes, between the ages of 2 and 24. This included 12,000 deaths from injuries between the ages of 1 and 14, 50 percent of all deaths in this age category,[1] and 6048 murders of victims under the age of 24, 30 percent of *all* murders in the United States in that year.[2]

Each of these deaths impacts with a tenacity that is difficult to comprehend. For some parents, years pass before they are able to resume their lives. Others never seem able to find their way out of the turmoil and disorganization of bereavement. These latter are the real tragedies of childhood death—the collapse of the family and the psychological and emotional destruction of parents in the face of the death of a child.

This book is written to shed some light on this ultimate human tragedy. We need to build an understanding of the various modes of death. We need to show how, when death strikes our children, parents and close family members are likely to respond, and how they are able to find their way through the long, dark tunnel of debilitating grief to the surrendering resolution at the end.

It should be noted that not only is the death of a child a debilitating experience for families to endure, but also the diagnosis of a fatal illness. This too can plunge a family into the pit of despair and hinder its functioning as a viable unit.

Three types of child death will be investigated: (1) Death which comes after a long illness where parents are able to anticipate the loss and, in some rudimentary way, prepare for the end. I will show that the greatest trauma for parents caught in the tangle of this event comes from the struggle to save the child sentenced to death by a dreaded disease. (2) Sudden or unexpected death, usually as a result of accident, where there is obviously no time to anticipate or prepare. Here I will primarily be concerned with the ravaging impact such losses have on a family's ability to hold itself together and to survive as a viable unit. And (3) death by murder—violent, sudden death— which attacks the family with such vehemence that recovery genuinely becomes questionable. With murder there is a variety of critical problems that families must face which serve as effective barriers to the resolution of grief.

These three types or modes of death leave different tracks as they march through the family. It is the purpose of the initial chapters of this book to describe these imprints and to try to understand, on the basis of an analysis of the way the families in the study group responded, how parents and families deal with them.

However, it should be noted that even though these three modes of death are quite different, the definitions that society places on death in general, and child death in particular, suggest that there is an array of commonalities that underlie the response patterns of parents to child death, regardless of how it occurs. Some of these commonalities are discussed in the remainder of the book.

It is important to keep in mind that the findings presented in this work are based on an assessment and analysis of in-depth interviews with 155 families—mothers and fathers—who had suffered the loss of a child ranging in age from 1 to 28. The interviews were conducted in five midwestern and southern cities during the winter, spring, and summer of 1982. The families suffered their losses anywhere from three months to five years prior to the interviews. All varieties of loss were included—anticipated after a long illness, unanticipated or sudden, and murder.

The actual "findings" reported in the following chapters are based on the interview results.

Let me make one last comment. I have never personally suffered the loss of a child. Therefore I cannot know, nor can I feel, the pain and agony in the same way that the parents in the study group have known and have felt it. However, in seven months of field work I have come to know something of the ordeal of child death in a way few others have. I have sat through 300 hours of the most intense, emotional, heartrending interview sessions of my life. I have listened intently as parents dredged up from the very depths of their beings the great emotional outpourings that became their step-by-step accounting of what they experienced. I have tried to "see" the events as they saw them. I have tried to "feel" the emotion as they felt it. I became essentially a "participant experiencer" in the ordeals they poured out to me during the interview sessions. So in a way I have come to know, to experience, if you will—vicariously to be sure—the trauma of child death. Nevertheless, the experience of "living through" these stories of agony and horror, of pain and sorrow, intense as they were, still does not permit me to live it as these parents have lived it.

Therefore I am writing this book as an outsider—I hope a knowledgeable outsider, but an outsider nonetheless. I consider myself analogous to a front-line "war correspondent" who is capable of presenting accurate information but who remains a nonparticipant in the "war" itself. To enhance my writing and improve my reporting I have therefore liberally sprinkled the text with excerpts from the actual interviews. I believe this adds an element of interest to the accounts and gives some validity to the reported findings.

It is my hope that mothers and fathers who have lost a child through illness, accident, or murder, or from any other cause, will find this work helpful and supportive in their struggle to survive.

It is also my hope that professionals—those who are called upon to render support services in the aftermath of child death—can find a source of information within this book that will facilitate their rehabilitative efforts.

In addition, it is my hope that the rest of us, who represent relatives, neighbors, friends, and acquaintances of those who have suffered the loss of a child, can use this material to develop a more sensitive, more humanistic, understanding of what the death of a child means in our modern society.

Personal Acknowledgments

There are many people to whom I owe a debt of gratitude and thanks. In fact, without the faith and assistance of the group coordinators in the five cities I visited, there would be no book. Therefore I specifically wish to extend my heartfelt thanks to Lucy Christopher of Charlotte, North Carolina, who arranged interviews with families from Kinder-Mourn, a mutual self-help organization in Charlotte, and from the surrounding area. Lucy is also the author of Chapter 12, on the Kinder-Mourn organization. Lucy, my sincere thanks and appreciation for your unselfish effort and your valuable contribution.

Special thanks are also extended to Sister Jane Marie Lamb, director of SHARE, St. John's Hospital, Springfield, Illinois, who arranged interviews with families, mostly members of the Compassionate Friends of central Illinois. Thank you, Sister Jane Marie, for your many hours of work on my behalf.

In addition, I must also thank Katherine Klein of Minneapolis, the mother of Mark, who died at the age of 12, and presently a grief counselor, who put forth what I define as heroic effort in arranging for a wide variety of families from the Minneapolis–St. Paul area to come forth to share their experiences with me. Thanks for your understanding and patience, Katherine.

I also wish to extend my sincere thanks and gratitude to Charlotte and Bob Hullinger of Cincinnati, Ohio, founders of Parents of Murdered Children, Inc., a Cincinnati-based organization devoted to helping parents of murdered children cope. This organization served as a source of families who agreed to participate in the study. Thank you, Charlotte and Bob, for your time and energy in arranging the interviews.

In addition I wish to express my sincere thanks to Judy Sturm and Cheryl Moellenhoff of St. Louis. These two leaders in Candlelighters—a hospital-based support group for parents of children suffering from leukemia—were instrumental in arranging the interviews with families who had lost children from this disease. Although I was unable to complete all the interviews in the St. Louis area (because of a violent snowstorm that blanketed the city during the last two days of my stay), I wish to thank Judy and Cheryl for their unfailing support and effort on my behalf.

To Margaret Gerner, also from St. Louis, then editor of *The Compassionate Friends Newsletter*, who arranged a series of interviews with families with whom I was unable to meet (again due to snow), I owe a debt of thanks for the work she put into this effort.

Certainly I cannot forget the parents and brothers and sisters who participated in the study. To them I am grateful for being allowed the privilege of sharing in this most intimate and painful ordeal in their lives. Thank you for your graciousness and kindnesses extended to me during the course of the interviews. I shall remember you always with fondness and appreciation.

Other individuals and organizations also deserve a note of thanks and appreciation. Special thanks to Dr. Richard F. Larson, Professor and Head of the Department of Sociology, Clemson University, for his conscientious and critical review of a portion of the manuscript. Also, I wish to extend my gratitude to Clemson University, the College of Liberal Arts, and the Department of Sociology for permitting and encouraging me to take a sabbatical leave during the spring semester of 1981. The sabbatical allowed me to devote full time to the project and released me for the necessary travel. In addition, I should also thank the Clemson University Faculty Research Committee for approving a research grant to help defray travel expenses.

In this same regard, I would like formally to extend my sincere thanks to my mother and father, Sally and Clyde Knapp of Largo, Florida, for their financial and moral support throughout the project.

In addition, although I mention this person among the last, she is by no means last in my eyes—my dear wife, Jane. Without her continuing confidence in this effort through the past two and a half years, I doubt that it would ever have seen the light of day! Also, I owe her a significant debt of gratitude and thanks for her careful and conscientious editing of the preliminary drafts as well as the final manuscript. She was always there when I needed her. She was my inspiration and support through the entire project.

Finally, I wish to express my appreciation to my son, Barry, and my daughter, Jennifer, for just being themselves. Throughout the work on this project I often thought how fortunate I was to have them alive and well. I hope and pray that neither my wife nor I will ever have to experience what this study revealed!

I of course take full responsibility for the final product. Any misrepresentations, errors, distortions, or omissions fall directly on my shoulders.

Clemson, South Carolina   R.J.K.
March 1985

Beyond
Endurance

1

Childhood and the Dying Experience

Although we know that after . . . a loss the acute state of mourning will subside, we also know we shall remain inconsolable and will never find a substitute. No matter what may fill the gap, even if it is filled completely, it nevertheless remains something else. And actually this is how it should be. It is the only way of perpetuating that love which we do not want to relinquish.
—*Letters of Sigmund Freud*

The Death of Billy

The sound of machinery laboring to keep alive an almost lifeless human form is frightening, particularly to the uninitiated. So is the sight. Complicated-looking equipment surrounds the individual and creates an intimidating picture. Tubes, IV bottles, wires, drainage jars, oscilloscopes, heart stimulators, blood-pressure monitors, and respirators are part of the scene and come together to create the awesome sight of life-support activity on the intensive-care ward of any hospital.

These sights and sounds were all part of the scene on the 19th of July 1978 on the intensive-care ward of Duke University Medical Center in Durham, North Carolina. On that date in Room 215, lying in a white-sheeted bed, quite small in comparison to the equipment and paraphernalia surrounding him, was the tiny figure of 4-year-old Billy Ausman.

To the uninitiated stranger the sight of any individual in these surroundings would have been disturbing, but when it is a child it becomes particularly heartrending.

Picture the following scene in your mind's eye: Tubes and wires run from Billy's frail body in a myriad of directions. Plasma and glucose drip steadily into both arms. Oxygen is being fed into both nostrils. A respirator tube down his throat stretches his mouth, creating an unnatural appearance. A blood-pressure cuff on his left arm is continuously feeding results to a digital monitor next to his bed. Electrocardiogram patches dot his little chest, which is exposed above the white sheet folded neatly at his waist. There are little gauze pads covering each eye.

The room is literally alive with the buzzing, hissing, wheezing, thumping noises of the support machinery. If you stand close to his bed with your head tilted toward his chest you can hear the air being pushed into and extracted from his lungs by the respirator. Billy is no longer able to breathe efficiently on his own.

Next to his bed is a physician, in his last year of residency. Dr. Brock is assigned here on a temporary basis, since Billy now needs round-the-clock attention. Dr. Brock is watching the heart rate and blood pressure, which are being registered automatically on an oscilloscope and monitor dial. A nurse is also present in the room. She is slowly wiping the tiny beads of perspiration from Billy's forehead.

It is apparent to anyone entering upon this scene that Billy Ausman is dying.

Suddenly a flood of light flashes into the room as the door opens and two additional people enter. The door is closed quietly and Martha and Jim, Billy's parents, carefully approach their son's bed.

Dr. Brock, momentarily distracted from his task of surveillance, looks at them intently and wonders how much longer these two fine but very ordinary people are going to be able to hold together. He has come to know them quite well during the last several weeks and has developed a healthy respect for their courage and fortitude. Yet, he wonders, how much longer can they possibly be expected to deal with the trauma that this tragedy is producing in their lives? He knows that they have been at their son's bedside continuously for the last several days, catching winks of sleep here and there between "crises," which now seem to come with increasing frequency. In the last 48 hours Billy has slipped very close to death on four occasions, only to rally again. In the last 24 hours he has suffered two cardiac arrests, only to be revived. How much longer, he wonders? How much longer?

Martha looks terribly pale and haggard. It is apparent that she has been without sleep for some time. She clearly shows the strain and stress of the last several days.

Jim looks no better. He is obviously tired and weak. His wrinkled clothes and unshaven face indicate that he has not been home in several days and that he probably has slept most of the time in a chair.

As Martha approaches the bed she looks squarely into the face of Dr. Brock, intensely searching for some sign that there has been some improvement so that her desperate hope for her son's ultimate survival can be rekindled. The doctor, unable to look her in the eye, simply shakes his head. Martha begins to tremble slightly. Jim turns and walks slowly to the window as he has done on so many occasions before and stares into the quiet darkness of the early morning. This seems to be the only way he can cope with the scene in that room.

Martha, standing at Billy's side, slowly but deliberately reaches both hands through the hanging tubes and wires and grasps her son's tiny hand in hers. It is so cold, she thinks! She rubs it tenderly, trying to warm it.

Her mind begins to wander back over the last several months.

What a fighter he has been, she thinks! He just would not surrender to this disease. Almost from the very beginning, after it became apparent to him that he was seriously ill, Billy had told her not to worry, that he would someday get well again. That was his promise to her.

Martha remembers the total devastation she and Jim had felt upon hearing the diagnosis, just five months before. In a matter of minutes, seconds really, their whole world was suddenly ripped in half, never to be the same again! A new life, a new way of living—totally unacceptable to both—was suddenly and viciously dumped on them from out of nowhere. They wondered then whether they would be able mentally, physically, and emotionally to survive the ordeal they imagined lay ahead of them. Little did they realize that absolutely nothing they could have dreamed of or imagined at that time could possibly have prepared them for what they actually experienced. It has been five months of hell-on-earth, an unbelievable ordeal of weekly clinic visits, hospital stays, traveling long distances to and from the medical center, intractable physical pain, emotional upheavals, as well as a tremendous financial burden—all of which they would gladly repeat, if only to spend a few more lucid hours with their son.

Myelofibrosis is a devastating disease for a child. Akin to leukemia, it is cancer of the bone marrow—replacement of the marrow by undifferentiated fibroblastic cells. Yet unlike leukemia, there are no effective and proven treatment protocols. Treatment of myelofibrosis is for the most part experimental. In fact up to the time of Billy's diagnosis, there were very few known cases of myelofibrosis reported in children. It is primarily a disease of the aged.

Martha and Jim were put in touch with the finest doctors at Duke University Medical Center, who in turn were in communication with the most progressive cancer-treatment centers in the United States. Facilities all over the country searched their medical files for some treatment, some technique, that might prove to have some positive results in arresting this disease in children. It was discovered that there were only approximately 30 cases of myelofibrosis actually reported in children in the United States since the 1950s. All were in older children.

Martha and Jim gave their permission to use any experimental technique in the raw hope that something would work, that some unique combination of procedures or drugs would be discovered that would halt the devastating progress of the disease and the destruction of the bone marrow.

The treatment regimens Billy endured had highly destructive side effects which created havoc in his life and in the lives of Martha and Jim, who had to watch their son suffer under the impact of the "treatment" he was receiving.

Throughout the five-month ordeal, however, Martha maintained a strong element of hope, and she communicated this to Billy during the long months of his illness. She clung to hope and would not allow herself or her son to consider any possibility other than a complete remission, or even better, an ultimate cure.

Martha hoped and prayed that, even though this was a rare and essentially untreatable disease for a child, through the experimental procedures they were trying, something would work and Billy would be the first to survive the disease and go on to make medical history through a remarkable recovery. She fantasized that the treatment protocol would then become established to help other children suffering similar maladies.

This was the scenario she envisioned in her fantasies which served to keep alive the desperate hope she clung to during the months of Billy's illness.

Through the course of his relatively short illness Billy had mentally and emotionally changed from the carefree, uncomplicated little boy that he was five months before to a wiser, more sensitive, and certainly more mature young man, although still only 4 years old.

During the months of clinic visits, with the needles, pricks, painful bone marrow tests, and harsh side effects of the drugs, Billy had observed and experienced death among many of his new-found friends from the cancer clinic. He knew that it was certainly possible to die from his disease. He talked about this with Martha from time to time, but he never dwelled on it. He talked about what it must be like to die, getting help in formulating and clarifying his conceptions from Martha and Jim. But behind all this he remained confident that he would survive. Thoughts of death were never really given much space in his day-to-day conversations with his parents.

These conversations, incidentally, became more and more frequent as the months passed. He kept telling them over and over not to worry about him. He was so sure the treatments would eventually prove successful. In a sense this positive attitude was a reflection of Martha's and Jim's own states of unflinching confidence.

They had learned so much from this little guy during these last months. In fact both Martha and Jim began to experience a change in their own philosophies of life and death through their conversations with Billy about his perception of his condition and about what he saw his future to be. His vibrant spirit, his tenacious will to survive, his unshakable confidence in his own ability to overcome this adversity, made this present circumstance hard to take. Children twice, three times, four times his age could not have developed a better or more positive attitude toward life and survival or a more complete conception of death than Billy had at the age of four.

Martha and Jim had grown as a result of this experience and had learned so much. They were so grateful to have had him even though the pain of now losing him was almost beyond human endurance.

Martha stands beside the bed looking down at Billy's face with his bandaged eyes. In spite of the long ordeal, tears still come easily to her and she begins to weep softly as she thinks of the unfairness of it all. Not one remission! Not one reprieve in the five-month fight to save Billy's life. She wonders if she will ever again see the color of his eyes or hear his voice. How she yearns for this!

As she stands there she very slowly begins to notice something. Billy's breathing seems a little less labored now. The respirator does not appear to be working as hard. She wonders what this means. Is it possible that perhaps he is beginning to breathe on his own? She is still clutching and warming his hand.

Suddenly Martha feels a strange sensation! She notices that for the first time in over 12 hours Billy is beginning to move. His head turns slightly to one side. But what startles her is the fact that the fingers of Billy's hand are beginning to close ever so slightly around the edge of hers! She motions to Jim, who returns from the window to her side. Yes, it is happening—Billy is actually gripping her hand!

Martha gestures to the doctor, who also noticed the movement. The doctor's eyes drift across the dials and gauges of the monitoring equipment. He remains silent for a moment, contemplating. The respirator has indeed decreased its activity. The doctor then admits that Billy might be rallying somewhat. He might, at least temporarily, be coming out of the coma, although they cannot be sure and there seem to be no other signs that this is in fact taking place.

However, that small happening is enough to give Martha the courage to do what she has been waiting to do for the last 48 hours.

Two days previously, when Billy slipped into his present coma, the doctors had told Martha and Jim that he probably would never come out, that his chances for even a temporary recovery from this episode were a thousand to one. At that point the character of Martha's hope changed from what it had been during the months of Billy's illness. At that point Martha resigned herself to Billy's death. She knew without question that within a very short period of time she would lose him forever. Consequently her hope changed from hoping for eventual survival or remission, or even some kind of spontaneous cure, to simply hoping for one last rally before his death because she knew what she had to do! Perhaps this rally, if it could be called that, would be the one last time she would have to reach her son before his death.

Martha, seizing the opportunity, turns to the doctor and asks if she can spend some time alone with her son. The doctor nods and he and the nurse step into the hall. Jim, with tears streaming down his face, knowing what Martha is about to do, turns again to face the window.

Martha, no tears now, looks down quietly at the face of her son.

She then begins to push some of the equipment to one side. She moves the IV bottles and pushes the tubes until she can actually lean on the bed next to Billy. Still gripping his hand, she gently stretches her other arm around him in such a way as to cradle his head, enabling her to stroke his forehead. She knows what she must do but fears that she has so little time to do it. He could at any moment slip back into a coma and die. With some anticipation, she moves her lips close to Billy's ear and begins to speak just above a whisper. This is what she says:

Billy, I feel very sure that Jesus is ready for you to die. I don't know how He will come and take you, but I know it will be a beautiful experience. Daddy and I want you to know that it is alright for you to go.

You will never ever hurt again, sweetheart. There will be no more IVs, no more shots, no more bone marrow tests. None of these things will ever happen to you again.

You will not need your body anymore. It is very sick. You will leave it here and we will take care of it.

Don't be afraid, Billy, it will be okay. You do not have to stay. Please go to Jesus. Daddy and I will remain here without you. But we will think about you every day, and say prayers to you every day, and love you every day. Billy, we know it is best that you go to heaven where you can never hurt again. You will be just fine, sweetheart. You will be okay without me and I will be okay without you.

Someday we will all be together again. When the time is right, Jesus will come and bring me to you, and also your daddy and your brothers. Then we will all be happy together. But, Billy, you must go first and prepare the way for the rest of us.

Don't be afraid. This is your reward, sweetheart. Please take it.

Martha continues, whispering in Billy's ear, saying that she and his daddy are here with him, that they will stay with him until he leaves, that they love him very much, and that they will see him again someday. Martha continues to stroke his brow, repeating these words to him.

Suddenly, just as quickly as he had gripped her hand a few minutes before, she now begins to feel his grasp weaken. Martha rises from his side. A sense of relief and satisfaction floods over her. She believes she has communicated with her son. She believes he heard what she was saying to him. The lessening of his grip, seeing his frail body relax and the twisted, tense look on his face dissipate, convinces her that he heard and understood what she was saying. Jim moves to her side. Something is happening! Both watch the monitors with a sense of anticipation. The readings are beginning to decline. Blood pressure begins falling steadily. Jim becomes alarmed and summons the doctor. Dr. Brock surveys the situation and indicates to Martha and Jim that the end is very near.

They continue to watch the monitors. Blood-pressure readings are now 60 over 48, now 55 over 42 and falling. They continue to watch, hardly moving, hardly even breathing themselves. All eyes are fixed on the gauges: 40 over 30, 20 over 10, 10 over 6. Suddenly an alarm—followed quickly by another—as blood pressure disappears and Billy lapses into cardiac arrest.

All stand motionless around Billy's bed. No effort is made to resuscitate. They continue to watch as heart rhythm disappears from the oscilloscope. Blood pressure is now at zero. The respirator is pumping at full volume. Alarms and buzzers continue to sound. Finally, after what seems like an eternity, the doctor reaches around those standing by the bed and quietly turns off the machinery. The room is suddenly pitched into an almost deafening silence. Martha and Jim stand there like two stone statues, as if transfixed in timeless space, seemingly trying to fathom what has just happened. Then both let out a deep sigh—a sigh of understandable relief and release. At last the ordeal is over! It is 5:47 A.M., still dark outside, and Billy is dead.

This short scenario represents the very last moments in the life of Billy Ausman, who in just a five-month period underwent a dramatic physical change from a robust, active, energetic 4-year-old to a weak, emaciated skeleton of a boy. The lives of his parents, Martha and Jim, were turned into a roller coaster of ups, when hopes were high and everything seemed to be going well, and downs, when hopes were shattered on the rocks of reality. An endless array of hospital stays, clinic visits, and medical tests dominated their existence. Their lives were in constant turmoil, filled with heartbreak, remorse, sadness, bitterness, and anger. Only a higher power could know how they survived.

But they *did* survive, and Martha even summoned the courage to surrender her son in the final moments to what she knew was his only fate. She gave him up. Through her words, she allayed his fighting spirit and encouraged him to die.

The months of tracking along behind Billy, following him down the long foreboding corridors of treatment regimens, was at times almost more than any human individual could bear. Martha and Jim plodded along, putting one foot in front of the other, taking every moment, every hour, every day, one at a time. Unable to plan for or anticipate the future in any sense, they lived for the moment, now, today, this hour! They stumbled, they faltered, they fell, over and over again, only to pick themselves up and somehow continue on.

As I was talking to Jim about their experiences, he said something very simple and yet profound in the sense that it seemed to sum up the attitudes and feelings of parents who undergo the trauma of dealing with a terminally ill child. Seeing Billy being carried down the hall of the cancer clinic after the diagnosis for the first of what was to become one of many episodes characterized at best by finger pricks and at worst by blood transfusions and bone marrow tests, Jim said:

As I watched Billy being carried away, looking over the shoulder of the nurse, with his big eyes open wide, crying, looking to me for help, I knew then that I could not help him. As much as I wanted to, there was absolutely nothing either I or his mother—people he depended on all his life to satisfy his needs—could possibly do for him now.

I felt a strange sensation come over me. I wanted to be with him, to go with him, but they said no. And as I watched Billy being carried away, I knew that we had lost control over him. He was in the hands now of this big, complex medical clinic. Billy would never be ours again. This big facility would direct his life and our life for as long as he remained with us.

This sense of loss of control, I think, dominates the feelings of parents in these situations. I know it had a significant impact on us. You become like a robot, being steered through the maze of life by outside forces over which you have no control.

Neither Martha and Jim's emotional experience nor the manner in which Billy died is unique. Thousands of parents face similar ordeals every year in the United States. Death of course can come in many ways and from many causes. And although there certainly is a uniqueness in every death, there are also, more important, similarities in the way each of us responds. Every year in the United States over 66,000 children between the ages of 2 and 24 die in various ways from a variety of causes. Over 11,000 of these deaths occur before the age of 14. Each time the death of a child occurs it leaves in its wake the broken bodies and hearts of surviving parents, brothers, and sisters. Parents and siblings are forced by the event into the roles of survivors. But survivors of a different sort from those created by the death of an elderly loved one. Survivors of child death have unique roles to fill because of the importance our society ascribes to the status of children. In order to handle the conflict, turmoil, and disruption that child death produces, survivors are forced to meet a different set of needs. They are forced to respond to life with no sense of a future commitment. Life becomes viewed through a different lens, one that distorts and misdirects efforts at successful adjustment.

The Value and Uniqueness of Children

Children in our society today of course are highly valued. The value we place on children, however, is not derived from their practical, economic usefulness, as once was the case, but from their esthetic, emotional, or symbolic value.[1]

Children are indeed wanted today for themselves; they satisfy the desire for love and the feeling of being a part of a family.[2] They fulfill the basic functions of parenthood and satisfy a wide range of needs for the individual.[3]

For many women, having a child is defined as their major role in life and the fulfillment of womanhood. Even in today's modern world motherhood is still conceived as being synonymous with virtue. And being a good father can bring a feeling of self-respect.[4] It can represent a sense of accomplishment in and of itself. In many quarters fatherhood is still viewed as synonymous with manhood.

Our society is in many respects a child-centered society. Even though on the average two children die every day from parental abuse,[5] the consistent view is that most parents are preoccupied with childrearing; they pamper their children and take great pride in their development. They take the task of parenthood very seriously.

Thus it must be assumed that children are indeed highly valued, highly desirable, and that great effort goes into their care, development, and protection.

In addition, childhood today, as Skolnick has pointed out, is "a separate stage of life, having its own psychology and requiring separate institutions."[6] This means that childhood stands apart from adulthood with separate and rather distinct normative expectations and behavioral requirements.

Each child is a unique individual. Each child makes a unique contribution. Each child has his or her own quality or aura which defines the person as a separate entity. Each child occupies a position in time and space, and impacts on the lives of others in many different and significant ways. As one author says, each child is a "sociological force" in the family, in school, and in the community,[7] a force that we cannot ignore.

Defining the child as a "sociological force" may well represent a modern approach that can be contrasted with the earlier view of childhood. This modern view implies that children occupy recognized roles and enter into genuine and meaningful relationships with adults. And since every relationship implies reciprocity,[8] adults come to be reciprocally involved in the lives of children around them. This in turn gives children an importance and significance today that they did not enjoy previously.

Childhood and Dying: The Ultimate Tragedy

Although there are many aspects of childhood that are problematic, none is so devastating to the parent as the loss of the child through death. Charles Garfield states:

It is to the parents of a [dead] child that fate delivers the severest blow. We fear for our children as we fear for ourselves. Never have we lived or loved enough. Death always comes too soon.[9]

In many ways the death of a child represents in a symbolic way the death of the self. Symbolically, a mother or father will die along with the child, only to survive in a damaged state with little or no desire to live today or plan for tomorrow.

In earlier times the death of a child was a rather frequent occurrence. In days when infectious diseases were rampant, child death was rather common since infectious diseases are far more destructive of the young than of the old. With the growth of modern medical technology and the virtual eradication of infectious diseases, and the consequent reduction in the death rate, child death now occurs very infrequently in America. Although accidents, unforeseen disasters, and unpredicted chronic diseases do strike today's youth on occasion, most deaths occur quite naturally and expectedly among the older segment of the population, those who have lived full lives. This is where death is most often observed and experienced in today's world.

Because of the expected and predictable nature of death among the elderly, American culture has been structured in such a way that preparation for the event has been to some extent defined. In addition, certain coping mechanisms available to survivors following the death of an elderly person have been defined. That is, societal norms, such as those pertaining to estate litigation, mourning rites and bereavement behavior, funeral preparations, the recording of wills, the purchasing of life insurance and grave plots on a preneed basis, are examples of a number of institutionalized practices defined as preparatory behavior in response to the eventual death of the elderly.

Youthful deaths, particuarly of infants and young children, in our society today are to be regarded as "ultimate tragedies." The concept of infant and child death in America is in fact quite alien. Nothing compares. It is inappropriate, unnatural, and unacceptable to the mother and to the father. Children are not supposed to die, certainly not before the parents. In fact child death is not only emotionally, psychologically, and physically the most painful experience one can encounter, it is also philosophically unintelligible in today's world; it defies the natural order of things. And, it seems, the younger the child is at death, the more incomprehensible and unintelligible the loss becomes.

Therefore the relatively infrequent, or thought-to-be-infrequent, occurrence of infant and child death is always regarded as infinitely more tragic and traumatic than the death of an older person. And because it is thought to be so rare, few norms have been developed, or have survived from the past, to guide loved ones—parents and others—in coping with the aftermath. This in turn has created significant adjustment problems associated with the loss of infants and children for grieving parents and others.

The loss of infants and children also poses a particular problem for parents in the way grief is expected to be expressed in our society. For example, Sheila Fox claims that expression of violent emotion is oddly out of place today.[10] We are taught to control our emotions. This complicates the situation because child death demands violent expression of emotion. In the past it was indeed legitimate to express our feelings openly. Today we find a different world. Who is there to provide support? Who will listen? Who will sympathize?[11]

Teresa Crout, writing in a recent issue of *Thanatos,* talks about how mothers mourn the loss of stillborn infants.[12] And I think what she says about how grief is expressed in regard to the loss of unborn children can be applied to the loss of young children in general. She points out that when we suffer the loss of an older loved person—that is, when death occurs at the end of life—the grief we experience is in a significant way a part of the actual memories we have of the person and the relationships and experiences we have had with them.

These memories may be rich and varied, and may span our entire lifetime. After an expected death we allow these memories to fade away. And as they fade, they take large portions of our grief along with them. The resolution of grief in response to the loss of an older loved person is significantly dependent on this process.[13]

When we suffer the loss of an unborn child, however, we essentially have no rich storehouse of memories that will serve as the vehicle to carry grief away. Teresa Crout says that the loss of an unborn child is the loss of *future dreams,* which do not fade.[14] It is my contention that with all young children we are always oriented to the future. The death of any child represents the loss of future dreams, future relationships, future experiences, future fantasies, which we have not yet enjoyed, or are not even able to place within the context of rational discussion. As Fran Northrup says, "The death of a child speaks poignantly of unfulfilled promises and destroyed hopes."[15]

This orientation and commitment to the future is characteristic of the dominant way we respond to all young children in our world today. Consequently the scarcity of memories associated with this future orientation leads to a situation where parents, upon the death of a child, refuse to surrender the few they are able to retain. Thus there are no memories that can be allowed to fade, and the feelings of empty loss remain long after they would ordinarily have dissipated. They linger on. The sorrow, the sadness, the despair, the depression, the anger and bitterness are much longer lasting, much more debilitating, and exceedingly difficult to resolve appropriately.

In many ways the grief expressed by parents in response to the death of a child resembles in exaggerated form that described by Lindemann:[16] a syndrome including somatic distress, preoccupation with thoughts, feelings of guilt, hostile reactions, and loss of previous patterns of conduct. How long this lasts depends on the resources a family can bring to bear upon the problem and on how quickly parents are able to break the powerful bond that binds them to the dead child.[17] Since the parental bond is so strong, it may endure for years. This brings into play elements of "shadow grief"[18]—remnants of powerful feelings which may remain intact for a very long period of time. These often encumber the individual's ability to resolve and work through the grief and sorrow.

"We Don't Miss the Water till the Well Runs Dry"

This simple cliché has a particular meaning for those who have suffered the loss of a son or daughter as compared to those who have not. If we live with and are closely related to a person in our daily lives we of course will come to know and accept that person, but in such a way that it may not become fully apparent until after the person is gone from our midst.

The full contribution a person makes in this world can only rarely be known while he or she is still alive and still contributing. We all seem to take for granted persons who, objectively, are very important to us. Our appreciation of them in terms of the enrichment they produce in our lives and their central place of importance in our worlds is simply not fully realized or understood. We cannot begin truly to miss these significant others until they are gone from us.

This is a lesson that so many parents have learned in such an agonizing way following the deaths of their children.

We tend to take our children for granted as we do other important persons in our environment. This is particularly true with children because we operate on the assumption that children are more or less permanent fixtures in our families, at least for 18 to 20 years. We unconsciously count on them as always being there. Children, on occasion, do leave the family for various reasons, but they certainly are not supposed to die—at least, as stated earlier, not before their parents.

We, the older generation, often do not understand youth; in fact, because of our tendency to take them for granted we often make little effort to do so. There is a conflict of generations inherent in many parent–child relationships. As Lewis Feuer says: "The conflict of generations is a universal theme in history."[19]

We define childhood as a rather haphazard yet carefree and uncaring time. To the older generation young people appear to be a different breed. We have difficulty relating to them on their level. This is particularly true as they move into their teen years and begin to drift free of parental influence. We become impatient. We become frustrated. We sometimes become infuriated with their "know-it-all" attitude, with their seeming unwillingness to learn from our own past mistakes, with their sometimes apparent resentment of authority and rejection of rules by which to live. We become upset and impatient with unkempt rooms, dirty towels, muddy shoes, torn clothes, smelly gym socks pitched here and there, ear-piercing rock music, back-talk, sarcasm, coming in late, etc., etc. We often toss up our hands and say "What's the use!" Or we look up at the heavens and exclaim for God and all His angels to hear: "What did I ever do to deserve this?"

But children are also our greatest joy! Children are what keep us young and give us, the older generation, our reasons to get up in the morning. They are our present and our future, and sometimes our only reason to exist. Yet we are not always consciously aware of their vital place in our lives nor capable of assessing their full impact on us until after we have lost them. So we take them for granted and do not appreciate fully what we have.

If our imaginations are vivid and rich, we of course can conjure up images of what life might be like without a person's presence. A husband or wife can *imagine* the loss of a spouse, a child can *imagine* the loss of a parent, and a parent can *imagine* the loss of a child. But how often do we allow ourselves to have these kinds of thoughts? And even if we do, such images and thoughts are just that—images and thoughts, figments, if you will, of our imaginations that bear little relationship to reality.

For example, I have a very vivid imagination which manifests itself in a rich fantasy life. I personally have tried several times when jogging or driving long distances—when my mind is wandering from one thought to the other and is more or less waiting for some stimulation—to imagine what it must be like to lose, through death, one of my children (I have an 18-year-old son and a 16-year-old daughter). I must say that on such occasions I have indeed been somewhat successful in conjuring up *images* of one of my children dying from a catastrophic disease or being killed in a gruesome auto accident. The emotional reaction and psychological response this thought-exercise creates have proven to be frightening and upsetting. However, the feelings I experience are momentary. They are fleeting. Because, as I am pulled deeper and deeper into this scenario created by my imagination, I tend to become more and more conscious of the fact that this is all an exercise of the mind and of course is not really happening. So as I come close to feeling a genuine sense of loss and remorse—as the total devastation that a real loss might produce begins to impact on my consciousness—I can draw away from it and the "experience" (if you want to call it that) becomes a simple exercise of the mind, a large step removed from the real world. This process of withdrawal, of pulling oneself free from this imaginary experience, is unconscious and unintentional. The mind has a way of protecting the self from exposure to thoughts that are too painful to contemplate.

But persons who have actually lost a child cannot pull themselves free. They're trapped! They must face this grueling, gut-wrenching reality every hour, every minute, every second of every day. There is no place to run, no place to hide. The reality of the situation presses down on their shoulders with increasing ferocity. They feel themselves crumbling under the weight and there is no escape. There are no breathing spells, no time-outs. They think they will go stark raving mad!

How can those of us who have never experienced grief of this magnitude think that we can even imagine such an experience?

I think that the process of unconscious withdrawal takes place within the minds of most people who try to experience through the imagination a loss that in reality they have never had. In fact we can't even come close. Having never experienced such a tragedy, we can never truly achieve a feeling for, or an understanding of, the real thing.

To repeat, we tend to take our children for granted and cannot really miss them or truly understand their influence on our lives until they are gone from us. Only those who have "been there" can possibly "miss the water before the well runs dry." Others can only guess. Others can only rely on their imaginations and fantasies, which are never sufficient.

This does not mean that those who have never actually experienced such a loss can be of no help to those who have. It does mean that the kind of assistance others can give is limited. True, genuine help can come only from those who have had similar experiences. This is one reason why support groups consisting of parents who have suffered the loss of a child are so important to other parents in the same situation. No other resource in the community is as effective in dealing with the aftermath of such losses. A discussion of these support groups is offered in Chapters 11 and 12.

Loss of the Future

Harriet Schiff, quoting from another source, has said that when one loses a parent one has lost the past; when one loses a child one has lost the future.[20] If we accept this statement at face value, how can one plan for the future when the most important thing in life is gone forever? There really is no universal solution to this problem. Having lost a child, the rest of one's life will seem to fall short of the months or years spent with that child. Grief can be so devastating, so overwhelming, that it can bombard one with thoughts of the past and make one fearful of the present and unable to face the future. This can produce an utterly hopeless feeling.

How are these feelings of hopelessness in regard to the future to be handled? Are the survivors simply to sit back and allow life to pass them by without trying to pick up the pieces and go on? The surprising thing about it is that parents *do* survive. They have no choice. Well, that's not entirely correct. Actually they do have a choice, of sorts.

When a child dies, parents have essentially *two* choices: (1) They can die themselves, emotionally or physically—virtually following their child to the grave. In reality this isn't a choice at all, although some parents do have a strong desire to do just that. Fortunately the majority do not have the courage to carry through with this desire. Or, (2) after floundering about aimlessly for a time, they can begin the long, hard struggle forward. Although the effort is extremely painful while it lasts, there is a light at the end of that long, dark, cold tunnel I will call the "healing adventure." That light—which symbolically represents survival—will go unnoticed at first, but given time will eventually come into focus for whoever has the courage to begin the journey. These are not easy choices, but they are all that is available. One can stay put—die, emotionally and, many may wish, physically as well—or one can move forward!

That's it. Only two choices. No other alternatives exist or are important enough to be defined. And the vast majority of parents intentionally or unintentionally choose the second alternative. Why? Because they see this as the *only* alternative. There simply is *no* choice but to go forward.

You can say to a parent who has suffered the loss of a child: "I don't know how you survived!" or "I just couldn't have handled it the way you did," or "I would have been a basket case for sure!" To such statements parents angrily respond: *"We had no choice! We had to do it! We had to get up each morning and begin each day by putting one foot in front of the other and move forward, painful, agonizing, and tortuous as this was!"*

So one does survive because there is no alternative. Although parents reject the cliché that "time heals"—no one believes this— they do accept the idea that time does make the situation a little more bearable. One can survive, given enough time. One can even find some new meaning in life, given enough time. One might even learn to laugh and enjoy life again, given enough time. How much time? Good question.

In the remainder of the book I will be devoting some time to the problem of survival, and will try to show that there is a light at the end of the tunnel for those who are willing and able to make the trek.

Background for the Book

I am writing this book essentially as an outsider, as one who has never personally experienced the tragedy of losing a child.

Yet over the last five years I have logged over 550 hours of in-depth, open-ended interviews with more than 300 parents— mothers and fathers—who have suffered the death of an infant or child from an array of different causes. These parents were all middle- and working-class couples who placed high value on children and looked upon childbearing and -rearing as a rewarding endeavor.

By working closely with these individuals, trying to fathom the depths of feelings experienced, I feel that in a vicarious way I have come to a rudimentary understanding of what it is like for most to lose a child through death. I say "vicarious" because I, like others who have never had such an experience, even after interviewing several hundred who have, can only vaguely approach an understanding of such a reality.

What kind of death experience is this? What kind of social expectations are placed on behavior in the aftermath of such a loss? How does one mourn the death of an infant or child? What kind of impact does it have on a family's ability to survive?

In the first phase of the research, begun in 1977, my colleague and I interviewed over 150 parents, mostly mothers who had suffered the loss of an infant. These losses ranged from miscarriages (prenatal losses) to postnatal deaths from a myriad of causes, including deaths from Sudden Infant Death Syndrome. In most cases the pregnancies were planned. In all cases the infants were highly desired. The findings from this phase of the research, completed in 1980, were published in our book *Motherhood and Mourning*, released in July of that year.[21]

The second phase of the research is focused on reactions and responses of parents to the death of an *older* child, and represents the basis for the present book. This research endeavor has been underway since January of 1982 and is still continuing. Since that time I have completed over 300 hours of interviews with parents who have experienced the loss of an older child, ranging in age from 1 to as much as 28.

Since 1977 I have listened as parents unfolded for me the details of these tragic events in their lives. I have listened to stories reflecting the heartache of infant death. I have listened to stories of the sudden death of infants and children as a result of both accidents and suicide. I have listened to stories of almost incomprehensible tragedies, such as deaths from murder and violence. I have listened to stories of lingering illnesses, sometimes extending into months and years, only to be followed by death.

In many ways each of these stories had its unique aspects, illustrating the conclusion that we all experience death and grief differently. And yet each was also similar in many respects, pointing to the idea that, regardless of how different we all are, there is an underlying sameness or similarity with which each of us responds when death strikes down our most prized possessions—our children.

It is really this sameness or similarity that I want to dwell upon in this book. Because if we can come to understand the commonalities that underlie losses of this type, we may come to know better how to respond and how best to offer our help and assistance to families and parents undergoing the agony of losing a child. If we can understand the similarities, we might even come to be better prepared for our *own* losses should they occur, better prepared to predict some of our *own* responses, and even to seek help when our coping abilities become overburdened and the resources necessary to deal with these tragedies overextended.

Forthcoming Chapters

In Chapter 2, I present a brief discussion of the properties of the sample of parents on which this analysis is based. Also included is a summary of the major similarities or attributes characteristic of parents and families who have experienced the loss of an older child. These attributes are modal characteristics and not necessarily universal features of the families in the sample.

Chapter 3 deals exclusively with the "dying" child and how parents and families respond to this particular category of loss. By a dying child I am referring to one whose departure is slow and prolonged. Parents are forced into a situation of giving care and comfort over a period of several months to a child they know has no future. Although this can be a painful ordeal, they do have an opportunity to anticipate the end and, in a certain manner, find a way of lessening somewhat the emotional trauma accompanying death.

In Chapter 4, I discuss the problems faced by families experiencing the loss of a child through sudden or accidental death. I have included the few cases of suicide in this chapter since these are often defined as sudden and unexpected. Sudden deaths are characterized here as often violent, always unplanned and unintentional departures. Accidental deaths serve as the best example. Parents face enormous difficulties in resolving the grief and sorrow associated with these losses. They are prone to the development of long-term emotional upheavals that have a devastating impact on individual integrity and family organization.

Chapter 5 reflects some of the unique problems encountered by families in the aftermath of murder. Murder is a special type of death characterized not only by violence and suddenness but also by a deliberate or intentional feature. In regard to suicide, which may be violent and sudden, there is always the element of choice, and regardless of their personal feelings, parents eventually come to respect that choice. With murder, however, there is no choice and consequently it is often defined as the most wasteful of all deaths. Murder is the violent, sudden, intentional destruction of a human life by another human being. Therefore parents and survivors have the added problem of dealing not only with the devastating impact of the loss itself, but also with the murderer and the lack of concern for victims inherent in the criminal justice system as it is presently structured in American society.

Chapter 6 takes a broader view of child death, exploring the problem from the viewpoint of its impact on the family as the primary social unit having strategic importance in human life. This chapter provides us with a way of analyzing and explaining the adjustment capacities of families reacting to the stress of child loss.

In Chapter 7, I analyze some of the characteristics of grief and sorrow as expressed by parents and survivors involved in the three categories of loss—slow death, sudden death, and murder. Here I rely on "Stage Theory" as the model for arriving at the best and most complete explanation of the grief experiences of parents and other family survivors.

In Chapter 8, I look at some of the common yet special problems all survivor families seem to experience. These include (1) the lack of community support in trying to adjust to the aftermath of child death; (2) some of the unique problems encountered during the hospitalization of a child for a terminal illness, and also an assessment of some of the important needs of children during these times; (3) the physician and his or her reaction to parents suffering the tragedy of the death of a child (many doctors are untrained in dealing with the emotional upheavals such experiences cause); (4) the autopsy and the problems encountered with this procedure; (5) some ways of anticipating, planning for, and handling funeral arrangements and the funeral experience itself; (6) grave visits and the variable impact these events have on the family; (7) the child's room or special place in the home and what this means to the parent-survivors; and (8) special days and the stress these times produce for the family.

Chapter 9 is a short chapter on coping, emphasizing that in spite of the remnants of grief in shadow form which parents will most likely be forced to carry for a lifetime, there is a way out of the darkest part of the depths of sorrow and despair. One need not grieve for a lifetime, although many believe this will be the case. I wish to emphasize here that, for the most part, grief accompanying child loss can be resolved. The problem is that it must be accomplished from the inside out, which is a very painful and arduous ordeal.

I will also discuss the rekindling of religious commitment as a source of comfort and support for parents. Redefining one's religious perspective is an important way for many parents to cope with their loss and resolve their grief and sorrow, which many feel would be totally destructive without the ability to search for some meaning for the tragedy in their renewed commitment to a religious interpretation.

Chapter 10 outlines the variable responses to depression, a frequent component of grief. In this chapter I attempt to discuss some of the common characteristics of a depressive reaction and give some counsel on how to deal with manifestations of depression, both from the viewpoint of the individual experiencing it and from the point of view of friends and relatives as helpers and supporters. Depression and grief go hand-in-hand; therefore depression is important enough to merit a special chapter devoted to coping with it.

Chapter 11 is specifically devoted to a discussion of self-help support groups in general. Support groups are those collectivities of individuals—parents—who have suffered similar experiences and are available to assist others who have recently been bereaved. There are a number of such groups presently being formed in some of the larger urban communities around the country. The Compassionate Friends is probably the best known of these self-help support units. The value of, and the need for, these groups is discussed.

Chapter 12 consists of a discussion of a specific and uniquely structured support group which, I believe, is tailor-made for dealing with the unique and severe problems associated with the death of children. It is called Kinder-Mourn, and is presently headquartered in Charlotte, North Carolina. This group has a very different approach to dealing with the problem of child death, and I have chosen this group as the prototype of the kind of self-help group that could be started in any community by parents who have the will to survive and the motivation to overcome the tragic event of child death. Some of the organizational characteristics, goals and purposes, and philosophy of the group are discussed.

2

What Have We Learned?
Some Findings

What does one learn from talking intimately with 150 families about their experiences of and reactions to the loss of a child? How does one organize and present the array of information gained from two-hour in-depth interviews with each family?

This chapter attempts to present an overview of some general findings. These findings may be referred to as common characteristics or "similarities" shared by family survivors.

It has always been generally assumed that since death is a unique and personal experience for any family, it is not possible to characterize its impact on the survivors before the event has occurred. That is, there is no way to predict how a family or the individual members will respond, since each death will be experienced differently by each family and by each person. Each suffers grief in his or her own personal way and within his or her own time frame.

However, in the course of the present investigation it was discovered that in spite of, or in addition to, these differences, there were also several *similarities* in the way families, particularly parents, responded to the deaths of their children. The similarities presented here were of a general nature and pertained to certain behavior patterns and attitude sets which came to dominate the response patterns of a majority of families for various lengths of time and at various points during the after-death period. Certainly not all families or parents responded in these ways, but these similarities appeared in enough cases to warrant considering them as significant findings which may be useful to those who wish to serve as "helpers" to families undergoing the tragedy of child death.

Perhaps these similarities can best be put forth as hypotheses to be tested in other populations before firm generalizations are established. At present they pertain only to families with characteristics and attributes similar to those persons who participated in the study. Therefore, before I discuss some of these relevant findings, I should first define the populations from which the families for the present study were selected, as well as some of the demographic and social features of the respondents.

Families and Parents

What are some of the attributes of the parents who participated in the interviews and how were they selected? First of all, the majority of families—80 percent—belonged to various self-help support organizations in their respective communities. I interviewed in five cities (St. Louis, Minneapolis, Cincinnati, Charlotte, N.C., and Springfield, Ill.), selecting 25 to 40 families from each city. The support groups in these communities were known by various names: The Compassionate Friends, Candlelighters, Kinder-Mourn, SHARE, and Parents of Murdered Children. These support groups were the main source of the families for this study. The lay leaders in each of the groups in the five communities helped locate the parents within their organizations who were willing to be interviewed. The biases introduced into this selection procedure came from the self-selection process used. The selection procedure in each community was as follows: The group leader sent a personal letter to all current and past members of the group, in some cases numbering over a hundred, telling them something about myself and what I proposed to do in their areas, that is, to interview parents—mothers and fathers—about their experiences relative to the loss of their child. No pressure was applied; it was left entirely up to the individual family to determine whether or not they wished to participate. Times were then arranged on a first-call, first-served basis. As indicated, approximately 25 to 40 families from each city were secured in this manner.

In consultation with the various group leaders after the initial selection process was completed, these leaders all indicated to me that in looking over the parents from each group who had "selected themselves" to participate, they felt that a good cross section of the membership was achieved. Therefore, even though the generalizability of the findings may be questionable as far as the general population of families who have lost children is concerned, the findings or similarities I am about to discuss may be generalizable to the support groups that served as the populations that supplied the respondents, and also perhaps to other similar support groups in other areas of the country.

The families who agreed to be interviewed consisted of those suffering from four kinds of losses: (1) those attempting to fathom the aftermath of long-term, terminal illness where the family had had the opportunity to anticipate and, in a sense, plan for the subsequent death of the child; (2) those suffering from the aftermath of sudden or unexpected death where no planning or preparation was possible; (3) those responding to a suicide, which often was sudden and unexpected, and presented the family with the added burden of self-blame; and (4) those dealing with murder— the ultimate tragedy—presenting families with unique problems of adjustment and opening up conflicts with the criminal justice system. In some cases the losses had recently occurred, i.e., within the last year; in other cases the losses had occurred years before, some as long as 20 years before. The accompanying table presents a breakdown of the cases according to type of loss and age characteristics of victims.

Table 1 Breakdown of Cases

Type of Loss	% of Sample	Characteristic of Child Victim	
		Median Age	Age Range
Illness	34.1	8 years	1–24
Accident	45.6	16 years	2–25
Suicide	5.8	21 years	20–28
Murder	14.5	19 years	16–25

The parents interviewed were primarily from white, middle-class, success-striving, materialistically oriented families. Prior to experiencing their losses the families in the sample were very much involved in pursuing careers, heavily committed to material consumption, and oriented to personal development. The average income of these families was over $29,000 per year, and 35 percent earned over $40,000.

Some 97 percent of our respondents—both men and women— had at least a high school education. The typical father had completed at least two years of college and was employed in a white-collar job.

Less than 3 percent of the total sample were classified as laborers; 97 percent of the males were employed in semiskilled, skilled, white-collar service, or professional occupations. Nine out of ten were steadily employed. The typical mother also worked outside the home, usually in a clerical or pink-collar job, and had completed at least one year of college. Only 30 percent of the women were homemakers and did not work outside the home.

The findings to be reported therefore pertain only to white, generally middle-class Americans and are in no way representative of minority families or families of lower or upper socioeconomic status. In addition, 65 percent of these families were Protestant and 35 percent Catholic (there were no families of the Jewish faith represented), and 72 percent of the families expressed moderate to high religious participation in their respective churches.

Thus even though the social characteristics of the families in the study were not representative of all American families, they were representative of the "typical" American family. The families in our study displayed many of the standard features of the typical American family; they sought the traditional success goals that permeate American society; they emphasized personal accomplishments through home ownership and the accumulation of a new car and other material things; and they displayed typical middle-class "values" by sharing positive attitudes toward children and childrearing. In fact childrearing was often a devoted undertaking, an avocation, if you will. Therefore our families did seem to represent the majority of American families as they are usually idealized in American culture. And perhaps these findings might be said to be generally relevant to these types of families.

Six Findings

With this brief description of the characteristics of the families, let me now turn to a discussion of some of the common patterns that developed in response to the loss of a child through death. I make no attempt to separate findings according to category of loss, i.e., illness, accident, suicide, or murder. These are general findings that appeared in the majority of cases irrespective of the kind of loss suffered. In addition, as noted earlier, the findings discussed here are not universally distributed but rather represent modal characteristics. Some of these common patterns carried a positive or beneficial connotation for the families in which the feature appeared. Other characteristics, where they appeared, were highly detrimental to the well-being of the family and of the individual members. I will differentiate these two effects in the summaries that follow.

Here, then, is a short synopsis of some of the common modal response patterns—the similarities—that appeared in the present research. I will add some interpretive comments that may be important in explaining the features as they are discussed. In addition I will expand on some of these issues in the remainder of the book. They are discussed here in summary form. These findings in essence represent the breadth but not the depth of what was learned from the interviews.

TO NEVER FORGET

One important commonality that appeared to be characteristic of all parents who have suffered the loss of a child for whatever reason took the form of a need or desire: a need that makes the loss of a child different from other kinds of losses, and one that truly complicates the normal process of grieving. This is the need or desire never to forget—or to remember always!

The child is gone! Out of sight! And parents, mothers particularly, harbor a great fear that what memories they have of the child may eventually fade away. They fear that they will forget the sight of the child's face, the sound of his or her voice, the texture of the child's hair, the uniqueness of the hands, even the child's characteristic smell. Parents severely miss these sensual experiences and eventually come to wish to retain them in memory for as long as they live.

As a way of interpreting this, apparently many times there exists among parents an inability to discuss or talk about their losses and feelings at a time when such discussion would be most appreciated and needed, such as at the time of the death itself. In some cases this inability stems from the parents' reluctance to upset others, and in other cases from the refusal of other significant people (close friends, relatives, doctors) to enter into meaningful and helpful discussions of the events.

This inability or refusal to communicate often amplifies the emotional feelings and extends them over a much longer period of time. More important, the longer the silence continues, the harder it is to deal with. This "conspiracy of silence" that surrounds parents is what leads to the terrible fears manifested by parents that everyone is forgetting, that their memories are fading, and produces this burning desire to keep the memories alive by vowing never to forget. In fact it was discovered that the interview situation itself was, for many, the first time they had had that kind of in-depth opportunity to discuss openly the details, as well as the hurt, surrounding the loss of their child.

In regard to these kinds of losses, nothing hurts more than being ignored. Nothing hurts more than not being given the opportunities to express pent-up feelings and emotions, not being allowed to submit to the pain, not being allowed to cry and wail and rant when the feelings overtake one. Nothing hurts more than the deep fear that deceased sons and daughters are being forgotten because no one ever talks of them again.

When people outside the immediate family are encountered who do not allow these physical expressions of emotions and thoughts about deceased children, it creates a resentment that is difficult to control. Subsequently the time comes when parents begin to separate themselves from insensitive and uncaring people in their environments who insist on keeping channels of communication closed.

Many times a wedge is driven between those suffering the loss and very dear and close friends. We can refer to this as a "wedge of ignorance"—ignorance about the great importance of open and physical communication.

It was discovered that all parents eventually develop a primary and fundamental need to talk about this tragic experience and about what they can remember about their child. They develop an intense desire or need to reveal their sadness, to release their anger, to allay their guilt, and to have others understand their reactions. This is not only how they remember; this is also how they confront the reality of what has happened to them.

This is an important finding because it tells each of us who may someday find ourselves in a position of ministering to families or parents foundering in the aftermath of child death that what is important is not to help them forget, as we are inclined to do, but to help them keep what few memories they have alive and fresh. It also tells us that we must be tolerant of the many episodes of emotional behavior—outbursts—that are the safety valves for the rage that builds within them. The worst thing we can do is to continually tell them to stay calm and maintain control!

In listening to these parents express themselves, I have come to the conclusion that one can deal with the emptiness of the future produced by the death of a child only by filling these voids with images of the child they once had, through thoughts, memories, and open discussion. Only in this way does such a loss become a reality. Only in this way can one truly survive, and eventually overcome, such a tragedy.

Therefore talking and open discussion become essential. Talking is comforting. Talking is comprehending. Talking is healing. Talking is remembering. This parents must do. This they *will* do. Anyone standing between these parents and their need to express themselves about the experience of their loss and their feelings relative to it will be deeply resented, and eventually their friendship discarded or pushed aside.

THE WISH TO DIE

In addition to the intense need to "remember" and to express oneself about the loss, which, I might add, is characteristic of the aftermath of both infant and child death, there is another feature shared in common, especially by those suffering the sudden loss of older children—children over the age of infancy. The death of an older child, particularly a sudden death, is one of the few categories of loss where the closest survivors—mothers and fathers—actually contemplate their *own* deaths as a way of legitimizing the loss.

As I have said before, child death, from any cause and under any circumstances, is so inappropriate, unnatural, and unacceptable in our modern society that it often is not fully comprehended. This is particularly true where the death is sudden and unexpected. There simply is no context within which such an event can be fitted.

Consequently it appears to many parents—especially mothers, but many fathers too—that survival for themselves is at best questionable. There appears to be no hope, no way of justifying their lives, no way of continuing on with life without the deceased child. Many parents therefore come to the point where they sincerely want to die themselves; they want to follow their children to the grave in a blind but understandable desire to continue to see and caress and love them. Also, there is an intense drive to escape the pain, the devastation, and the agony that separation has caused them to experience.

This feeling and response is closely related to the "survivor syndrome," which is a fairly typical reaction of individuals to the sudden death of a loved one. The survivors can find no "reason" why they survived and the deceased did not, leading to intense feelings of guilt and vulnerability. However, whereas the survivor syndrome, as a psychological response pattern, is fairly short-lived and can be conceived of within a rational framework, parents who think of dying (who think of their own death) in response to the death of a child are unable to contemplate the irrationality of their desires, and remnants of these thoughts and desires extend over a much longer period of time. Fortunately, for the vast majority this desire is not carried into action. But it seems that almost all parents who suffer losses of this type at least contemplate their own deaths, and for most it is a genuine desperate feeling and a very revealing experience.

Let us not condemn this response, but simply understand it. When one is plunged into the pit of intense despair and depression, certainly one would tend to lose the zest for living. After undergoing such an experience, what, in life, could possibly make sense anymore? Why struggle to remain alive? Death becomes an escape from what is defined as an intolerable life situation, while at the same time, and perhaps equally important, a means of reunification with their beloved deceased child.

I found two phases at work in this process. The *acute phase* of these feelings of desolation and wanting to escape from life, where the individual teeters on the brink of self-destruction, will generally last from two weeks to three months. The *chronic phase,* which is of longer duration but characterized by less intense feelings, may last up to a year or more after the loss. During this latter phase the parents' response to death is to take it or leave it. They tend to develop a nonchalant attitude toward it. They tend to have no overt fear of death or dying in any form. And even though they may no longer contemplate taking their lives, they would still consider allowing death to occur if it was pending.

What really keeps these parents moving forward is the recognition that one's own death would probably compound the hurt already experienced by other family members. Their own death would require that they leave behind a spouse, perhaps other children, maybe even their own parents. They may still prefer death, but at the same time they recognize their responsibilities to others. So they hang on to life and simply hope for the best.

Listen to how five mothers, all of whom lost sons or daughters under the age of 10 through some sudden, unexpected event, typically relate their feelings on this issue:

I had no reason to live. I didn't really *want* to live. I thought about it often. . . . How easy it would be to simply "lose control" of the car while driving on the freeway. . . .

I wanted to die . . . to escape . . . the pain! It was the worst pain I had ever experienced! I kept thinking, "Why Susan? Why Susan? Why not me? . . ."

Oh, God, yes! . . . Definitely! . . . I did *not* want to live! No way! I thought about suicide constantly for the first three weeks or so. . . . It was so, so hard! . . .

I stared at that gun for the longest time! . . . It would have been so easy. . . . I think I was ready for it . . . I don't know why I didn't do it. . . .

Yes, I wanted to die . . . I wanted to be with Billy again. . . . I thought if I died, I would be able to see him and touch him and hold him again . . . I . . . I . . . [she begins to cry] I couldn't think of anything else for weeks. . . .

It might be said of the period following significant losses that true happiness and contentment can return only if one *works* to make it happen. Some parents make the effort and are relatively successful. Others (about half the mothers who have experienced these feelings) simply can no longer muster such motivation; instead they prefer to sit quietly, watch the world go by, and no longer participate. These are the real social tragedies left in the aftermath of the sudden unexpected loss of a child.

There is a positive side to this, however, and that is that few parents—both mothers and fathers—ever again feared death in the same way they did before the tragedy. In the majority of cases this feeling or attitude usually continued for many years, long after the chronic phase of this reaction had passed. In fact I believe that living with *no fear* of death or dying may become a permanent characteristic of the after-death period for a majority of parent-survivors.

A RELIGIOUS EXPERIENCE

Many parents, whether or not they have experienced a "death wish," inevitably attempted to search for some cause or rational reason for the loss. For some this effort became a genuine "search" for a reason to survive. For others it represented a simple need to make the loss intelligible.

In fact all survivors seemed to have a need to fit death into some kind of recognizable context. It was the rare family indeed who could simply accept the loss of a child as an act of "fate." They had to develop a sense of control over the event. Parents needed a way of justifying the death in their own minds. This was true for all categories of loss—after an illness, sudden death, suicide, and murder. However, with sudden death, suicide, and murder, the search for reasons seemed to be longer in developing. It took these parents a longer period of time—sometimes extending into months—to get over the shock, anger, and resentment that such losses characteristically produce.

Nevertheless, in time even these parents often began their search for logical reasons for the death—reasons they could accept, reasons they could feel comfortable with. In essence they searched for assurances that the loss was not in vain, for some "meaning" for the event.

In their sometimes frantic search for meaning and justification, a majority of these parents, roughly 70 percent, turned to their religious faiths for answers and for comfort.

Thus this represents the third important commonality: the death of a child ultimately tends to change the religious orientation of parents in a positive direction.

This finding, incidentally, appeared to hold true even in those cases where parents did not place much credence in religion prior to the loss. This included parents who for one reason or another had drifted away from their churches in recent years, agnostic parents who considered the existence of a God to be questionable, and those who were unsure of the existence of an afterlife.

It seemed, again, that the tragedy was so overpowering, so initially incomprehensible, that parents, plunged into the depths of bottomless despair and finding no other way of justifying the loss, turned—in some cases in desperation—to a religious interpretation and a religious explanation in an effort to make some sense of their situation. This became their way of dealing with the incomprehensibleness of the loss in their own minds.

In some cases (in about 30 percent of the families that responded in this way) the response took the form of a genuine religious revitalization or conversion experience. In the other cases it took the form of a growth or rekindling of the belief in some sort of reunification with the child after the parent's own death.

The growth of this latter belief was accompanied by a rekindling or revitalization of the belief in an afterlife of sorts. I say "of sorts" because these conceptions as they were recharged in the minds of parents after experiencing a devastating loss did not always correspond to the traditional conceptions of a "heaven" in the Christian sense. In some cases, of course, they did, reflecting the early learning of parents having grown up in "God-fearing" Christian families. In most cases, however, the idea of an afterlife was merely conceived of as a "place" of an existential nature. And it was here that the "reuniting" would take place. There were many inconsistencies in the way these conceptions were expressed. For example, following the death of her daughter one mother said:

I'm really not a religious person. I didn't fall back on religion as support when she died, but the thing that helped me get through it was knowing that we would be together again, that our separation was not permanent. . . .

Another, following the death of her son:

In my mind, my son is in a better place. Call it heaven or whatever, I don't know. I do not believe in God but I do accept some kind of existence after death. I have to believe this, otherwise I don't think I could go on. . . .

A father after the death of his son:

I always thought religion was a myth. But since Mike's death I have come to think of it as a nice myth, a comforting myth. If it's not true, after I die it won't matter anyway. But right now, it's kind of nice to hang on to.

Many parents thus felt that they had achieved some sense of satisfaction, however temporary it may indeed have been. For now at least they had found some peace. And for those who were able to orient themselves in this way, it seems they were indeed able to deal more effectively with their losses.

How do we interpret this response? It became very apparent during the interview sessions that parents who were able to stoke up their religious fires had found a way of making the loss less "final," and therefore ultimately less painful. Many parents could not accept the idea that they would *never* be able to see and caress their child again. Accepting this aspect of reality was so painful that they just refused to consider it. So, very gradually at first, they came to accept this vague idea of an afterlife and began to envision their child residing *there* in a state of peace and comfort.

As stated earlier, even those bereaved parents who before the loss rejected the idea of a heavenly God, who rejected belief in an afterlife, who believed firmly in the reality of life and the finality of death, after suffering for a period of time were unable to sustain these attitudes. It was just too discomforting, too painful, to do so. They simply could not fathom the idea of their child being totally obliterated, having no substance anywhere. So they allowed their orientation to change. They began to search their backgrounds and experiences for some evidence that death was not the finality they had thought it to be. They found their answers in their early religious beliefs and experiences, which they now actively rekindled in one form or another.

I do not know, at this point, precisely how firmly these new conceptions were held; however, I did find that, for many, even after several years these new commitments continued to hold sway over their existence.

Let me say again that these changes in the patterns of parents' religious responses were important because they led to the establishment of effective personal remedies for dealing quite effectively with the loss and helped parents find some answers and comprehend the events they were experiencing. In fact this religious reorientation, where successfully implemented, was an important key to the partial resolution of the acute phase of grief.

A CHANGE OF VALUES

In addition to an emphasis on the religious experiences of parents, I also observed a rather significant change in their value perspectives. Again, this was particularly true for those who struggled through a long terminal illness with the child. The value changes were very evident in these cases. A change of values might also occur in the aftermath of sudden death; however, I do not believe the changes would be so immediately evident. It takes a much longer time to adjust to such losses, and any change in values would probably be slow in developing.

In regard to anticipated vs. sudden loss, I did notice a more significant and clear-cut change in those families who had recently surrendered a child to death after a long illness. As for families experiencing sudden death, there was often still a high level of anger and resentment present and it was difficult to determine any real alterations in values. However, I believe that a significant value change will occur in response to all types of child death. It simply takes a longer time to manifest itself in the aftermath of sudden death.

To explain this change in values relative to anticipated death, it seems that, prior to the death of the child, many of these families were very much involved in worldly affairs. However, the death itself, coupled with months of heroic effort in ministering to the needs of a dying child, tended to shake parental attachments to traditional values and goals of success and personal achievement, and brought into play new commitments to more intangible values.

Having experienced and survived such an ordeal, many families no longer seemed to have a *need* to strive in the way they were accustomed to in the past. Granted, I do not know how valid this finding is in regard to families in other socioeconomic strata; however, for these middle-class families there appeared to be a definite deemphasis on worldly values and worldly things. Family, as opposed to individual, goals become primary.

This change in the direction of one's life manifested itself in various ways. For one thing, parents tended to become more concerned with cultivating and strengthening family relationships. Remaining family members gradually began to be viewed in a new light, with renewed emphasis on their importance as people who have needs that must be met and concerns that must be addressed. Doing things *with* the family rather than *for* the family, and taking a genuine interest in each other, eventually came to be defined as more important than trying to "keep up with the Joneses"—perhaps a common behavior pattern in the "predeath" family.

Fathers, for instance, in the aftermath of the loss, tended to become less interested in their jobs, less career motivated, less interested in simply making "more money," and more interested in establishing better, more stable, higher quality interpersonal relationships with other members of the family.

One mother said of this change in their lives, which is also reflective of the views of others:

We have learned what is important in this world as a result of what happened to Sandra. My husband has consistently refused promotions and pay raises because they mean leaving the area and moving. . . . We have simply decided that our family now comes first. . . . My husband and I are very close to our parents and brother and sisters. We want to preserve these relationships. They became so very important to us after Sandra's death. Prior to that time, we, like all our friends, were on the "fast track." . . . We just never gave much thought to what relationships really meant.

Mothers too became more caring, more tuned-in to other family members, and less concerned with appearances, less concerned with "things" such as clothes, furniture, and keeping the house cleaned. It is not that such things lost all importance, it is rather that they were now put in perspective relative to the experience of losing their most important possession. Another mother said:

I used to worry about all the little things in life, just like everyone else: how to pay for this or that; keeping the house clean; making sure the yard is mowed, and so on. I still hear my friends complain about these things. And I think "How silly!" What a waste to occupy your mind with such trivia! Today I am happy to say that I am more concerned with the larger issues— my family's health, my family's happiness. . . .

For parents suffering through such tragedies, it seemed that everything in life—everything remaining in life—was suddenly reduced in importance and significance to what it was before.

A sense of vulnerability came to dominate family life. For each family member left behind, life itself now seemed so fragile. Life came to be viewed as something that could be snatched away at any moment, without warning. One father commented:

Time became very precious to us. When you face few threats, you tend to take what is important in life for granted—such as family and friends. When you are faced, however, with losing something precious, time suddenly becomes so very important. It becomes something not to be wasted. . . .

Certainly these feelings did not come immediately or all at once. There were always the many long months of agony, turmoil, and confusion as parents desperately attempted to work through the acute phase of their grief. However, once this acute phase began to subside, parents could then begin the arduous task of putting their lives back together. This always seemed to take place in different ways for different individuals, and each life would never be the same again. It was at these times that one's values and ideas of importance began to change. As stated earlier, I believe these changes would be a longer time in coming in the case of sudden death; however, I do believe that they will occur, after the shock and anger have begun to subside and a clearer image of the consequences of such losses begins to pervade the family.

In many respects I think this change of values is one of the positive or redeeming effects of such an experience. The loss of a child is such a monumental event in the lives of most families that it causes them to reevaluate their whole life situation and results in a significant alteration in their value patterns and personal commitments.

It must be recalled that even though our sample is *not* representative of all families, in my interviews with these parents in the aftermath of the death of their children, many of them indicated that they had become more compassionate in their dealings with others, more understanding of the problems of others, more forgiving of the transgressions of others, more open with their own feelings, more patient, and more loving. All are very positive changes, and are recognized as such by the parents. They too eventually come to accept the loss as having some redeeming value in their lives. Again, these feelings do not arrive all at once; they take time to cultivate.

MORE TOLERANCE

Another common finding emerging from the interviews, which is perhaps related to the others discussed here, is that the event of child loss tends to make a person more tolerant of other people and more sensitive to and understanding of the problems and suffering of others.

It appears that bereaved parents are more willing to listen to others express their problems, more willing to try to develop a sense of understanding, more willing to respond in a personal sort of way to the expressed needs and concerns of others.

I do not know at this point just how generalized this apparent tolerant attitude might be. I cannot yet say whether this increased tolerance might be extended to actual reduction in "prejudicial" feelings toward other ethnic, racial, or religious groups. However, in many respects this might be concluded if such groups are defined by the bereaved parents as suffering from hardships over which they have little or no control.

I wish to state this finding in hypothesis form to be tested in subsequent groups of bereaved parents from different socioeconomic levels who have suffered the loss of a child under an array of different circumstances.

At present about all that can be concluded is that the experience of losing a child does seem to produce a liberalizing effect on attitudes toward other people and the problems they are experiencing. Like the alteration of values, this finding also seems to carry a positive connotation.

Personally I find it unfortunate that the rest of us—those who have never suffered a tragedy of such magnitude—cannot learn some lesson from what these bereaved families have experienced. We have seen that such tragedies can in time produce positive results for those experiencing them, and can teach important lessons to us all about the true meaning of life in this world.

SHADOW GRIEF

One last finding I wish to discuss pertains to the discovery of the existence of what has come to be defined as "shadow grief" among the majority of families in our study. By this I mean that parental grief may never be totally resolved!

The concept of shadow grief was first revealed in the book titled *Motherhood and Mourning: Perinatal Death* by Larry G. Peppers and Ronald J. Knapp (New York: Praeger Special Studies, 1980). These authors found the lingering effects of grief to be quite prominent among mothers who suffered perinatal losses. That is, these mothers never seemed to be completely able to shake off the vestiges of grief; in some cases remnants remained for years.

Generally I found this to be true also for parents in the present study. Parents who suffer the loss of an older child have also shown that the emotions, feelings, and thoughts surrounding the loss persist, in some cases for as long as 20 years, with no relief of the feelings in sight. This does not mean that grief continued to dominate their existence as it once did, but rather that the experience of child death and many of the attendant feelings do remain, ever so subtly, and perhaps are never entirely forgotten or resolved.

Shadow grief is a form of "chronic" grief, and can be a burden that parents—mothers especially—sometimes must bear for most of their lives. Shadow grief does not manifest itself overtly; it does not debilitate; no effort is required to cope with it. On the surface most observers would say that the "grief work" has been accomplished. But this is not the case. Shadow grief reveals itself more in the form of an emotional "dullness," where the person is unable to respond fully and completely to outer stimulation and where normal activity is moderately inhibited. It is characterized as a dull ache in the background of one's feelings that remains fairly constant and that, under certain circumstances and on certain occasions, comes bubbling to the surface, sometimes in the form of tears, sometimes not, but always accompanied by a feeling of sadness and a mild sense of anxiety. Shadow grief will vary in intensity depending on the person and the unique factors involved. It is more emotional for some than for others.

Where shadow grief exists, the individual can never remember the events surrounding the loss without feeling some kind of emotional reaction, regardless of how mild.

The difference between "normal" grief and "shadow" grief is similar to the difference between pneumonia and the common cold. The latter is less serious, less disruptive to life, more of a nuisance than anything else.

Here are some short excerpts from the interviews which graphically portray the vestiges of grief in shadow form. In each case the losses occurred 12 years or more before:

I still remember everything, and I can still feel all the pain. I never *want* to forget. Even though it's been 17 years, it's like it happened yesterday. . . .

I shall always remember Bill with both happiness and remorse. This is the way Bill's memories will always be for me—a bittersweet encounter. . . .

When Mike was killed, I died too. . . . I will never again be as alive as I was before. . . . Oh, I get by okay today. But I am not whole and never will be again! . . .

There are no words to describe the heartache and pain I felt when Sandra died. . . . It's been 12 years, and if I live to be 80 I'll never entirely get over it. . . .

You know I can't ever forget it. I never *want* to forget Paul, nor do I *want* to forget the accident. . . . I guess I need to suffer. . . .

My son died 13 years ago. . . . Although I don't cry anymore as often as I used to, my life is not the same. . . . It will never be the same . . . nor do I expect it to be. . . .

In conclusion, it appears that there are many factors and variables that make the loss of a child a unique experience for most parents. However, in saying this I do not wish to leave the wrong impression. In our assessment of the way parents respond to the death of a child we must be very careful not to equate "unique" with what is "abnormal" or "bizarre." The reactions—the commonalities reported here—must be defined as quite *normal*, perhaps even routine, when viewed from the perspective of those experiencing them.

Thus the findings revealed in this study are very important for the parents themselves, in that by having knowledge of and sharing this kind of information they can come to realize that their deepest feelings and their most "personally" bizarre behaviors are in no way abnormal or dissimilar to what other parents have felt and experienced when faced with the same tragedies.

Such findings are important also because they result in an array of knowledge that might prove useful to the many people in the community—professionals as well as relatives, friends, and neighbors—who might be called upon to offer assistance to grief-stricken families.

In the next chapter I begin a discussion of the dying child and attempt to show how parents very gradually come to accept the inevitable. Death after a long illness often produces a significant long-term impact on the family in terms of a change in orientation toward life and death. Many of the findings revealed in the present chapter pertain to those undergoing the trauma of separation after a long illness.

3

The Dying Child:
Someone Special

Those of us who have never been through the heartrending task of caring for a terminally ill child, only to have the months of intense sacrifice and hope draw to an empty, despairing close with the child's death, cannot possibly know or understand the depths of emotional anguish such an ordeal can extract. Here are a few remarks from parents as they describe the trauma of caring for their terminally ill children:

Nothing that I can imagine could have been any worse for us. You take it one day at a time. If only you can make it through today.

It took a gigantic amount of energy just to make it through each day. My God, how we survived those times is still a mystery to me! The pain was simply indescribable.

There is nothing in this world that could have prepared us for what we subsequently experienced. You have no idea what we went through.

The hurt is so unbearable, it's hard to describe. I'm talking about the physical hurt, not really our emotions—they were shot already! The physical pain was so excruciating.

Our life stood still. We actually hoped tomorrow would never come for fear of what new crisis would emerge.

As the end approached we tended to become very bitter. What did all the months of heartache and turmoil really accomplish? What a waste!

To lose this beautiful child, after fighting for his life for three years, was more than I could bear. I wanted to follow him to his grave!

You really wish tomorrow would never come. You are content to spend the rest of your life living today because you know you can live with it. You may not be able to live with what tomorrow brings.

To this day, I really don't know how we managed to live through all those months. It was a nightmare—an absolute nightmare!

A Change in Priorities

Terminally ill children are in many respects special—special certainly to their parents in that as they progress through an illness their relationships with their parents, and in turn their parents' view of them, becomes redefined. Terminal illness forces the child into a new role in the family, and in some ways in the community as well. This new role is characterized by a new set of needs and expectations which demand attention and must be addressed. As a result the usual every-day activities of family members must be modified or curtailed as attention is increasingly focused on the child's situation and on meeting the needs of his or her new role.

This modification or curtailment of parental and family activities must occur because in the normal world activities are geared to the future. Most of us tend to view life from a "future" perspective, and parenthood intensifies this future orientation. In many respects children are the personifications of their parents' dreams and plans. They represent goals and purpose for their parents, and in many ways are reflections of them.

When a child is defined as dying, priorities change. The parental future orientation becomes modified. Parents see their future dreams and plans placed in dire jeopardy. They are no longer able to adhere to these commitments; consequently the *present* takes on a deeper meaning.

All effort and attention now become concentrated on the moment at hand. Moment-to-moment happenings become primary to parent and child. The time, *now*, becomes vital. Life begins to revolve around the present and acquires a quality that is rarely understood by those not undergoing these experiences. This redirection of focus tends to magnify the importance of present relationships and current experiences parents have with their children, and in many ways amplifies the richness of every moment spent with them.

Not only is there no effort to see beyond the present, but the future is now regarded with dread. The future becomes filled with unknowns that parents would just as soon avoid.

Each of the following fathers and mothers suffered the loss of their child after a long illness. Listen to what they say about the present and the future at the time they were struggling with their dying child:

A mother whose 17-year-old son died of bone cancer:

There was no future for us. We were afraid of what tomorrow and the next day might bring. We learned to savor every good moment, every good day. We didn't allow ourselves to even think beyond that day. The future was a frightening place for us.

A mother whose 8-year-old son died of leukemia:

You concentrate on the good days and live for those. You have to grasp them as they come. You have to take the bad days too, but you want to get them over quickly. When you have a good day, you want it to last forever. You never want to let it go.

A father whose 4-year-old son died of leukemia:

We had to readjust our whole life when Sam became ill. All our future plans had to be shelved. I didn't even want to think about the future because I knew it held Sam's death. It was just too unbearable to think about.

A mother whose 6-year-old daughter died of leukemia:

Her death was not imminent to me. This was something in the future; it was far away. I lived only for today. I didn't even think about tomorrow, let alone plan for it.

A father whose 10-year-old son died of a brain tumor:

You know, we cared for Ricky for two years before he died. Toward the end he was nothing more than a vegetable. But we'd do it all over again if we could have just a little more time with him. He was the pride of my life—God, how I miss him! I savored each day—treasured them, really. And if it was a good day, that made it all the better. I could not have cared less about tomorrow. Today I had my son and that was all that was important to me.

So when a child is dying, future plans are cancelled. The focus is shifted to the present. The relationship between parent and child becomes laden with rich overtones of feelings, both positive and negative. Worry, concern, ambiguity, uncertainty, anxiety, respect, admiration, and love come to dominate the parent's present feelings and attitudes toward the child. There is also a great amount of fear and anger generated by the situation, which parents often find difficult to control.

The Maturity of the Dying Child

Children who are dying often know that they are dying. This creates a unique problem in that they must deal with not only their own feelings and reactions to this knowledge, but also the feelings and reactions of others, particularly their parents.

To maintain a mutual sense of understanding and support, parents and children must maintain open lines of communication. This is difficult to do because of the complexity of feelings that arise in a child aware of his or her coming death. As with adults, children too have a need to protect others from the coming harsh reality. They too maintain false facades. Like adults, they suffer from fear, resentment, and puzzlement. They suffer from denial. They fear loneliness. They resent and fear isolation. They suffer from separation anxiety, just as adults do. They fear being deserted and abandoned. And they also need to begin the process of detaching themselves from others as death approaches.

All this complicates the development of good communication, which is essential if both parent and child are to reach the final stage of "acceptance" of death *before* it occurs.

The child's knowledge of his or her impending death often comes while the parents are still in a stage of denial. The child, sensing the reluctance of the parents, refrains from any discussion of his or her true feelings so as to protect the parents from the trauma of such encounters. This prevents open communication between parent and child when it would be so beneficial to both. About the best that can be achieved is a facade of communication in which both parties know what the outcome will be but refrain from talking about it openly. This "pretense awareness" may dominate to the very end unless the child makes a special effort to break through the resistance of the parents. In my interviews with parents, I have found that the situation is seldom reversed. It is the parent who resists confrontation, at least in the beginning.

The fact that children develop a knowledge of their impending death so soon contributes in part to the development of the very rapid maturity of children under sentence of death. Parents claim that as the illness progresses their children develop a maturity far beyond their years. Dying children tend to display wisdom and understanding far advanced from what one would normally expect. As death approaches, there is usually no hysteria, no agitation, no hostility. Rather, a calmness seems to overtake them, along with a sense of revered wisdom and maturity. Such changes have been noted in children as young as 3 years of age.

Parents often find themselves in a state of awe over the way these young people handle themselves as death approaches. In fact parents are usually surprised that young people can approach death without being overcome by fear and uncertainty and consumed by anxiety.

Parents are also usually very impressed by their child's unique understanding of what others in the family are going through. The dying child seems to know how this event will affect others, and by their words and actions they do try to make it easier, more bearable, for others to endure. In one case a dying child of 7 willingly shared with his brother and sister gifts given to him. In another case a child of 12 was overheard by his parents, one week before his death, explaining to a younger brother that he was not afraid to die and that the younger brother should not feel bad about his leaving, that he was going to heaven and this was far better than being sick all the time!

Listen to how some of our parents expressed themselves about their perceptions of their child's rapid psychological maturation:

A father whose 6-year-old son died of leukemia:

I don't know what it was or where it came from. I only know that Jimmy was not the same little boy at the end that he was in the beginning. I mean he grew up so fast! He had a maturity about him that far surpassed his six years. He was a grown-up man in the body of a little boy!

A father whose 9-year-old daughter died of leukemia:

I can't tell you how reassuring it was to us to see this change take place in Paula over the two years she struggled with this thing. We were awed by the things she would say and by the depths of her insights. I think her ability to comprehend what was happening in her life exceeded that of many adults.

A mother whose 7-year-old son died of bone cancer:

Billy grew up rapidly; he matured far ahead of his chronological age. I think children who are fighting a losing battle with a terminal condition come to know this very early on. And in order to deal with it, they tend to develop rapidly beyond their years. I think the realization that they are dying forces them to grow up—fast!

A mother whose 12-year-old son died of Ewing's tumor:

I saw a very real change take place in Rico, particularly during the last six months when it became apparent to him that he was fighting a losing battle. It was like a calmness enveloped him. He wasn't what you would call moody, but more contemplative. He seemed to set aside boyish things and boyish behavior. He never cried anymore after that. I can't really say he was depressed either. I think he displayed more control and wisdom during those last six months than most people do in a lifetime. He became my main support during that time.

We should make it clear that the interrelationship between parent and child during the living–dying period is complex. Often the psychological and emotional changes that take place in the child are influenced, or in part determined, by the actions and attitudes of the parents. In fact some parents may themselves be primarily responsible for the rapid psychological maturation of their child without being fully aware of their participation in this development.

For example, parents often operate under the conscious assumption that all will be well, although they may know *unconsciously* that this is a fiction. That is, they never allow themselves openly to express the view that their child may not live, either to their spouses or even to themselves. Until the very last moments they consciously reject the thought that their child is in fact dying.

This attitude of conscious denial covers an unconscious knowledge of reality and leads to behavior on the part of the parent which may contribute to the development of maturity on the part of the child.

As indicated, the sense of awe and admiration that is characteristic of the parents' attitude toward their children as they begin to observe the maturational changes occurring in them, in turn draws parents physically closer to the child. They begin to spend more time with the child; they listen more intently to the child's words and how she or he expresses them; they begin to read meanings and interpretations into the child's expressions. In fact, during this time parents often come to the point where they actually begin to respond to the child more as an adult than as a child. They begin to share an array of rather technical information with their children about their condition and the treatment regimens they are undergoing. They communicate with them more nearly as equals.

Many parents reveal that they allow a role reversal to take place. Many begin to think of their child as their mentor or teacher, quite the reverse of the usual parent–child relationship. And they allow the child to control large segments of their lives. These changes can occur even with very young children.

This attitude and behavior toward the child can lead to a change or alteration in the child's self-concept and self-definition which in turn contributes to the subsequent rapid evolution of maturity on the child's part.

In fact, although our discussion pertains to changes taking place in the child, it might be noted that parents also tend to reach a new level of maturity as a result of their close relationship with a dying child. Parental maturity, however, takes time to achieve, and these new levels may not appear for weeks or even months after the death of the child, when the parents begin the process of assessing the impact of the loss on their values and philosophies of life.

Anticipation of Death Can Be Helpful

Dealing with a terminally ill child is without doubt one of the hardest ordeals any family will experience. Even so, there are redeeming aspects to this experience.

It should be apparent to the reader that in the case of dying children some parents have an opportunity to adjust to the impending death of their child. Through the process of "anticipatory grief," the end can become somewhat less debilitating for these parents, something which is not possible in the case of sudden or accidental death. However, there are many varieties of parental responses to impending death. Anticipatory grieving may be possible only if the parent is able to *face* potential death and does not deny its approach.

The opportunity for anticipatory grieving is vitally important, and structures the way grief and mourning behavior is usually expressed in those cases where there is time to adjust.

In my interviews with parents I have found that I tend to agree with Murray Parkes, who in his study of unexpected and untimely deaths pointed out that there is a difference between the "no-preparation" group and the "long-preparation" group.[1] Although Parkes was defining the reactions of widows and widowers to the loss of a spouse, his conclusions are very similar to the findings of this study.

Like Parkes, this study also revealed that in the "long-preparation" group, where survivors had time to anticipate the loss, there appeared to be less difficulty accepting the loss, little evidence of guilt or self-blame, little extreme emotional or stressful reaction at the time of death, less anger involved, far fewer depressive symptoms, a greater tendency to formulate some way of handling the event that made it more real, less likelihood of reacting with disbelief and shock, greater tendency to involve oneself in such after-death ceremonies as grave visits, fewer problems with role functioning, and less likelihood of developing a fixation to the past.

Relationship Between Husband and Wife

I should note that the husband—wife relationship was often assaulted during the months of following along behind a terminally ill child, in spite of the apparent differences between the "long-preparation" and "short-preparation" groups. The long-term and continuous support functions demanded by terminal illness placed unique strains on the marital relationship.

Parents—both mothers and fathers—often indicated that they did not always receive support and understanding from their spouse during the months of care, and this compounded all the other problems that impinged on the situation.

In fact the main source of support for parents often was their close friends, at least for a time, and particularly during the interim period. This was especially true for the mother, who was often given the primary responsibility for the care of the child during the middle stage of the terminal illness. The father was there, but not continuously. Therefore the mother and father often proceeded through the illness, and experienced the emotional ravages of the encounter, at different rates and with differing degrees of intensity. At any given time they were often at different stages in their own preparatory or anticipatory grief responses. This resulted in the collapse of effective communication channels between mother and father and led to the tendency for both parents to reach beyond the family unit for support.

I might add that unless support outside the family can be found for parents who have difficulty responding to each other's needs, they will approach the death of the child with a sense of loneliness and isolation and may find themselves totally ill-prepared for this tragic event when it occurs.

Inability to draw support from a spouse when one needs it can lead to a feeling of resentment and even hostility, which in turn can permanently affect the relationship in a way that may be detrimental to the marriage.

The death of the child is indeed a difficult time for parents to endure, particularly after having spent weeks and months of ups and downs through the illness. However, contrary to what common sense might tell us, if the relationship between the parents has not been fraught with difficulty, the *hardest times* come at other points along the path from diagnosis to termination and do not come at the time of death itself! In fact, for most parents who were able to keep channels of communication open and who were able to rely on each other during the ordeal of caring for the child, there was an element of relief when death finally came, following a drawn-out, debilitating illness.

Parents indicated that of the time spent in the care of terminally ill children, the greatest emotional upheaval and anguish were experienced at the beginning of the ordeal and as the end drew near—*not* at the time of death. These were the times that were remembered most vividly as being associated with the greatest stress.

By the "beginning," I am referring to the diagnosis itself and the time immediately surrounding that event. This without question was the most excruciating period for parents. By "as the end drew near," I am referring to that time—the final moments—*before* death, when all hope for survival had vanished and parents came face to face with the reality of losing their child.

We can divide the process of following a child from diagnosis to death into three phases: the diagnosis, the interim period, and the final moments.

The Devastation of Diagnosis

It appears that when parents learn their child has a terminal illness, their reaction is very similar to those parents who have learned of their child's sudden death. Shock and disbelief are common initial responses, accompanied frequently by anger and expressed hostility. Unlike the response to a sudden death, there is usually an eventual relief after the shock of diagnosis. Initially, however, it is a devastating experience.

Friedman and his colleagues found the same thing in a study of the reactions of parents responding to the diagnosis of a terminal illness in their child. They report that it sometimes takes days for the meaning of a diagnosis to sink in.[2] Even though the majority of parents said that they expected it and anticipated it, they were still shocked and stunned when the words were actually pronounced. One mother said—and this seems to reflect the feelings of all—"it was like being stabbed through the heart with cold steel!" One is simply never prepared for this kind of encounter. Here are what other parents said about their reaction to the initial diagnosis:

A father whose 18-year-old son was diagnosed as having lymphosarcoma:

I had heard of Hodgkin's disease but not lymphosarcoma. I didn't understand, or perhaps didn't *want* to understand, what he was saying to me. I just couldn't reconcile that with what was happening to our son. He had just graduated from high school! How could this be happening now? I couldn't accept what the doctor was saying. I told him he was wrong and I would not listen anymore. I just couldn't deal with it at that time. He seemed to understand and said he would talk to me again later. I remember almost running from his office. I wanted to get away from him and those things he was saying.

A mother whose 7-year-old daughter was diagnosed has having acute lymphoblastic leukemia:

I think nature prepares you for these times. You can only absorb a small amount of information at one time. You hear the words but they don't sink in. The true reality comes to you over a span of time—a little at a time. I know it was several hours before I was able to grasp the full weight of what was said to me and several days for the emotional impact to ripple through me.

A mother whose 12-year-old daughter was diagnosed as having chronic myelocytic leukemia:

When you first hear that horrible word "leukemia," it strikes like a bolt out of the blue! I felt weak and sick inside. Why was this happening to us? The whole situation quickly turns into a bad dream from which you desperately want to escape. The doctor kept talking about survival rates but I couldn't listen—I couldn't accept the possibility of her dying at that time.

A mother whose 10-year-old son was diagnosed on the operating table as having a malignant growth in his nasal passage:

We took Mark to a specialist who put him in the hospital for surgery the next day. We were confident of the outcome. I think I developed an optimism which supported me at that time. I went to the hospital alone with Mark and was waiting in the reception area when they called me into the hall. The doctor was standing there with his hands in his surgical gloves raised in front of him just like you see on TV. He had come out of surgery halfway through to talk with me. All he said was "I've got some bad news—it's cancer!" I just stood there. I don't think I ever in my life experienced that kind of feeling of shock! No preparation! Everything stopped! It was as if I was stuck to the floor! I couldn't move! I couldn't speak! I knew that hospital well but I couldn't even think what floor Mark's room was on. I walked up and down the corridors aimlessly. Those ugly words—"it's cancer"—were repeated over and over in my mind. I tried to call home but I couldn't even remember my own phone number!

Although shock and disbelief were initial reactions, these were often closely followed by anger and hostility. And although these latter feelings were often initially overpowered by the numbness that overtakes one at these critical times, it was not long before intense anger revealed itself.

Anger manifests itself differently with mothers and fathers. With some fathers it may be expressed outward in the form of hostile actions directed toward the spouse, other children, and even the doctor. With others it may take the form of reckless driving or excessive drinking. It is culturally more acceptable for men than for women to express anger in these ways. The background and previous response patterns of the individual often are good indicators of the specific type of reactions one might expect.

Whereas fathers often direct anger outward, mothers often turn anger inward. It often takes the form of sarcasm, silence, withdrawal, demanding love and affection, and sometimes is also directed at other children. It also takes the form of guilt or self-blame for not having paid adequate attention to early warning signs or not having gone sooner to seek medical advice. This is understandable, since it is the mother who traditionally is given the role in the family of caretaker of the children's health. Mothers can find ample reasons to blame themselves for allowing this terrible illness to strike their child. After all, isn't it the job of all mothers to protect their children and keep them out of harm's way?

Fortunately, this sense of self-blame, which at first may constitute a very powerful and uncomfortable feeling, does not manifest itself openly for very long. Mothers usually find ways of dealing with their initial sense of blame by seeking reassurance from doctors and other experts that they were not responsible for their child's illness and that nothing they could have done would have prevented it. In fact, at the time of the diagnosis doctors often stress that nothing the mother, or father for that matter, did or did not do could in any way have prevented the outcome. Once parents are able to grasp hold of the reality of what the doctor is telling them, many are able to allay the outward feelings of guilt and self-blame. I say "outward" because many still carry remnants of guilt through most of the illness as well as for long periods after death. These remnants appear during the course of the illness as a kind of overindulgence, where discipline becomes lax and the child is perceived as being incapable of any wrong doing.

Friedman also points out that overindulgence and overprotective behavior on the part of the parents during the dying process may be a way of making up for early imagined neglect that parents—particularly mothers—believe they are responsible for.[3] (This point will be discussed in more detail later.)

Needless to say, the time of the diagnosis is a difficult event for parents to endure. Fortunately, for most it is not a lengthy ordeal. Within a relatively short period of time the initial feelings of shock, numbness, disbelief, anger, and hostility begin to get under rational control as physicians build treatment scenarios and as parents hear what modern medicine with all its wonders really has to offer.

At this point parents, with the doctor's input, begin to consider the odds for long-term survival and a unique hopeful change occurs in the parents' attitude toward the illness as well as an assessment of their own ability to deal with it. Thus begins another phase or period, as parents move from the diagnosis of the illness to the death of their child. This phase I will call the "interim" period, and it is this period that is usually the longest of the three phases I will discuss.

The Interim Period

As parents begin to recover from the devastating encounter with the diagnosis, their thinking undergoes a significant change. Generally by the next session with the doctor, when he or she begins to explain the full details of what this diagnosis means to them and to the child, the shock and numbness have begun to subside. The parents are ready now to take on this beast in full battle! At this point, thoughts of death and dying which may have been dominant earlier are no longer allowed to penetrate into their consciousness. Instead their thoughts now become filled with hope and visions of survival. They will not allow themselves consciously to contemplate what might occur should this disease take hold and fail to respond to treatment. They do not, and cannot, allow themselves to think in terms of the death of this child since that would mean surrendering to defeat.

During this interim period parents come to think of their child's condition in very positive terms. They operate under the assumption that all will be well. It is at this time that they rearrange their priorities and change their focus so as to concentrate on the present situation. They discard all future plans and future commitments. They live on a day-to-day basis, relying on whatever treatment protocol is recommended, and maintain a tenacious hope for their child's ultimate survival.

It is during this interim period that parents develop a tremendous need to know everything possible. They question, analyze, and search for information. This was a finding also revealed by Friedman.[4] Parents search for books, for other parents who may be experiencing similar problems; they shop for other specialists, other opinions—anyone or anything that may help clarify the situation as it is unfolding before them. They grope for anything that will help them understand what is happening to them and to their child. They search medical publications for survival rates, new treatment protocols, experimental drugs that may have been successful in other cases, even evidence of miraculous or spontaneous cures. Parents seem to develop an unbounded determination to lick this disease.

In many cases this unbridled optimism coupled with a sense of determined hope is passed on to the child, who becomes a reflection of the parents. This leads to a determination to survive that is difficult to penetrate even during the very last moments when death is pending.

As Guimond points out, parents are simply unprepared to deal with a terminal condition; therefore they are *unable* to think through the implications of its full meaning.[5] This is probably a good thing since it leads to a sense of confidence and support that makes treatment regimens, with their horrendous side effects, a bearable ordeal. A confidence in the future is necessary if one is mentally and physically to survive the adverse effects of chemotherapy.

Without hope in ultimate survival, families might assume that a cruel and inhumane hoax is being played on them by the medical profession, who for the sake of experimentation extract a "pound of flesh" before death is "allowed" to overtake their victims. Parents willingly agree to almost any treatment regimen suggested. And as each treatment regimen is begun, parents enter the situation with renewed vigor and renewed hope.

It is also during the interim period that parents enter a stage of emotional disengagement, where their emotional attachment to the child and his or her condition is moderated. In fact Friedman has indicated that while parents reduce their emotional involvement, at the same time they tend to increase their intellectual awareness. This may be due to the fact that parents are continuously surrounded by "concentric circles of disbelief," by grandparents, other relatives outside the family, close friends, and acquaintances.[6] Parents must control their emotional involvement; they are forced to assume the supportive role in the extended family and must present a unified front of confidence in order to stem a possible chaotic confrontation with other relatives and family. They must also assume the role of liaison with the school, teachers, and school friends.

Parents are at the forefront of the action, so to speak. They are in the trenches; they know what the situation is and must continually convey what they know to others who seek information from them. They are the only ones who really know what is going on. They recognize this; others recognize this. Parents do not really care for this role that has been thrust upon them by circumstances, but at the same time they assume it as their responsibility. Therefore they learn to be supportive and confident in their dealings with others. This requires an admirable amount of emotional control and an increase in intellectual awareness so that information can be transmitted reliably.

Most parents are unable to express their deepest feelings during this interim period. Even though some may feel great anxiety over what is happening to them and the events as they are unfolding, they will not allow themselves to think about the worst that could happen. Parents will make genuine, sometimes heroic, efforts to keep such thoughts from creeping into their consciousness. They try to keep their minds filled with positive thoughts of cures, remissions, and survival. The child becomes a precious commodity to be comforted, consoled, and protected.

Among these positive thoughts will be the belief that somewhere along the way a *new* treatment will be discovered or a *new* cure found that will result in a permanent remission or a spontaneous recovery. This was a modal characteristic of the parents who shared their experiences with me. It demonstrates the vitality of the kind of hope that parents displayed. In some cases parents even envisioned miraculous cures after all else failed. One mother prepared her 4-year-old daughter to receive her first communion two years ahead of schedule because she felt that a "healing" might occur at this time.

Nor was it unusual for parents to assume that their child would be the exception in a long line of failures. This, incidentally, was the kind of hope that sustained Martha over the seven months of Billy's downhill fight against the overwhelming odds of beating myelofibrosis. If you recall, Martha and Jim were told initially that only 30 cases had been reported in the United States since the 1950s; all were older and all died. There were no treatment protocols for children available at that time. Yet in spite of these gloomy predictions Martha's hope was beyond compare. She in turn passed on this confidence to Billy with such commitment that at the very end she had to persuade him to let go—she had to convince him that it was alright to die!

During the interim period parents suffer from a sense of helplessness but not necessarily a sense of failure. The helplessness is understandable since there is little one can personally do to make the situation less painful or more bearable. Helplessness is a common feeling that is shared by all who surrender their child to the trauma of treatment of a terminal illness. The child is taken from the parents and placed under the control of the large medical facility. This facility and the impersonal forces that drive it dominate not only the life of the patient but the lives of the parents as well. Jim Ausman, in Chapter 1, has commented on the feelings of helplessness and loss of control that dominate the attitudes of many parents as they begin the long journey forward.

Even though helplessness is a common feature of parents as they move through the interim period, a sense of failure is *not*, as long as parents are satisfied that they are doing all that is humanly possible. It is interesting to note that this is largely determined by their attitude toward their child's doctor and their judgment as to the quality of medical care the child is getting. To avoid a feeling of failure, the parents must believe that they have available to them the best medical care in the country. The knowledge that their child's doctors are in touch with the best treatment centers in the United States and Western Europe is invaluable in their efforts to remain optimistic.

The parents who talked with me were generally very satisfied with the physicians, nurses, office receptionists, treatment centers, and the various regimens recommended. All were important in building trust and confidence in the outcome. Many came ultimately to believe that their doctor would not let them down. They depended on him or her as a source of vital information about their child's condition. They believed that the doctor was doing his or her best and that modern medicine had a great deal to offer. Parents trusted the doctors so implicitly that they believed, with the vast storehouse of treatment techniques, remedies, and medicines, that he or she would not allow anything bad to happen to their child. It was not unusual for the parents to put all their eggs in the doctor's basket, which the physician then had to carry ever so delicately.

One might suspect that this overwhelming confidence in the doctor would prove to be detrimental to the doctor–parent relationship once it became apparent that the doctor could not save the child. However, even after death parents still upheld the efforts made on behalf of their child as remarkable, and could find no fault either with the doctor's efforts or with their own sustained determination to beat the disease. The fact that they failed in this regard was seen as not within their control. Hence a sense of confidence replaced a sense of failure—confidence that everyone did everything that could possibly have been done.

As parents enter the interim period and doctors begin to explain treatment protocols, parents hear what they want to hear. They pick out the best of what they hear. They grasp at rays of hope. Hope becomes their source of emotional support during this interim period.

As an example, parents of leukemic children literally live for remissions. It should be noted that leukemia is the nation's number one killer of children under age 12. The mere mention of the word itself can strike terror into the hearts and souls of parents. However, even though the diagnosis of leukemia can generate an intense emotional reaction, as doctors begin to explain the various treatment protocols and as parents begin to consider survival rates, they usually become highly encouraged and begin to hope, and plan for, a remission.

A remission is a period of time when drug therapies produce a virtual disappearance of all symptoms and the child appears cured. Remissions can last from a month or two to, in some cases, years. Some remissions have lasted as long as five years with children continuing in a state of remission and presumed cured.

During such a period parents often treat their children with a guarded optimism in the beginning. As the remission continues they grasp hold of the belief that the child is cured and no thoughts of death or even the possibility of dying are entertained. Leukemia is one of the few kinds of cancer where patients can be entirely symptom free for long periods of time.

What contributes to the parents' optimism and tenacious adherence to hope at such critical times is the doctor's explanation that with a remission chances of recovery improve dramatically. What parents may not understand is that once a relapse occurs—that is, when the patient comes out of remission or when the drug therapies fail to keep the patient in remission—chances for long-term survival fall drastically: from a 70–80 percent chance for survival for a leukemic child in a first remission to less than a 20 percent chance after relapse.

Although many doctors explain this to parents, as indicated, parents are selective in what they hear and a 70–80 percent survival rate after the first remission sounds pretty darn good!

The reason for this fall-off in rates of survival between the first remission and after relapse is easy to understand. In 70–80 percent of the leukemia cases a remission is achieved. Once the patient is in remission, the task is to keep him or her there. This is attempted through a vigorous drug and/or radiation treatment program. However, once a relapse occurs, modern medicine, at least the chemical therapies available, has little more to offer.

A remission of course relieves a lot of tension on the part of parents and patient. The patient's symptoms disappear. He or she feels good again, perhaps for the first time in weeks. The patient and family begin to return to normal activity. Many parents will not allow themselves to think beyond the remission. They live one day at a time, proceeding very cautiously at first, continuing to hope that it will be permanent. As the days drift into weeks and the weeks into months, both patient and parents may begin to allow themselves to believe that a cure is imminent. Their spirit and attitude continue to improve. Eventually, after several months with the remission still holding, they return to what life was before the diagnosis. Thoughts of fatal diseases, dying, and death are now farthest from their minds.

A relapse is devastating. At this point the parents and child are shocked back to the real world. Parents can indeed understand the difference now between an 80 percent chance of survival and a 20 percent chance. In fact many parents have said that the relapse is as emotionally traumatic to accept as the diagnosis, since at this point they are forced into a confrontation with the real possibility of losing the child, possibly very soon.

Perhaps surprisingly, though, hope is again rekindled as secondary treatment protocols are discussed. There is still faith in the ultimate cure—the miraculous cure. Parents continue to cling to this "possibility" with a tenacity that is difficult to understand. Perhaps it is all that sustains them during these critical times.

Nevertheless it becomes exceedingly difficult to keep thoughts of their child's death from seeping into their consciousnesses. They become less and less successful in avoiding confrontation with this possibility. Thoughts of the child's death do penetrate their hope with increasingly greater frequency than ever before.

During this time parents will use all sorts of ways to avoid a confrontation with the truth, as its threat is so great. These ways may be incorporated in what June Lowenberg calls "coping behavior,"[7] a phrase pertaining to all mechanisms used by an individual to meet a threat to his or her emotional stability and which allow the person to continue to function effectively.[8] Lowenberg divides coping behavior into two categories: (1) approach behaviors, designed to be effective in confronting reality; and (2) avoidance behaviors, designed to escape or deny reality.[9] The second of these—avoidance behaviors— seem to be a reaction of parents to the diagnosis of a fatal illness. Such behaviors carry a protective function. They allow the individual to escape—to deny—a reality that is too harsh to accept. Avoidance behaviors that extend into the interim period can, during this period, include a physical avoidance of everything that reminds one of the fact that the disease is fatal. Avoidance behaviors on the part of parents may in part explain the persistent adherence to intractable hope even after the odds for survival have dropped so drastically after the advent of a relapse.

During a remission, when parents are dealing with a symptom-free child and trying to reconcile this with conditions as they appeared earlier, avoidance behaviors may enter the area of "cognitive" distortion. Once parents begin cognitively to avoid the implications of this potentially fatal illness, there is no longer any reason to "cope." The person can feel comfortable and continue his or her daily routine without significant emotional disruption. Cognitive avoidance behaviors are the most extreme forms of coping behaviors.

Of course there can be no anticipatory grief work accomplished as long as denial and avoidance behaviors are operative. Only when avoidance behaviors are abandoned can the individual move through the process of grieving and emotionally *accept* the impending loss.[10]

As the condition of the child begins to deteriorate, which often occurs after relapse—sometimes very rapidly—and with survival rates so low, it becomes exceedingly difficult to maintain the facade of confidence that dominated the family's existence up to this time. And the unconscious conviction or knowledge that their child will die leads them to begin the slow and deliberate process of preparing the child for his or her ultimate demise. Even though this is done unconsciously at first, it is quite effective in its impact on the child.

Many parents are not entirely aware of just how they were able to prepare their child for his or her death until later, when they were able to assess their previous behavior more objectively.

How do parents accomplish this task of preparing their child for his or her own death? By various means. Let me briefly describe one way.

Children suffering from various forms of cancer usually attend local cancer clinics where their treatment and progress are closely and regularly monitored. There are always other children and other families involved. Many of the child's friends, particularly if he or she is young, are other children suffering from a similar malady.

Many parents begin here in preparing their child for his or her coming rendezvous with death. For example, one parent (a mother) talked with her 6-year-old son about "how neat heaven is." Heaven was defined as "a place where a lot of your little friends have gone. . . . It's a good place and your friends are very happy there. . . ." This mother also read to her son memorials of other children from the clinic who had died. She took him to the funerals of other children and then would spend considerable time talking with him about what he was feeling and what he was experiencing. The mother talked with him about how, in heaven, his friends would have no more pain, no more finger "sticks," no more sickness from the drugs. This mother said: "I really didn't fully realize what I was doing at the time. Looking back, I think I knew down deep that he was dying, although I would not openly admit it. I just knew I had to do something; I had to help him across the threshold. . . . I guess I was preparing Jimmy for his eventual death and, I guess, even myself." Through this kind of preparation, this mother managed to succeed in her endeavor.

There are other ways of preparing a child for death. For instance, as the child's condition worsens, parents often feel a sense of helplessness in that they cannot make it any better. They cannot alter the course of the disease. They cannot save their child from pain and discomfort, and they know unconsciously that they cannot save their child from death. So they adopt the view that it is up to them—the parents—to make the time remaining, however short it may be, the best ever! They will go to great lengths to make these times—the final days—as meaningful as possible. When such an effort is made, the final days will usually turn out to be times filled with sharing and love for the whole family. Taking that one "last" trip together to a favorite vacation spot is one example of how to make the last days meaningful while preparing the child to accept the end with a modicum of dignity. Even though it sometimes takes heroic effort on the part of parents to undergo these experiences at these critical times, there can be great rewards for both patient and family.

The Final Moments

As a parent, one is never really prepared for the end. One can never be. But this does not mean that the end has to be the devastation and destruction that it could be. As treatment protocols are worked through and the child continues to lose ground, one reaches a point where resignation begins to replace hope for survival. And the inevitable end comes slowly into focus.

It should be apparent that parental hope is not attached exclusively to survival but also to the way life is brought to an end. Lipton reports that the way the final moments of life are handled by parents, and the assurance that they can have some control over the final event, is also a part of the complex of hope that parents display.[11]

Therefore, when it finally becomes blatantly obvious to the parents that the child is fighting a losing battle, the character of their hope changes from hoping for survival to hoping for a full range of living in the time they have available and for a comfortable, pain-free death.

When the time comes, as it always does, when parents *consciously* accept the fact that death is imminent, when they know without any real doubt that their child is dying, they become totally absorbed in the life of that child. The dying child, now openly recognized by the family as dying, tends to dominate the family's time and interest.

Treatment regimens become unimportant and may even be stopped completely as parents come to the realization that nothing they can do will stave off the inevitable. Parents throw themselves into the task of making each day a memorable occasion. As one mother said: "You want each day to be neat; you want to make as many good memories as possible. . . . There is the realization that soon all you will have will be your memories! You somehow know that they should be good ones."

As parents develop a conscious awareness that the end is near, they find themselves "living" over and over in their imaginations their child's death. They are able to "see" in their mind's eye their child's actual death; they see themselves making funeral arrangements, selecting the casket, the clothes the child will wear, and the cemetery plot. They can imagine themselves at the funeral and can envision the sight of the child lying in the casket. All of these experiences are a part of the imaginary scenario that comes into focus as parents come to accept the truth that they are indeed losing forever this precious child.

As the end approaches, parents may wish to keep the child at home so he or she will not die in strange surroundings. This takes great courage and dedicated planning. However, this is a wish that is easier to verbalize than to actually satisfy. The decision to keep a child at home is so important that it should never be made until questions have been answered and potential problems anticipated and discussed.

When to stop all treatment and life support falls into this category. This is a decision that is enormously difficult for parents to make. But it is a necessary one if death is to overtake the child without the stress of artificial support. Ideally, the best way to make the decision is by means of a "team effort," with the parents an active and important part of that team. However, the physician will usually make the "final" decision.

Parents have a strong desire to have these few precious final moments alone with the child in the quiet and privacy of their home. Some parents are unprepared for events as they subsequently develop, with a result that can be very unsatisfactory.

As the child begins to struggle as death approaches, parents who have not been properly prepared may become frightened, and in their effort to respond with what they think is compassion may call in the rescue squad. Such a maneuver inevitably prolongs the end. The rescue team will do everything within their power to *forestall* death, which may include a painful tracheotomy, respirators, oxygen supplementation, and so on. The hospital, upon receiving the patient from a rescue unit, by law is usually required to continue these procedures. Thus the parents who, out of love and concern, initially made the decision to keep the child at home now find themselves back where they started.

They thought they had resigned themselves to their child's death but find now that they were unprepared for the experience. And now their child is being artificially maintained. It is not usual in these cases for a child to remain in a living-dying state—a comatose condition—for a much longer period of time than would have been the case had he or she remained in the home. This has the effect of prolonging the agony of separation for the parents as well as the agony of dying for the child.

The decision to keep a child at home during the final moments should not be made lightly. It can be a frightening experience for those unprepared. However, when proper procedures have been followed and where parents are adequately informed on what to expect and how to deal with problems as they arise, it can be an intimate experience for the parents and other children as well as a peaceful death for the child.

A time is reached in the struggle to keep alive their child when parents begin to ask "What are we doing to this child? What quality of life are we prolonging here?"

As we noted earlier, children exposed to the hostile side effects of chemical and radiation therapy often change dramatically in appearance and vitality. As the disease progresses they deteriorate badly, physically and sometimes mentally. Sometimes the drugs he or she is receiving become the child's worst enemy. One father discussing the treatment protocols his 13-year-old daughter went through talked about what he referred to as "recall," in which a "last-resort" medication brought back—recalled—all side effects the child had experienced in the past.

It appears that in some cases the child's death may be more difficult due to the devastating effects of prolonged treatment regimens, maintained in the blind hope that something will work in spite of overwhelming odds against it.

So parents come to the point where it becomes increasingly more difficult for them to continue this assault on the child's body with no real hope for survival. Parents begin to ask themselves "Why are we trying so hard to prolong the life of this child? Are we doing it for him/her or for us?" The hope for a "new" cure or a miraculous cure becomes defined as senseless and selfish.

Contemplations and thoughts of the child's death begin to enter into their consciousness. How will it happen? Will the child know when it is approaching? Will the child be in any discomfort or pain? Will he or she be frightened? These become inescapable concerns. Many tears will be shed as this time approaches. The stress and strain will be overpowering. Many parents will begin the tortuous process of consciously thinking about making some sort of preliminary arrangements. They will now begin to contemplate selecting the casket, the gravesite, and the funeral itself. Such contemplations cause visible, excruciating pain, but they are inescapable.

As the child continues to deteriorate physically, parents lament on the quality of life that is being prolonged. They ask the question "What kind of life are we sustaining?" When parents reach the point where they can ask such a question, the answer is quickly at hand! Inevitably a decision is made to terminate all but pain-relieving medication. The result is that death, by now more a friend than an enemy, approaches rapidly.

When one finally reaches this stage and is able to make the decision to terminate all further treatment and let the disease take its course, there is a peace felt—a sense of tranquility—that is difficult to understand by those not experiencing this kind of dilemma. It is the peace and tranquility that come when parents accept whatever God or fate deals them.

It is at this point in the process that parents and other family members openly begin to grieve and mourn for the child, as they have truly accepted the inevitable. There is no more pretense, no more denying, no more hope for survival. The only hope one has now is hope for a peaceful death. It is now that parents actually begin to make the final arrangements, to buy the casket and the gravesite, and to plan the details of the funeral ceremony itself—who will give the sermon, who will serve as pallbearers, etc.

Others, who have not been a part of the long process of care, who have never suffered the emotional upheavals that parents have as they followed their children down the long, dark, corridors toward death, often do not understand this response. It is only when you hurt so badly and when your child hurts so badly that you can make the decision to end treatment and begin to make final plans for surrendering this child to death. It is not "giving up," as some outside the situation might say; it is instead "giving in" to what is ultimately the best course for the child and for the family.

When parent-survivors are able to face the inevitable and follow through with what needs to be done, the oft-repeated cliché "God never takes a child without the parents' consent" becomes somewhat accepted and understood. They are ready to release their hold.

As has already been indicated, sometimes parents must take on the painfully hard task of telling the child that it is alright to let go, it is alright to stop fighting, it is alright to die! Sometimes parents must encourage their child to die, as Martha did with Billy at the very last. They must help them achieve a release from this life.

We know that people can control the time of their departure and even postpone death because they simply have not received *permission* to die. We all have it within our power to delay death, at least to some extent, if we are not ready to give up. It is no different for children. They too can postpone the inevitable if they think their parents and other important people in their lives are not ready for them to die.

Giving permission to die is not hard to do. Sometimes all it takes is gentle encouragement from parents, gentle persuasion that all has been done that there is to do, that nothing more remains.

One mother told of the way she handled the final days in the life of her 4-year-old daughter, Cindy, suffering from leukemia, and how she found a way to prepare her for death and in fact to give her permission to die. It was the hardest task she had to face during the two years of Cindy's illness. But she felt that she needed to do this, she needed to help her daughter confront this inevitable event in her short life. This mother said:

One day I was alone with her. She was so sick and weak. I knew I had to do it soon. But how to do it? That was the question! How do I prepare a four-year-old child to die? She was lying on her bed in her room. I sat down next to her and said, "Cindy, I have something I want to tell you." She turned and looked at me with tears in her eyes. I said, "I know you have been feeling bad for quite a few months now. You can't play anymore; you can't go to nursery school anymore; you can't go to Sunday school anymore; you can't dance anymore. But there is a real special place you can go and pretty soon you will be going there. Do you know where that place is, Cindy?" She thought for a moment, then said "Heaven?" I said, "That's right!" Then I told her about all the people she would see there, all her little friends, and her grandparents. "They will be waiting for you," I told her. She had been listening very intently. Then, forcing back my own tears, I said, "But before you go to heaven, Cindy, you first have to die!" She just looked at me and said, "Oh, Mommy, I know that!" And I got the feeling she really *did* know and was now so glad that I knew too! It was no longer a secret that she had to keep. She seemed so relieved that she no longer had to protect me.

I saw a definite change in her after that. She became less agitated and seemed more comfortable. We talked a lot about heaven and about what she would shortly experience. She died four days later, and I am so glad now that I found the strength to do what I did. She seemed to experience a freedom upon discovering that at last I knew what she had apparently known for a long time.

In the next chapter the reader will be introduced to a profound event in the lives of parents—the sudden death of a child. The chapter will attempt to show how the trauma of sudden death produces devastating effects on parents as well as on the family organization.

4

Sudden Death: A Study in Disbelief

Impossible to Find the Words

How can parental response to the sudden and unexpected death of a child be defined? The event is so dramatic that it almost defies description. Parents who had been through the agony of sudden loss experienced great difficulty describing their reactions. They pointed to the inability to find the "right" words to convey the depth of their responses. They used such phrases as: "It was hell!" "It was insane!" "It was unbelievable!" "It was numbing!" Or they said: "I don't have the words!" "I was in a daze!" "I was in shock!" "I can't comprehend what happened!" "I can't feel anything!"

Questions also appeared: "How can we cope with this?" "What am I going to do?" "Can you help me?" "Can anyone help me?" "Is this what life is going to be like?" "How can I possibly go on?" "How am I going to survive?" And of course the inevitable "Why me?" "Why my child?" These were desperate questions! And the answers they were able to conjure up were weak and unsatisfactory compared to the power and strength of the questions. The rage from within was overwhelming—"If only someone will help me find an answer!!"

It was true, as the parents themselves admitted, that they really did *not* have the words to relate their precise feelings and emotions at the time of the sudden and surprising deaths of their children, or even now, after some months or years have passed. These events were so devastating that even after they had had some time to reconstruct the sequence of happenings in their minds, they were still unable to describe fully their emotional responses. It is as if they were continuing to protect themselves by being unable to recall precisely their reactions, since these reactions were so debilitating to their psychological stability.

By sudden death, I mean generally any death that occurs without warning, such as by accident, where death follows rather quickly and where there is no anticipation.

It should be noted that in 1976 in the United States 12,000 children between the ages of 1 and 14 died from injuries. This represents 50 percent of all deaths in this age range.[1] Thus it was not surprising that accidental deaths represented the largest category of loss in the study group. Over 45 percent of the sample reported that their losses were due to accidents resulting in fatal injuries.

However, "sudden death" as a category can also include cases where the child has died from an acute illness such as Reye's Syndrome, or from unexpected heart seizure or stroke or any other type of acute critical disorder. Homicide may also, quite obviously, be a form of sudden death.

The determining factor is whether the death is in any way expected or anticipated. Generally in the case of sudden death there was no time to anticipate, no time to plan. Such losses, therefore, always extracted more severe forms of response. They took families by surprise. Suddenly their world was turned upside down. Life would never be the same again. *They* would never be the same again. And since all this happened suddenly—striking like a tornado—leaving the family in shambles, there was no time for a careful accounting of resources that under other circumstances might have been available to families to help them rebuild their shattered form.

As was noted in a previous chapter, in the case of death after a long illness, parents were more successful in their attempt to describe and work through consequences of their loss. Such losses were still bitter experiences, but the element of anticipation and the ability to plan softened the impact. Parents had a period of time—in some cases a long period—to work through their feelings. They were usually better able to verbalize their reactions.

For many parents experiencing death after a protracted illness, there were weeks, sometimes months of anticipatory mourning so that they gradually prepared themselves for their loss. Their behaviors appeared less disorganized and confused, and lent themselves more to later scrutiny and analysis. Words, indeed, could be found to describe the anticipated feelings and emotional reactions of those who had the opportunity to prepare.

With sudden death, this was never the case. As stated, there was no preparation possible. There was no lead time. There was no anticipatory mourning involved. It was rather a "surprise" attack on one's psyche, a frontal assault on one's ego. Parental responses were disorganized, inappropriate, confused, defying adequate and meaningful description.

The situation did not improve with time. The more time that passed, the more difficult it became to remember the confusion and disorganization and emotions, and the harder it became to put it all into words.

Piecing It Together

Listening to parents freely associating about what sudden death meant to them really did not tell us much. Their verbal responses did not really convey the depth of emotion felt. It was apparent that behind their utterances was a hotbed of smoldering pent-up disbelief, anguish, despair, anger, pain, and guilt. These emotions appeared to lie just out of view or out of reach, revealed only at fleeting times above the controlled exteriors portrayed for the sake of the interview. However, if perceptive, one could catch glimpses of the boiling caldron within. Faces were stern and blotched, with clenched teeth and an ocean of tears just behind glazed eyes, creating a glassy, puffy appearance.

It would have been apparent to anyone sitting across a table from these parents that they were indeed suffering intense *pain*, emotional and physical.

Most were there because they believed that the project was important. Besides, someone had agreed to listen and they felt that they would at last have an opportunity to talk.

However, when it came to questioning them about how they reacted to the death, to describing the state of their emotions and how they felt and what they experienced at the time of the loss, they had difficulty responding. It was as if they were forced to relive those scenes again. This was something they simply could not or would not do. So they resorted to statements described earlier—meaningful, but helpful only by inference—in building an understanding of how the sudden loss of a child affected those left behind.

Apparently the mind has a way of protecting the self from too harsh a reality. We all have the ability, through the operation of the psychological defense mechanism of denial, to reject something that is too threatening to our system to absorb all at once. Denial is a very prominent defensive reaction in the case of sudden death. Even months later this coping mechanism was still operating, as manifested in the continuing inability to "remember" precisely the pain and anguish experienced at the time.

Thus many parents seemed to lose the ability to communicate accurately about this initial period. Even after a reasonable length of time they still could not recall or relate how they handled the situation at the time of the loss itself. The usual response was: "I really can't recall what I experienced"; or "I think about it every day but I simply can't tell how I felt"; or "I guess I was in a state of shock—I don't really know"; or "I think you can imagine what we went through, can't you?" or "I can't really put it into words"; and so on.

Such responses were very similar to the reactions of parents to the murder of their children, a problem to be investigated in the next chapter.

The sudden death of a child is so unbelievable, so utterly shocking, so devastating, so traumatic, that denial, characterized by a numbing of the emotions and a dulling of the senses, becomes the dominant reaction, which in turn leaves the individual at a later time with little recall of his or her emotional state.

One mother, whose 14-year-old son was killed in a hunting accident, illustrates the general inability of many parents to express themselves. Her response is typical of others in similar circumstances:

The days and weeks following Pete's death are all a hazy blur—a horrible nightmare that I now can only catch glimpses of. We were so unprepared! This grief, which we had never known before, was inescapable. It followed us everywhere—every moment of every day. Absolutely nothing would dull the pain. This is really all that I can recall, all that I can remember—that terrible unrelenting pain!

I do not mean to imply that the inability to relate and describe accurately one's emotional response to the death of a child was a universal feature of all who suffered such losses, only that it was a common or modal characteristic and something that had to be interpreted.

In order to weave together the loose threads of feelings and experiences into a tapestry of meaning that might be relevant for understanding the aftermath of sudden death, it was necessary to try to extrapolate from other information. We had to *infer* how parents responded and how they felt and what they experienced from the way they described what they believed took place at the time of the loss and in the aftermath. Talking with different family members and questioning them about what they *observed* at the time—rather than how they *felt* or what they personally experienced—helped reconstruct a scenario of events and inferred emotional reactions as these unfolded among the various participants at the time of the loss itself.

Listening and Learning

There is something we need to remember about the event of child death. Even though the sudden death of a child was so traumatic that it masked the parents' ability to see and understand their own responses and feelings, it nevertheless left an indelible imprint on them. The eyes and ears forever recorded the sights and sounds of the events and situations in which they were enmeshed. They saw and remembered every detail of this horrendous occurrence. My interviews with these families left no doubt about this. Individuals could recall every detail of what they *saw* and what they *heard,* even though they could not adequately describe how they *felt.*

Thus I received valuable information from spouses and siblings relative to what they observed. Even though they were in a state of shock and denial regarding their own emotional states, and could seldom recall their own behavior and reactions, they had little difficulty recalling the behavior and, through inference, the feelings and emotional responses of others.

For example, here is another excerpt from interviews with two parents—a father and a mother, interviewed on separate occasions—describing their own reactions and the reactions of the spouse at the time of receiving the news of the accidental death of their son two years before. Here are their responses to the questions "What was your first feeling or reaction upon hearing of the death of your son?" and "How would you describe your wife's (husband's) response?"

[*Husband, regarding himself*] It's hard to say . . . disbelief, I guess . . . shock. . . . I was numb, I know that! I don't really know what I did or what I said. It's so hard to think about that time. It was so painful!

[*Husband, regarding his wife*] I know she went absolutely berserk! I have never seen Edith in such a state. I had to hold her up. She couldn't seem to get her balance. . . . I remember her just screaming at the sheriff's deputy who was standing in the doorway. . . . She kept saying, "No! No! No!—it's not true, it's not true!" It must have been at least twenty minutes before she was able to get control of herself. . . .

[*Wife, regarding herself*] I remember saying something to the officer upon hearing the news. . . . To this day I don't know what it was. . . . I couldn't think—I couldn't do anything! It's really hard to describe. . . .

[*Wife, regarding husband*] Van cried—he just started to weep, heavily. . . . I remember him hanging on to me. . . . I felt I needed to support him. . . . He was so broken up. He didn't say anything—he just cried and cried. In fact, for most of the evening he just paced the floor, crying on and off. . . .

Here we see two somewhat different views of each other's behavior upon hearing the news of their son's death. Although these quotes are taken out of context, they do tell us something of the way these parents reacted to the news—not from their personal accounts, which did not tell us much, but from a description of the observations each makes of the other. Much of what we know about the way parents handle the sudden death of children is gleaned through this type of accounting and reporting.

Written Accounts

There is another source of information available that helps us obtain an understanding of the parental response to sudden death. Some parents turned to pen and paper to express what could not be expressed in any other way. These written accounts were not available from all who experienced sudden losses, but the few that I had access to proved to be a rich source of data.

It is hard to generalize to the larger issues on the basis of the relatively small sample of writings that came to my attention in the course of the interviews. However, I feel that they are important and should be accepted as valid. They were produced after careful thought and assessment, and many were written very close in time to the actual death, when thoughts and perceptions were fresher. There is also another reason to accept these writings as valid accounts of feelings and reactions: when one sits down to write about a painful tragedy, one is obviously *trying* to remember—trying to recall—and is most likely making every effort to circumvent denial.

Judith was able to respond in writing to the tragedy of losing her 16-year-old son in an automobile accident. She said she felt that this was the only way she could adequately express herself. She would often write late into the evening. She said that it was still too painful to talk about but she could put in on paper. Here are some rather lengthy excerpts from her writings, which filled over 30 pages, expressing her recollection of the accident. As you read this account, you can almost feel the pain just as she must have felt it at the time. She wrote:

As I drove down the familiar narrow road about a mile from our home, I came upon what appeared to be a very serious automobile accident, which had apparently just occurred minutes before. My heart pounded and my breath was literally taken away as I sat in my car, my maternal instincts telling me that my son was involved. . . .

Running toward the scene, I became aware of several familiar faces who were trying to stop me. I knew from the looks on their faces what had happened. As I approached the wreck, I thought "Is that our car?" My God, it was our car! It was our car! I began to feel very light-headed and sick at the same time. A policeman was standing there looking through a wallet. I knew! I knew! Oh, Howard! Howie!! My beautiful boy—just 16 years, 8 months, and 10 days into his life—was dead! He was dead!! Killed instantly, coming home from school! . . .

I vaguely remember the officer telling me how his wheels had gone off the deep shoulder on this rough stretch of road. He lost control, hit a culvert, and the car overturned, throwing him onto the road, the impact snuffing out his precious life! Howard was dead! But how could that be true? It must be a mistake! Then the officer said again, "Your son is dead!" Oh God, it was no mistake! My beautiful son is dead! . . .

The officer asked me how to contact my husband and I took a crumpled piece of paper with the telephone number on it from my billfold. I remember picking up Howard's school papers and books which were blowing all over the the road. I remember a TV camera focusing on my face to get a story for the evening news. I remember some dear friends trying desperately to give some morsel of support. I also remember my thoughts: "Dear Lord, please let me die! This is the one thing I cannot handle and You know it. Why couldn't it have been me?" These must be the thoughts of all parents who lose a child in this way. I wondered how I was ever going to live without him! . . .

I wondered how my dear husband could ever handle the loss of this precious boy—his firstborn child and one of the loves of his life. And how Keith, our 14-year-old, could lose his constant lifetime companion. . . .

Somehow I got myself home, and as I was opening the back door the phone was ringing. It was my husband, Howard, wanting to speak with Howie! My numb silence betrayed me, and my husband asked, "Honey, has Howie been killed?" The call he received from the highway patrol had made him suspicious. I could not keep it from him, even with the distance between us. I will never forget his cries of anguish and how I wanted to hold him and say it wasn't true! His friend brought him home about the same time our son Keith arrived. For the next several hours, Howard, Keith, and I lay together on the bed, holding each other in total silence. The tears would be a long time coming as the pain was so, so intense. . . .

The next few weeks were so difficult for us all. I would mentally picture the three of us as the main supports of a teepee, all leaning together and each one dependent on the others for support. The days were such an effort to get through and the nights were sleepless exhaustion. Each 24-hour period we went through was a victory. I was totally convinced that life would never again hold any of the happiness and joy I had known, and that *death* would be the only way out! I remember thinking of the terrible labor pains I had felt at Howie's birth—the worst pain I had ever felt in my life—until his death! Then I found out what pain really was! Pain inflicted on the heart is far worse than pain inflicted on the body. . . .[2]

Reading what Judith experienced helps us to understand the depth of her reactions and feelings. She was trying to relate to us the impact that this death had on her life—a task she found difficult to do without the aid of pen and paper.

Another mother attempted to relate in writing her feeling about the sudden death of her teenage son. She writes about a *word*—a word we all have used and one we all assume we know the meaning of. The word is *pain;* this mother tells what pain means to her. She writes:

There are certain words used over and over in reading material, lectures, and conversations to describe what we, as bereaved parents, are going through. You know—"pain," "anger," "hurt"—you hear them everywhere. I've heard them so often they have become patronizing. They are just cardboard words stuck on paper pages. Let's bring them alive again. Let's dust off the metaphors and try to express what they *really* mean. . . .

Take *pain*, a four-letter word, and you know what that means. Pain to me is symbolized by a crystal knife and a pot of fire! They assault my body every night as my mind searches for peace. It has been two years and four months since my son—my "sonshine"—was brutally put to death when his motorcycle carried him unknowingly into the side of a large boat being transported on a dark road on a dark night at 45 miles an hour. A large object, totally unseen, just appearing out of nowhere abruptly halting his trip home, two blocks away. Just two blocks to safety. . . .

Two years and four months of feeling my body in his body, flying—surprised—through the air. Every night I feel the sticky warmth of my blood draining on the pavement. Every night I feel my bones break; I hear my bones—his bones—break. My foot, which has lost its boot, grows cold in the cool air. The crystal knife turns its jagged edges in my heart and the fire pot explodes in my gut as I try not to shake the bed as I cry so as not to disturb my husband's sleep. The crystal knife keeps turning as I hear the siren screaming like a frightened child through the cool southern air racing its way to the depository to have my beloved son's toe tagged DOA. . . .

I leave my bed to walk the quiet streets . . . or to look out some window on the cool night air—the cool, once-friendly, southern air that has since become my enemy—a constant reminder of that other night two years and four months ago. The simple question "Why?" keeps raping my mind again and again! That jagged crystal knife, that hellish fire pot is still with me. It's a living thing—killing me from the inside out. It has ravaged my beliefs and destroyed my personality. . . .[3]

This mother, in her writings, also indicated that she eventually found some peace from the ordeal of her loss. Her salvation came in the form of a self-help support group which she joined soon after her son's death. This group, consisting of parents like herself, became her weapon in the war she waged in her battle for survival. And although she wrote vividly of the agony and pain of loss, she was among the fortunate few who found new friends who care.

Why?

One of the problems parents had with sudden death was to find answers to the question "Why?" One of the reasons these deaths were so difficult to deal with was the fact that they were so incomprehensible. Such deaths are defined as senseless and even avoidable. *If* the child had been at a different place or had left the house a minute or two earlier or later, or *if* the parent had been more observant of developing symptoms, or *if* the child had done this or that instead of what was done, parents reasoned, he or she might still be alive. Accidents, particularly, were not always defined as unavoidable. It was also easy to attach blame in case of sudden death if some fulminating disease process was involved—blame for not recognizing early symptoms. Therefore "Why—why did this happen to my child?"

and "Could I have prevented this?" became questions every parent asked.

Even though such questions were basically unanswerable, they seemed to impinge upon, if not dominate, the thought patterns of many parents for weeks, months, and sometimes years. They riddled the mind and complicated the grieving process.

The Character of Grief

As stated earlier, sudden death generated a different kind of grief—a harsher variety—than in the case of a death after a long-term illness. Accidental deaths and other kinds of sudden loss were particularly difficult to handle because there was no anticipatory mourning involved which had the effect of softening the blow. In cases of sudden death, parents often reacted with intense shock, numbness, disbelief, total confusion, and denial. These represented essentially "insulating" emotions; they tended to insulate or protect the individual from facing the reality of the loss all at once. Parents were not fully cognizant of what was happening, and therefore were at the time, and are now, still incapable of describing their place in the events.

As parents moved through the experience, other feelings and emotions came to dominate. Helplessness, intense anxiety, feelings of impending doom came into sharp focus. These were followed by feelings of emptiness, aimlessness, hollowness. Within a short period came additional sensations of intense irritability, bitterness, and gut-wrenching sadness and sorrow. Anger—intense anger—also appeared, sometimes directed at the child. Parents began to experience a loss of patterns of conduct. Interpersonal relationships became disrupted. Feelings of "coming apart" and "falling to pieces" were also common. They could find no solid ground. There were no anchorages in this wild storm that swept in from nowhere.

Physical symptoms soon appeared, taking the form of a loss of appetite or loss of sleep or constant fatigue. Somatic complaints became common: headaches, heart palpitations, stomach problems, and agonizing pain in the chest.

Guilt and self-blame often consumed parents throughout the entire ordeal. Later on, depression coupled with a deep sense of loneliness, accompanied by thoughts of death and self-destruction, became the mode of response.

These symptoms became overpowering and stretched into weeks and months. Parents were so inundated by the ferociousness of the onslaught that they often thought they were becoming mentally unstable, that they were losing their minds!

Fay Harden, co-leader of the Tuscaloosa, Alabama, chapter of The Compassionate Friends and editor of its newsletter, has written on her conceptions of what many parents experience in the aftermath of sudden death. I would like to quote a section of her writing that appeared in a recent issue of *The Compassionate Friends Newsletter*, St. Louis Chapter. Fay recently lost her 21-year-old son in a motorcycle accident, so she is writing a firsthand account. She said that in sudden death:

Emotional or psychological shock is . . . of unfathomable proportions. Initially, there is alarm because in an instant our whole lives are changed; there is disbelief, the overwhelming reality is more than we can comprehend, we think there must be a mistake! Often we experience a numbness and later we go through this feeling of numbness again and it may last for weeks or months. We feel dazed and sometimes this is a blessing; it prevents our having to face all the consequences of the death at once; it is as if we are under an anesthetic. If we had to face our total pain all at once, how could we survive? . . .

There are tears and depression; we relive the events surrounding the death over and over. Usually, by this time our family and friends have gone back to their own lives and we are alone with this awful burden of grief. At this time, the highly emotional experience may cause us to think we are mentally unstable, that we are losing our minds! . . .

With sudden death, there is usually a feeling of guilt. It may be self-imposed or real. We remember punishments that were unresolved, arguments that were not reconciled, and there is always the question of: could I have prevented it? We ask ourselves the question "Why?" over and over, sometimes for years, sometimes for a lifetime. The question is unanswerable and, being unanswered, we go on pursuing it. Why did my child die? Why did this happen to me? . . .

In sudden death, we have no chance for closure, no chance to say goodbye. This adds to the burden as we think of what we could have or should have done. Recovery and identification of the body is an important part of closure. . . . I know that in the area of Portland there are still people missing and presumed dead from the Mt. St. Helens eruption, leaving those parents with an added factor to their grief. This is also true of survivors of war tragedies. "Seeing for yourself" is a needed part of . . . closure. Without it, we fantasize that someday we will find the child. Grief is intensified when no body is found. . . .

The circumstances of sudden death cause loneliness. Few people can identify with us because our circumstances are practically unique. This uniqueness isolates us. Therefore, persons suffering traumatic grief [of sudden death] have greater need for fellowship with other people. We must reach out and find people to be with. . . .

Another of our severe problems is often anger, which might better be described as rage! It can be focused anger—focused on individuals who were responsible for the death of our child, at medical personnel whom we feel did not do the right things to save our child, at God for letting this happen to our child, even at people around us whose lives are happy and whose children are healthy. . . . You may even feel anger at your child for dying and leaving you with such a burden. . . .

Or it may be unfocused anger. This type of anger usually turns into depression, anger turned inward. Combine this anger/depression and isolation and you have the makings of a suicidal personality! . . .

With the [sudden] death of a child, we as parents experience the ultimate failure—we are supposed to be invincible where our children are concerned and now *we have failed to keep our child alive*! Suddenly our belief system is shattered. The suddenness of the death has robbed us of our confidence in ourselves, we have . . . [lost our] self-esteem. . . . We have nothing left to believe in, not even God for some. We are totally insecure. . . .[4]

This excerpt from Fay's writing places in perspective the agonizing ordeal that parents encounter with the sudden death of a child.

The idea of closure, noted in the above quotation, is especially important in resolving the grief of sudden death. Parents must be given the opportunity to see and touch the child before burial. As Fay pointed out, the family must "see for themselves"; they must have the opportunity to stroke the child and say their good-byes; otherwise the resolution of grief will be difficult to achieve.

Parents who suffer the shock of sudden death pay their dues all at once, rather than a little at a time! As another mother stated:

That's a big chunk of reality to deal with *all at once*. . . . It's like a vicious tornado that sweeps in out of the blue and devastates your life before you realize what has happened! It's no wonder why so many cannot handle it. . . . You feel as though you're losing your mind and there's not a damn thing you can do about it! . . .

Such a momentous "chunk of reality"—this "vicious tornado"—was many times impossible for families to swallow. This is what led to the tendency to *deny*. They actually developed a "protective shield" around themselves and did not allow anything or anyone to penetrate it, sometimes for weeks and even months. The big chunk of reality was also what led to the zombie-like behavior so characteristic at these critical times. Family members walked around in a daze, unable to respond to outer stimuli, unable to fulfill their normal roles. Often, many of the family's needs went unmet. Parents were simply too preoccupied with maintaining, unconsciously, this protective wall. They failed to perform their required activities relative to other members of the family. Child-care functions collapsed. Sexual incompatibilities were encountered due to the inability of each spouse to penetrate the protective membrane within which the other functioned. Nothing really worked anymore. Everything—all family activities—seemed to come to a halt as long as this shielding was in place. As one father said:

I was in a world all my own . . . and I would not allow *anyone* to enter it! Looking back now, I can see what I was doing. I was trying to comprehend— trying to find some meaning to it all. And until I came to terms with the questions that flooded my mind, I was not about to let anyone enter that special sphere within which I functioned.

This reaction was indeed typical. And it was a part of the "normal" patterns of prebereavement behavior associated with sudden death. I say "pre"-bereavement because such responses actually *preceded* the grief experience. In fact there can really be no grief expressed until one is able to rid oneself of this "protective cocoon." Parents cannot reach to the depths of feelings required to begin to express emotion until shock and disbelief are dissipated, until the event becomes "believable" and comprehensible to them.

Obstacles to Recovery

It was not uncommon for the phase of shock and disbelief to last for months. In fact in my conversations with some families it was suspected that certain members still—at the time of the interview—were unable to deal with the reality of the loss even though in some cases years had passed since the death.

It seemed that certain kinds of behavior served as protective barriers to dealing with the reality of sudden death. Perhaps I can ennumerate some of them:

1. Parents sometimes found it impossible to disturb in any way the child's room or favorite place in the home. They also had enormous difficulty disposing of personal belongings. Many times personal things and the room were kept intact and parents came to view them as having an almost sacred quality. They surrounded themselves with many reminders of the child, in many cases turning the home into a kind of shrine. The child was conceived of as still "living" in the home; his or her "presence" was felt everywhere.

Of course such a response is *normal* for a time and should not be viewed with alarm. When carried beyond several months, however, it often interfered with the development of effective behaviors necessary to complete the grief work. I think that for some parents the child never dies.

2. Parents sometimes avoided all reminders of the child. Clothes were packed away, out of sight; pictures were placed in drawers; rooms were sealed; the child's school and friends were avoided. Sometimes even a new residence was sought. Anything and anyplace that might have contained a memory was avoided. Parents often felt that this was the only way they could handle the situation. And as long as such an avoidance reaction was in place, there could be no way effective grief work could be accomplished.

So, whereas some parents tried to live in the past, as noted above, by attempting to keep every aspect of the home just as it was at the time of death, others tended to *reject* the past. Either case proved to be a barrier to the resolution of grief.

3. Another obstacle was the tendency on the part of parents to idealize or "canonize" the child, refusing to recognize faults. Under these circumstances the child became bigger than life and came to occupy a "saintly" place in the family. This reaction often created and intensified other family problems, such as the tendency to reevaluate the place of other siblings in the family. Parents often took a highly critical view of sibling behavior when placed in comparison with that of the dead child. This caused great consternation and resentment from siblings and resulted in important incongruencies in the "family" response to child death.

4. Sometimes for months after a sudden loss parents refused to be comforted. They tended to seek ways to prolong the sadness and pain. Although on the surface this appeared to be a way of "working

through" the grief experience, this was *not* the intent of this deliberate refusal to surrender the pain and agony. For some parents, "suffering" was their way of maintaining a linkage with the dead child! When they felt pain and sadness, when they cried, when they experienced the agony—they were remembering! And as pointed out in Chapter 2, the need to remember was paramount. However, the refusal to be comforted, the refusal to allow the pain to subside, the refusal to smile and enjoy some aspects of life, even after months had passed, represented an obstacle to the resolution of grief. A few even said that they wanted to grieve for a lifetime!

5. Sometimes the pain was so great that, rather than develop essential coping mechanisms, the parent turned to drugs or alcohol for relief and escape. Only a small number of parents in the study group actually responded in this way, and in most of these cases it was a temporary reaction. In those few cases where this response pattern became long term, it served as an effective block to grief work. Parents believed that they were coping while engaging in this kind of escape; however, this was always a myth. There was no progress until they were able to rid themselves of this very destructive form of behavior. In fact, where it persisted as a behavior, it often destroyed the family system.

Existing Somewhere Else

Before closing this chapter, it is important to note one additional response pattern associated with the death of a child. This reaction was also found among those parents responding to death after a long illness, but it was especially noticeable after sudden loss. It could be construed as a way of coping.

A significant number of parents tended to reject the idea of total annihilation of children. This revealed itself in the ability of parents to conceive of deceased sons or daughters as "existing somewhere else." In this way death, in the sense of final separation, was avoided.

Conceiving of the child as "living" or existing somewhere else seemed to place a lighter burden on the parent, making the whole affair somewhat easier to fathom. The ability to formulate these conceptions usually did not come until after the initial shock of the loss had passed; that is, the idea was formed gradually during the months and, in some cases, years that followed the sudden death.

Children were "not really dead," at least not in the profoundest sense, but were simply existing elsewhere! They were away from the home, to be sure, but many times children leave home, sometimes for prolonged periods. The survivor's grief becomes bearable under this kind of conceptualization. Just as the family will accept that a son or daughter will spend the summer at the grandparents' or the winter at a boarding school or a year away at college, so they accepted departure and separation brought about by death and allowed it to be defined in the same way. By conceptualizing the child as existing—"living," if you will—someplace else, death became bearable!

Let me give a concrete example of how this myth manifested itself. In two independent cases I encountered fathers who were emotionally unable to accept the deaths of their sons, even though two and three years respectively had passed. Both boys were killed in auto accidents, one at the age of 18 and the other at 19. The fathers admitted to me their inability to accept the losses. Intellectually they knew their sons were dead and would never return, and they could live with that on the intellectual level. Emotionally, however, they were unable to fathom the losses. One of the fathers said that he simply thinks of his son as being away at college. He of course misses his son terribly, but could deal with his absence from the home only by considering him to be at another "place." This father recognized this "fiction" as being "not very healthy," as he put it, but at the same time he indicated that it was the "only way" he could handle it. The other father also thought of his son as simply "being away" from home. He said that his son was old enough to be "on his own" and that this is how he conceptualized the loss. Both fathers would not allow themselves to even *think* consciously of the possibility that they would never again see their sons. It was as if they did not allow themselves to think that far ahead! They could deal only with the *present* and that seemed to be the way they preferred it.

One may wonder how much longer such a myth can be perpetuated, and the kind of explosive reaction likely to follow when it is finally dissipated and these fathers come face to face with reality.

As I talked with these fathers, I could feel the growing emotional pain that hovered behind their controlled exteriors. The very fact that they came forward and agreed to share with me indicated an increasing inability to adhere to this myth.

Generally, the most common "place" where the child was conceived to be existing was defined in religious terms. The place was "heaven" or an "afterlife" of sorts, and the son or daughter was defined by the parent as "living" there. Grandmother or grandfather or "my brother who died last year" was also conceived of as "being there" and as looking after the deceased child.

In addition, associated with this conceptualization was evidence of the revival of a definite religious orientation on the part of the parents—a renewal or intensification of their faith. (Some evidence of this was discussed in Chapter 2, and will be discussed again, as a way of coping, in Chapter 9.) Incorporated within this revitalization of faith was the firm belief that the parents would be *reunited* with the child someday.

Parents who dealt with the loss in this way expressed the belief that they would actually "see" their children again, perhaps at some distant time when they were able to join them in the place where the children were now residing. Those parents who expressed this view generally held firmly to it, and, I must admit, it did seem to bring comfort to them in their mourning.

In the next chapter, another kind of sudden death is discussed— death by murder. In many ways homicide, because of its violence and intentional nature, is the ultimate disaster to strike a family. The initial response of parents to such tragedies is not different from that to sudden death. However, with murder, parents are faced with additional burdens, such as the presence of a murderer and an insensitive criminal justice system, which complicate their ability to cope.

5

The Murdered Child: A Tragedy Beyond Compare

When we are forced by circumstances to think about the death of children, we can sometimes conjure up images of how a child might die. Most of us think of a hospital setting where the child, after a long struggle with a fatal disease, surrounded in the final moments by loved ones, slips into a coma and dies quietly. Or we may bring forth images of sudden, unexpected death, such as under the wheels of car or by drowning in the neighborhood swimming pool. These images are justified because they represent the usual ways that children die today—after an illness or by accident.

We are seldom able, however, to conjure up images of children being murdered. It is difficult to comprehend this type of destructive act. In many respects the murder of any human being represents an act that is uniformly condemned by all. The violent and wanton destruction of the human body, particularly when it is a child, is often too gruesome for the mind to grasp without engendering a severe emotional reaction accompanied by denial and perhaps repression of such thoughts.

Just how do we describe a "murdered" child? I think it is accurate to say that such a child is like any other child—a boy or girl, a teenager perhaps—who happened to be in the wrong place at the wrong time. These are not wayward children in any sense. They are not juvenile delinquents who lose their lives in gang fights, although some are indeed killed by their peers. They are ordinary, normal, everyday, "run-of-the-mill" kids who are picked up after school or at other times by perverts, who become involved in one-of-a-kind arguments over silly things with aggressive youths, who break off relationships with jealous partners, who inadvertently become associated with the "wrong kind of people," or who are the innocent bystanders while crimes are being committed. What happened to these children could happen to any child, anywhere, anytime.

There does seem to be one common characteristic shared by the murdered children in the present analysis. They were all older. This is not to say that younger children are not murdered. However, younger children are usually sufficiently protected by the family so that they escape the kinds of situations where murder is most likely to occur. The median age of the murdered child in the present sample was 19 years (the youngest was 16; the oldest, 25). So in this sense they are not "children" at all but young adults. However, I will continue to call them children, since this is how they were referred to by their parents.

A Most Painful Loss

Of all the ways a child might die, murder is surely the most devastating and painful for a family to endure. For one thing, murder represents a *sudden* loss, which in itself throws the family into violent turmoil. There is no time to prepare; it cuts deep and swift, like being run through with a cold blade. The whole family's equilibrium is shattered—suddenly. And it usually takes a very long time to fit all the pieces together again.

In addition it is a *violent* death, which presents the family with the very real problem of coming to terms with the fact that the child may have suffered before dying. This one aspect, perhaps more than any other, greatly complicates the family's ability to resolve its grief. Parents will often dwell on this aspect for months, unable to escape the thoughts or the horror that the thoughts conjure up.

There is another important aspect of murder which deserves mention, and that is its deliberate nature. Accidental deaths, for example, are often sudden and violent, but never planned; there is no element of "intent" involved. And this is really what distinguishes murder from accidental deaths. Murder is not only sudden and violent, but *intentional* as well! With murder, there is always a perpetrator who has intentionally committed an act against the victim. Therefore a murder is defined by those immediately affected as potentially "preventable." For example, survivors will reason that if the law was strict enough and vengeful enough to act as a true deterrent, or if the police had been active in their patrols, or if the perpetrator had not received an early parole, or if they themselves had been more vigilant or more mindful of their role as protector of their children, the act might have been prevented. There is nothing "rational" in this kind of reasoning, but it is fairly typical in the case of murder and tends to complicate one's effort to resolve the grief.

Another factor that makes murder more difficult to deal with is the absence of *choice*. "Choice" can stand for the main difference between murder and suicide, both of which may be sudden, violent, intentional acts. In the case of suicide, however, a choice was involved when the victim made a decision to carry out an act of self-destruction. Regardless of how we, as survivors, feel about it, we are bound at least to try to understand, and/or perhaps even respect, that choice, even though we may certainly not agree with it. In the case of murder, however, the victim had no choice, and therefore under no circumstances can such an act be respected or understood. Thus murder, because of its suddenness, violence, intentional nature, and lack of choice, becomes one of the most devastating types of loss any family can possibly endure.

"Did My Child Suffer?"

The fact that murder, by anyone's definition, entails pain and suffering is enormously difficult for families to deal with. The anger and pain the parents experience over such an act tend to dominate their emotions for a very long period of time. They find that they can think of nothing else. They become obsessed with the thought of their child lying somewhere bruised, bleeding, crying out, and in great pain. The mental imagery is very acute and extorts an enormous price in terms of their emotional well-being. If they could only be sure that death occurred quickly, they believe, this would make it a little easier to bear. However, because of the uncooperativeness of police authorities in these cases, parents can neither confirm nor deny these fears.

Parents therefore become obsessed with the desire to find out everything there is to know about the case, which leads to the revelation of many gruesome details that they would perhaps be better off not knowing. The brutal honesty of the coroner's report, which is written for official consumption and designed to reveal all details of how death occurred, but nothing concerning the probability of suffering, is usually all they have available. In addition there generally is no one to interpret or soften the impact of these blatantly revealing reports.

This intense concern that parents have over whether their child suffered physical pain before he or she died extends to emotional "pain" as well. Did the child feel any fear or was he or she terrorized before being killed by the murderer? Did the child realize that he or she was about to die? These questions also plague parents' minds, and their inability to supply or find adequate answers perhaps becomes the most troublesome aspect of the entire grief process.

Again, there is no adequate resource that will satisfy the parents' need for this kind of knowledge. Coroners' reports reveal nothing in this area, leaving parents guessing as to the emotional state of their child as well as to the occurrence of physical suffering prior to his or her death.

The impact that this has on the survivors can best be illustrated by listening to some of the reactions of parents as they express fears and concerns over how their sons and daughters died:

A mother whose *two* sons were killed during the holdup of a convenience store where they were innocent shoppers:

The hardest thing for me to cope with has been the fear and terror that our sons may have felt before they were shot. Did they know what was coming? Were they afraid? My son, Keith, was shot with two guns—a .22 and a .38 caliber. My stepson, Kent, only with the .38. The autopsy said either bullet was instant death. But today I read an account of a recent murder where it said that the victim was shot twice with a .22 and then run over by a car to finish killing him! I immediately reacted—did the .22 not kill Keith? Is that why they shot him [again] with the .38? Did he suffer between the shots? All of these questions torment us and . . . you wake up in the night and it hits you and you feel you are living a bad dream or losing your mind.

A father describing the murder of his 24-year-old daughter and 4-year-old granddaughter by the father and estranged husband:

He literally kidnapped them! Took them both under threat of physical harm from my son's apartment where they had been staying. They were driving through Pennsylvania when they pulled off the road and stopped. A highway patrol car drove by a few minutes later, saw them sitting in the car, and stopped a couple of hundred feet up the road. Apparently when my daughter saw the patrol car stop, she got out of the car and began to run toward it. Bill got out of his side of the car with gun in hand and very calmly rested his arm on the roof of the car and fired three shots, two of which struck my daughter in the back, between the shoulder blades. He then shot inside the car, killing our granddaughter, then turned the gun on himself, killing himself with one bullet through the brain. My daughter died almost instantly. She collapsed in the mud alongside the road. I did not actually witness any of this—the story was related to me by the highway patrolman who stopped to give assistance. But to this day I can still "see" her lying in the mud. I can't get that image out of my mind! My only daughter, lying dead in the mud alongside some lonely highway! . . . How can I possibly live with this? . . . I literally come apart every time the thought crosses my mind!

A mother whose 17-year-old son was killed in a street fight:

He died of multiple stab wounds, and I lie awake every night thinking of him lying on the street bleeding to death. I'm afraid to sleep because my dreams are so terrible. They said he did not die right away. He must have been in terrible pain! [She begins to cry.] I just can't handle it anymore. I can't get it out of my mind! . . .

A father whose 23-year-old daughter was raped and then murdered by drowning in a creek:

They say that drowning is the least painful of all deaths. But you can't tell me my daughter did not suffer enormously before she died! She was mutilated by that beast! This is the hardest thing for me to deal with—the fact that she suffered painfully before she died. She was such a gentle person; she must have been terror-stricken! If she had been killed in a car crash, I think I could have handled that. I can't handle this. No one could handle this!

A father whose 17-year-old daughter was killed the night of her senior prom by an estranged boyfriend:

All I can think about these days is revenge! I know it's un-Christian, but it dominates my mind. If he beats this [the crime] and gets off [is acquitted], I think now I will kill him myself! The coroner told us that Susan lived for probably 20 minutes. She was stabbed repeatedly in the chest and abdomen with a short, dull blade of some sort! Can you imagine how painful that must have been! I just keep thinking of this over and over. I can't seem to get away from it. . . . It's very hard for me to deal with the rest of my feelings because my emotions are overloaded with these thoughts of her suffering!

The agony of living the event over and over in one's mind, unable to think of anything else for days at a time, can only be guessed at. Those of us who have never experienced losses of this type cannot in our wildest imaginations conceive the kind of experience this really is.

Parents of Murdered Children, Inc.

An organization, the first of its kind in the country, has been established in Cincinnati, Ohio, to help parents cope with the murders of their children. This is a self-help group offering friendship, understanding, and physical support to parents surviving these tragedies. Called Parents of Murdered Children (POMC), it was founded in 1978 by Charlotte and Robert Hullinger, three months after their daughter Lisa died from injuries inflicted by her former boyfriend. The organization is based on two principles:

> First, a person who has recovered from a problem can be far more helpful than a professional using only theoretical knowledge. Second, when an individual helps another without charge, they both benefit.[1]

Charlotte Hullinger talks about the need for such an organization and how it can help those grieving over the murder of a child. She points out that survivors have a need to talk and relate to those who are not afraid of the intensity of feelings being expressed, and who do not react in a negative or judgmental fashion. This need can best be met by establishing some common ground where individuals who are suffering such tragedies can find understanding and support from those who have already been through it. Such a group can be set up in any community where there is interest and motivation on the part of one or two individuals who have already been through it and who recognize that there is something they can do for others. Charlotte Hullinger has said:

> The anger felt by the parent of a murdered child is too threatening to many people, and so they try to calm us down and discourage us from fully experiencing the intensity of our emotions. And yet if healing is to take place, it must be by expressing and working through our feelings, no matter how negative or destructive they may seem to others, rather than by denying and repressing them. . . . Why can't we express these feelings to a psychiatrist, a social worker, a friend? [Because] . . . some of us . . . find we need to talk to those who truly understand what we've been through

because they themselves have had a similar experience. . . . Many people said to me after Lisa's death, "I just can't imagine what you are going through." These are people [in this organization] who don't have to imagine; they know![2]

POMC provides ongoing physical and emotional support to parents, by phone, by mail, through person-to-person contact, in group meetings, and through literature. As of this writing there are chapters in 37 states, centering mostly in the larger urban areas. A brochure available through the parent organization in Cincinnati makes the following statement, which further serves to document the trauma that parents experience:

> When a child dies, bereaved parents go through intense personal grief. When a child is murdered, the grief process is complicated by intrusions into the parents' grief. Police, lawyers, and other members of the criminal justice system need information, evidence, and testimony. Television and newspapers focus on the victim and the grieving family.
>
> Sometimes a murder suspect is apprehended, sometimes not. In either case, there is additional pain. Trials and sentencing, preliminary hearings, and postponements force grieving parents to face what may seem to be a lack of justice. What, they wonder, was my son's or daughter's life worth?[3]

Problems with the System

In addition to the intense problems families of murder victims have in reconciling themselves to these types of death and the many complications introduced into the grief process by the sudden, violent, intentional nature of these losses, the survivors of victims of murder face another kind of problem not encountered in other types of death.

This problem is specifically emphasized in the above quotation, and involves parents' dealings with the police investigators and the criminal justice system as well as with the murderers themselves. It seems that our criminal justice system in this country is geared to protect the rights of the accused and gives little attention to the rights of the victims and practically no attention to the rights of the survivors of the victims. This is particularly true when the victim is a murdered child. Police agencies and personnel do not fully realize the terrible impact child murder has on a family, and that many families feel victimized by the *system* as well as by the perpetrators of the crime. The problems become very clear only to those who are left behind as survivors to deal with the criminal justice system.

One of the recurrent needs of survivors of murder victims is to see justice done through the apprehension of the guilty party and his or her punishment for the crime. The survivors of the murder victims I talked with could find little peace of mind—little resolution of grief—until punishment had been extracted. In fact, survivors were *not able* to experience grief; often they did *not allow* themselves to grieve and to express the intensity of emotion required to resolve grief as long as the investigation was continuing.

It is therefore important that survivors be kept informed of the status of the police investigation, kept informed when arrests are made, and kept informed of trial dates. It is also important from the standpoint of bringing some resolution to the bottled-up feelings of remorse and the agony of grief that the system exact punishment corresponding to the seriousness of the act. These events seldom occur, however.

One mother said:

We can hardly stand to think about the murderer's never being caught. It injures me greatly for people to say, "You may never know!"

Another mother:

I am violently upset with the police! They seem to have forgotten this case . . . . There is just no sense of closure—no real end to the whole agonizing experience.

And another:

Will I ever have peace inside about this? Will the police ever get a lead? Do they even still care? I think that the police and the public at large have forgotten this tragedy. They just don't give a damn anymore! I think this hurts maybe [even] more than my daughter's murder!

A father said:

We naïvely believed that the right to life was an inalienable right; the killer would certainly be caught. The coldness and suspicion received from the sheriff's office in response to queries baffled our family, for it was impossible to understand how such a crime could seemingly be forgotten so quickly.

Another mother:

We received progress reports at first, because one nice detective with the sheriff's department has been very kind and compassionate, and we called him many times. However, *we* had to do the calling; no one called us. Now the sheriff has ordered him not to give out any more information to us. What are we to do now? How are we ever to know anything?

The fact of the loss itself is therefore compounded by the survivors' encounters with an essentially insensitive and uncaring criminal justice system. The experiences they have with police investigators, prosecuting attorneys, and the court system so traumatize them that it becomes virtually impossible for parents of murdered children to feel the emotional and mental reactions to the loss in a legitimate and meaningful manner. As one father put it:

The grieving process is disrupted by the criminal justice procedures. As a result, one's emotional system goes on hold while one is dealing with the police and the prosecutors and the courts.

Thus grief tends to become complicated and prolonged. For many, feelings of anger, hostility, bitterness, and resentment toward the criminal justice system—very negative emotions—come to dominate their existence. These feelings and reactions remain for as long as their frustrating experiences with the criminal justice system remain, or for as long as the killer remains at large.

Robert Hullinger, the father of a murdered child and co-founder of POMC, in speaking of the needs of the group, said:

One of the things we discovered is that the whole way that survivors are treated in this country at the hands of the criminal justice system tends to be one of the greatest protracters of grief in the whole process in which we are involved.

We know that someone is out there who has murdered our son or daughter. We want that person caught—for several reasons: one, we don't think *anyone* should get away with it; two, we don't think anyone else should have to go through what we have; and three, we have a *right* to bring that person to justice! However, the system doesn't respect these needs. Many of us eventually come to ask, "Is there no one who cares? . . . Is there no one who is going to continue to try to find the person who killed my son or daughter?"

PLEA BARGAINING

Probably the most difficult aspect of the entire criminal justice system for these parents to deal with is plea bargaining.

When the murderer is finally apprehended, the process parents go through is almost as painful as during the search because it is at this time that parents discover what their child's life is worth! Plea bargaining, without doubt, is a concept that is most damaging to parents.

Plea bargaining works in this way. When a murderer is caught, usually one or two pieces of evidence will be lacking to bring about a first-degree murder charge. In the criminal court system today it is very difficult to get a first-degree murder conviction unless there are eyewitnesses or the accused confesses. Even with a confession, plea bargaining may have been an element in bringing about the confession. Therefore because it is so difficult to get first-degree murder convictions, and in order to bring the accused to some kind of justice, the prosecutor will plea-bargain. The accused will agree to be tried on a lesser charge, which means, if he or she is convicted, less time in prison and usually a quicker parole time.

It is at this point that parents find out the value of their child's life. Perhaps it is worth only seven years in prison! Or if the defense attorney can arrange it, the accused may be able to plead temporary insanity and get off with a lesser sentence or even no sentence! As one father said in response to plea bargaining in the case of the alleged murderer of his daughter: "We raised that child and then found that her life was worth only three years!" Robert Hullinger said:

This is one of the most painful things parents must endure: to discover the price that our society places on the human life of someone for whom we would be willing to die!

Oftentimes a person convicted of robbery will receive a sentence of 15 years, but a person convicted of killing another human being will receive only a five-year sentence! Tell me, where is the justice here?

Even if the convicted killer gets a life sentence, a life sentence does not mean what it used to. In fact there is no such thing as a "life" sentence anymore. In most states life means 7–10 years at most. That is, a convicted killer sentenced to "life in prison" *must* come up for parole in 7–10 years. Parole can of course be denied, but this usually occurs only in the more publicized cases, such as with Charles Manson, Sirhan Sirhan, and other such "celebrity" killers. The usual "lifer" coming up for parole, more likely than not, will get it! In fact we can be sure that even the celebrity killers will eventually be successful in achieving their freedom as well.

Parents of murdered children experience a tremendous sense of frustration and outrage over plea bargaining as it is presently structured within the criminal justice system in the United States. There may well be a great loss of incentive and ability on the part of parents to continue in their normal patterns and functioning, and a significantly equal loss of faith in the system of justice in this country as a result of this one quirk or flaw in our criminal justice system.

Plea bargaining is only one of the problems parents encounter in the aftermath of murder. There are others just as sinister and just as damaging.

Some Special Kinds of Problems

IS SOMEONE WATCHING US

When the murderer is not apprehended, parents often live in fear that it could happen again. They grow suspicious of strangers. They grow apprehensive and fearful of new situations and new places. They become overprotective of other family members, often venturing out only when accompanied by others.

Some of the parents interviewed actually believed that they were being watched or even pursued by the murderer! This was particularly the case if the family had been the subject of an inordinate amount of media publicity. When this occurs, they realize that they are now known entities in the community. They may have reacted in a violent way through the media, expressing their wish for an arrest and punishment for the murderer. Consequently they develop fears that the murderer will return and somehow exact revenge!

Such fears can become overpowering, leading to much avoidance behavior on the part of the family. Some families even go to the expense of installing expensive alarm systems. Others buy attack dogs. Many family survivors refuse to go out at night. They become hyper-suspicious when in a crowd and usually try to avoid such encounters.

These fears and anxieties sometimes persist until the killer is apprehended and imprisoned. Only then do they truly feel safe—at least, until the killer's parole!

FEAR OF FAMILY REVENGE

Another aspect of the problem emerges *within* the families of the victims. There is often the fear expressed by parents that someone— some member of their own family—may try to avenge the death of their son or daughter by seeking out and taking some action against the alleged or accused murderer. This becomes a particular problem if an arrest has been made and if the family gets word that the "murderer" has plea-bargained his way into a reduced sentence. It is not unusual for an older brother or another male relative of the victim to vow to "get the bastard" when he walks out of jail. This becomes another burden for parents to bear. They have lost one child to murder and now they are faced with the possibility that another child or close relative might become a murderer himself. They have lost one, there is now the possibility of losing two! Many parents have expressed a fear that this would indeed happen if the murderer escaped the maximum sentence.

PARENTAL REVENGE

In addition to expressing fear of family revenge, there is another dimension to the problem of revenge. Sometimes a parent—usually a father—will experience such hatred of the murderer that he himself will begin the process of "avenging" the killing of his son or daughter by mentally planning to "get" the murderer. I found this to be relatively rare among the families I interviewed, but in a few cases it was evident, and it becomes a double burden for the family to bear.

Why some fathers react this way and others do not is somewhat of a mystery, probably having something to do with the way they have been socialized to deal with violence. For those few who respond in this way, their anger and hatred often become overpowering and consume virtually all their time and energies.

As an example of these emotions, one father, whose daughter was raped and murdered by an 18-year-old neighbor boy, said:

There is some talk about diminished capacity; I don't buy that! If he beats this, so help me God, I'll get him if it's the last thing I do on this earth! He killed the only thing that mattered to me, and I'll be damned if he's going to get away with it!

This is a rather powerful statement by one father that really expressed the sentiments of many who were afraid to say so because they recognized that such feelings violated expected behavior in our "civilized" society.

Another father could hardly contain himself as he was relating his feelings of hatred for the murderer of his 19-year-old son. He said:

That son-of-a-bitch shot him down in cold blood! Didn't give him a chance! . . . And he's not going to walk away from this, not if I can help it! I'm not a violent man . . . but . . . [he begins to weep] I'll do it! . . . I'll do it!

Another father, whose daughter, he believes, was intentionally killed by her boyfriend in a "so-called auto accident," said in a very calm and calculated fashion:

I am definitely going to settle the score someday. . . . He knows I'm waiting for him. . . . I have intentionally allowed him to see me watching him, and he knows I'm after him. . . . It may take some time to find the right time, but I'll get him for what he did to my daughter!

These reactions, although evident in only a few isolated cases, illustrate the intensity of emotion that can impinge upon some survivors. This obviously creates enormous additional problems with which the family must deal. They have to work through not only their grief and fears, but their own personal revenge as well.

POMC can sometimes help allay feelings of revenge. One mother said of her experience with the organization in trying to deal with her feelings of revenge and hatred:

The idea [behind the organization]is to permit outbursts of feelings. You can scream and cuss and swear and cry all you want and no one will say "Why don't you shape up?" . . . There's a healing in that. It's alright to hate the person who killed your child. We don't teach turning the other cheek. The hope is [with support from those who truly understand] that after the hate, you learn to forgive yourself and others around you and, hopefully, the murderer.[4]

ANGER AND HELPLESSNESS

Survivors of homicide deaths find that news coverage, police investigations, the search for the perpetrator, and the trial greatly strain their ability to adjust to the loss. The impatience, disorganization, anxiety, and uncertainty are often extended far beyond usual limits, complicating efforts to complete the grief work.

A common characteristic shared by most (but not all) parents of murdered children is anger—anger directed at the event itself and toward the murderer, but also anger over what is *not* being done to apprehend and prosecute the guilty. Although I have commented on these feelings earlier, they bear repeating in light of the significance of anger as a legitimate response to losses of this type.

Many parents indicated that they carry so much anger and hostility that it is hard, if not impossible, to get down to the grief and mourn their loss in an appropriate manner. The hostile feelings that dominate their existence tend to block any efforts at reacting in a "normal" fashion to the loss itself. Anger and hostility, when experienced with such intensity, tend to hide genuine feelings of grief and remorse. Parents, to be sure, feel an intense sadness. They experience pain, heartache, and anguish. But these feelings are coupled with anger and hostility, which become the dominant emotions, particularly in the immediate aftermath of the loss. Consequently many parents cannot adequately mourn their loss in a way that would be beneficial and lead to a resolution of their grief. There are simply too many hostile and angry feelings in the communication channels.

Associated with anger are feelings of helplessness, which can become overpowering at times. There is also bewilderment and frustration, as indicated earlier, over being kept ill-informed by police investigators, and even open outrage over their experiences with the judicial system and with all the events in which they become involved in the aftermath of the death.

Charlotte Hullinger tries to put these attitudes of helplessness, frustration, and bewilderment into perspective. Commenting on some of the specific experiences parents have with the criminal justice system, she says:

> Try to imagine . . . :
> . . . the agony of sitting through a trial in which a defense attorney—and later the media—tries to cast aspersions on your daughter's character and paint a completely false picture of her, intimating that she somehow brought it on herself;
> . . . the sense of utter helplessness while waiting outside in the hall as the trial is being conducted because the defense attorney does not want the jury to see the grieving parents, and so

uses the ploy that he "may" call them as witnesses and then never does;

. . . the bewilderment of never having anyone from the prosecutor's office contact you to let you know when the trial will be held, and so you never find out; or of being told, "You're not important to our case; it wasn't a crime against you; I don't have time to talk to you";

. . . the frustration of having a trial postponed three times and finally learning that the confession was thrown out of court by a judge because of a technicality, with no possibility of appealing this one judge's decision; and finally,

. . . the outrage at being told by an insensitive policeman when asking if anyone has been arrested yet for the murder of your child, "Lady, if anybody is charged, you'll see it on TV."[5]

Such experiences outrage parents and stoke the fires of anger, resentment, bitterness, and hostility. These are negative emotions which must be nullified before parents can get down to the task of working through the normal vestiges of grief.

GUILT

Another emotion felt by survivors of homicide victims which tends to complicate the grief process is guilt—guilt for not having protected the victim. In fact, guilt can and often does become stultifying. It can consume one like a superheated flame. It can become overpowering to the point where one loses the ability to function. Just as excessive concern over whether the child suffered physically or emotionally can dominate one's existence, guilt can also become debilitating.

Although the intentional nature of murder leads one to *believe* that, unlike accidents, these crimes could perhaps have been prevented, in reality no one could have prevented these deeds. So guilt is often irrationally based.

In this study the typical case was a rape-murder. But there were also cases involving random murders where the person just happened to be in the wrong place at the wrong time. There were cases of mistaken identity, where the murderer thought the victim was someone else. There were several cases of murder following a fight or argument, where such an outcome would have been impossible to predict. Looking at what was known about these cases at the time revealed that there was nothing anyone could have done to prevent them from happening. Certainly parents were not to blame. But many parents did in fact blame themselves for what happened, using the argument "if only . . . " as the basis for their guilt. Listen to how several mothers and fathers expressed personal guilt over what happened to their children:

A father:

If only we had insisted that John be home at an early hour! . . . [son shot and killed at 3 A.M. while returning home from his girlfriend's—no suspects]

A father:

If only we had been home that night, Virginia might have decided to stay in! . . . [daughter raped and strangled]

A mother:

If only I had cautioned him more diligently about riding with strangers! . . . [16-year-old son brutally beaten and murdered while hitchhiking home from school]

A mother:

If only I had listened to what Peter was telling me about this guy, perhaps we could have prevented this! . . . [17-year-old son killed by a "friend"—no apparent motive]

A father:

If only I had been more receptive, I could have seen this coming! . . . [daughter involved in drug culture, murdered by her boyfriend]

A mother:

If only I had insisted on his taking our car that night instead of his, he would not have stopped at that station! . . . [19-year-old son randomly shot down as an innocent bystander during a service station holdup]

A mother:

If only we hadn't raised her to be so trusting and friendly! . . . [daughter apparently picked up by a stranger, raped, and murdered]

A mother:

If only we had been more vigilant and concerned about the kinds of friends Bill had! . . . [son shot and killed by a friend during an argument]

They felt that they had failed as parents. By "allowing" this to happen—and many parents believed that they were ultimately responsible—they felt that they had committed the worst sin imaginable.

Fathers, particularly, harbored guilt. It is commonly accepted in our culture that the male, in addition to being the breadwinner in the family, is also its protector. It greatly disturbed fathers that they were not "there" when needed. Consequently many blamed themselves for the murder, knowing full well the irrational nature of this feeling but nevertheless being unable to rid themselves of it. It some cases it becomes a burden so heavy that the individual simply collapses under its weight and withdraws from contact with the world. The person escapes into the dark void of depression.

Of course if one can survive long enough, guilt and depression eventually subside. But it sometimes takes a long, long time. And in some cases it will take a heavy psychological toll, leaving an indelible and tender scar.

Not all parents suffered guilt, however. Those who in the immediate aftermath of the death received the most information on precisely what happened were often better able to work through feelings of self-blame more easily and more quickly than those whose information was sketchy and incomplete. Apparently, being fully informed of as many of the details as possible does help one deal more effectively with any guilt that is otherwise engendered.

STRAIN ON THE MARRIAGE

Statistics show that in approximately 70 percent of the families of children killed violently, the parents end up in the divorce courts or become separated.[6] Marriages hit rock bottom. Although less than 20 percent of the families in the present study experienced family dissolution at the time of the interview, almost all knew of others, through their support groups, who had experienced disintegration. And in about a third of the remaining families taking part in the interviews, although intact at the time, dissolution seemed inevitable.

Generally it was found that a breakdown in the ability to communicate effectively and the inability to draw support from one's spouse were the important causes of the collapse in family organization. Each parent is so devastated by the loss, and suffers such massive disorganization and confusion, that neither can possibly help the other in a way that is supportive and comforting. The guilt both parents feel is often translated into hatred of the murderer, but also hatred of themselves as well. Minor family problems that were perhaps more of a pest than anything else before the murder became blown into exaggerated major concerns after the murder. In addition, parents are often maligned by their own parents, their neighbors, their friends, who find them somehow at fault. Many times parents are at different points or stages in the grieving process and suddenly find that they can no longer offer support to or even communicate with the spouse since neither knows where the other is coming from. And there seems to be no way out of these dilemmas.

Perhaps I should note that in *The Courage to Grieve*, Judy Tatlebaum refers to Simonton's formula for an effective support system:

25 percent of your support comes from inner resources (from yourself);

20 percent from your spouse; and

55 percent from the environment or community.[7]

This is important to realize since couples seem to expect 100 percent from each other and this leads to difficulties.

There is an old cliché that "grief halved is grief diminished." Where both parties are grieving but in different ways and functioning in different stages, where they are bewildered and filled with fear and hostility and bitterness, this cliché becomes a myth. There can be no sharing, no supporting, no comforting, no communication between two people who are themselves coming apart at the seams. How can one help the other? How can one be of assistance to the other when that person is struggling desperately just to keep himself or herself afloat? We cannot really expect one to keep the other from drowning!

So they lose confidence in their ability to keep the family functioning. Parents lose their spontaneity. They say that they feel old and worn out. They are constantly exhausted. They lose their ability to function effectively within their assigned family roles. Parents lose interest in their jobs. Homemaking activities come to a standstill. Mothers and fathers lose faith in their ability to survive as a unit. They feel that they can no longer accept the responsibility for someone else. They feel that they need to get their act together, and perhaps they can do it better on their own. Thus divorce or separation becomes an inviting alternative.

Where strong family ties and good communication patterns existed prior to the loss, where the family was close knit and mutually supportive, there was a much better chance that the family would not be negatively affected. In fact, for some families the experience actually produced a positive effect, strengthening primary ties between members and bringing them closer together. The experience actually bonded some families into a rigid unit, increasing their ability to survive any crisis. We will investigate further some of the differences in the way families responded to all types of tragedies in a later chapter.

Other Concerns

Additional concerns faced by survivors which compound and complicate the grief process include the following (in the words of Charlotte Hullinger):

- Isolation, helplessness in a world that is seen as hostile and uncaring, and that frequently blames the victims.
- Growing public sympathy for perpetrators of crimes of passion (Jean Harris, etc.).
- Sensational and inaccurate media coverage.
- Financial burden of funeral and medical expenses, of professional counseling for surviving family members, of hiring private investigators when they feel that law enforcement officers are not doing an adequate job or when there are too many unanswered questions.
- The memory of a mutilated body at the morgue.
- The feeling that the murderer, if he's found gets all the help; that as parents of murdered children you don't have any rights.
- Getting back the personal effects of a murder victim, even those that are not essential to a trial, or after the trial is over.
- The effect on the other children in the family, especially the bitterness and loss of faith in the American criminal justice system.

Any one of these concerns can become overpowering for the parents, rendering the family incapable of resolving it. It takes enormous effort by the members to keep these concerns from breaking the back of the family as a viable unit.

Is All This Normal?

It should be noted that the feelings and emotions experienced by parents in the aftermath of these losses are in no way to be defined as "abnormal" reactions. Robert Hullinger points out:

Anger, hostility, helplessness, frustration, and guilt, although very negative feelings, are nevertheless genuine emotions experienced by all who suffer losses of this type. One cannot get rid of these feelings and emotions by going through some kind of counseling.

Seeking out a therapist for help leaves one with the notion that what one is suffering is something abnormal, something we should be rid of! The only help—the only real help—available to these parents are those who will live through the pain and the hurt with them, those who are now themselves going through the same kind of pain!

Although we recognize the "normality" of feelings and responses generated by the murder of a child, perhaps we might add that nondirective counseling, i.e., simply lending a receptive ear—allowing the parents the opportunity to talk and work through the myriad of feelings they are experiencing—can be beneficial. Structured in this way, professional counseling may indeed be very helpful in resolving some of the critical personal problems that losses generate. This may be particularly true where the individual does not have access to a support group and where he or she can find no one available in the community in the form of friends, neighbors, or relatives who are interested in serving in the capacity of "helper."

Perhaps I should also note that some do not allow themselves to feel the pain. They do not allow themselves to grieve openly or, for that matter, to express any emotion. This too is normal. The experience is too unbelievable for them to grasp all at once. It will take more time for these individuals. They should not be rushed or hurried. It will take time for the mind and body to unravel the mysterious details of what has happened to them.

Just What Kind of People Are the Parents of Murdered Children?

In summary, how do we describe the parents of a murdered child? First, we must not be deceived into thinking that all want to go out and return the favor! Some of course feel enormous revenge; but most victims are not vengeful people. They are instead *scared* people—scared of possible revenge inflicted upon them by a murderer still at large. They are *hurt* people—hurt severely by having their most prized possession ripped from their grasp in a most gruesome way. They are people in *pain*—great pain—more pain than those of us who have never been through it can imagine, a pain so deep that for many there appears to be no surface to it. They are *frustrated* people—frustrated by the layers of bureaucracy known as the criminal justice system, which essentially treats them as nonentities, with no rights. They are also people *alone*—alone in a world where they can find few others in the immediate environment who really understand their torment and who are willing to allow them to share their deepest feelings and sensations.

It seems that only when they encounter others who are like themselves in terms of sharing a similar experience in life can they find contentment and some sense of security in realizing that what they feel and experience is indeed *normal,* and that they are not insane or rapidly becoming so.

In the next chapter the discussion will turn to the family as the unit of analysis and an attempt will be made to examine a number of characteristics of the modern family that contribute to defining child death as a crisis. This discussion will be somewhat theoretical in nature. This chapter can be skipped over without loss of continuity, if the reader so desires.

6

The Family in Crisis

At this point in the discussion I turn to the social group—the family—within which the parent-survivors of child death function.

Here I will try to show that not every family is the same. Some families are structured as true support systems for the individual members while others do not possess these qualities. Instead they may even create an aberrant atmosphere where the stress associated with loss is exaggerated. Having knowledge of the *kind* of family that surrounds the individual parent is important in understanding both the impact of child death on the parent as well as how the parent responds to child death and other stressful events.

I believe that families can actually be categorized in terms of characteristics or attributes that either *protect* members from the stress of child loss, or *compound* or *intensify* the stress of such an event. By searching out and defining these characteristics, we should be able to predict how parents will respond to stress-provoking events.

The Family as a Unit

Social scientists define the family as a *primary group*, a group somewhat independent of other groups in the community. It is a social system with its own internal structure of positions, norms, roles, values, and beliefs. It also has its own set of defensive techniques for coping with problems that it encounters.

The family is often seen as the most basic unit or group in society. Each of us is a member of a family of one sort or another, and each of us spends much time in the family setting. The family's influence on our lives even in today's so-called impersonal world is substantial.

It became apparent in my interviews with individual family members—mothers, fathers, and in some cases siblings—that *each* member responded in a unique way to child death or a terminal diagnosis. Yet I noted that when these stress-provoking events were viewed from the perspective of the family, there appeared to be similarities in the way some families responded. Within certain families, members seemed to define the event as a "family" problem and a "family" experience. In these families, members were very much affected by the reactions of other members.

In other families the child death or terminal diagnosis was seen an individual problem, and members were forced to respond alone without the support of other participants.

Some families therefore were truly organized as "units" in that there was less of a tendency for individuals to respond alone and independently. And individuals saw their own responses as occurring within the organizational context of this unit.

This "family response" was observed quite frequently in the members' use of the personal pronouns "we" and "us" in referring to their responses. They would say "we grieved heavily" or "we were devastated by this thing" or "it had an enormous impact on us." "We" and "us" meant the *family*.

One mother, for example, voluntarily translated her "individual" response into a "family" response, in her answer to a question on how "she" handled the death of her 11-year-old son. She said:

In the weeks immediately following Mike's death we were like a subway train traveling through a busy station with the doors closed! We were a family surrounded by people, but could neither touch them nor communicate with them in the way we needed! *They* were out there! *We* were in here! This tiny unit—our family—trying desperately to survive. . . . During that time I received all my strength from them; I got nothing from outside. . . .

This view of the family expressed by this mother—as a "tiny unit . . . trying desperately to survive" the aftermath of child death—was typical of only some families in the study.

Incidentally, this is often the way *outside observers* see the situation. Even though "individual" responses to a loss can be discerned, what is often observed is a "family" response. In fact we are thinking of, or responding to, the family as a *unit* when we as outsiders make such statements as "It was really hard on the family" or "The family suffered greatly" or "We must pay condolences to the family." As outside observers, we group individuals together and define "the family" as our unit of focus.

The Family and the Management of Stress

Ideally, what is the role of the family in the management of personal stress?

Because of the ongoing change and transition that are characteristic of today's society, the modern family is much affected and seems to reflect a greater state of tension, facing problems that were unknown a few decades ago. Unlike the larger families of the past, the nuclear family of today is small and does not have the emotional support of an extended kinship group. Since it exists in isolation from the larger kin group and since it receives little support from the surrounding community, it has become virtually a "closed" system,[1] and a more fragile unit than the family of the past. Consequently if the modern nuclear family is to do what it is designed to do in these times, each member must fill a wider range of functions and each must share a greater responsibility for the welfare of others than was necessary in earlier families. Therefore the significance and participation of each member is greatly intensified in today's world. Reuben Hill, in his classic work *Families Under Stress*, said on this point:

> In a society of rapid social change, problems outnumber solutions, and the resulting uncertainties are absorbed by the members of society, who are for the most part also members of families. . . . Because the family is the bottleneck through which all troubles pass, no other association so reflects the strains and stresses of life.[2]

However, even though the modern family may indeed reflect "the strains and stresses of life," it is also the institution which, in modern society, should best function to alleviate these strains and stresses. In fact the "best" family units today may be not only the focal points of problems, but, ideally, the sources through which tensions caused by problems are released.

Thus the best or "ideal" families have as their goal the task of "preserving" the personalities of their members. In fact this is probably the most important function that the modern family can perform. As Hill stated:

> Through its capacity for sympathy, understanding, and unlimited loyal support, the family rehabilitates personalities bruised in the course of competitive daily living.[3]

And as Lawrence and Frank stated:

> Only the family can guard the emerging personality and protect the mental health of individuals through the quality of its interpersonal relationships, the provision of reassurance and comforting, the releases and encouragements each needs to keep on striving for orderly living and fulfillment of his or her aspirations.[4]

The family *as a unit* seems to have inherited, ideally at least, the underlying fundamental task of maintaining the mental health and stability of its members, of protecting its members, of guarding their egos, and of helping them overcome their difficulties. By supporting these functions, the ideal family, as a unit, becomes the source through which personal tensions caused by the stresses and strains of life are relieved.

Thus in the ideal family "individual" crises become "family" crises, since any attack on the individual's stability or sense of security will result in a "family" response. The ideal family should recognize that it must protect its own; it must insulate its members from outside hurt and rejection; it must serve the function of rehabilitating "personalities bruised in the course of competitive daily living." Any stressful encounter becomes a "family" problem. And individuals in turn are able to rely on their families as sources of help, with the expectation that the units are adaptable and integrated enough to support them in the midst of adversity.

FAMILIES AT RISK

When a diagnosis of a potentially fatal disease of a member is presented to the family, or when the death of a member occurs, the family is put "at risk." Death of a member and/or diagnosis of a potentially fatal illness are both experienced as intensely stressful events.

Caroff and Dobrof refer to the "family at risk" as an apt phrase depicting a family trying to cope with the impact of life-threatening illness and/or subsequent death.[5] It is a family under the impact of change. From the very moment the assault takes place, significant alterations begin to occur in its functions and in its organization. As each family member reacts to the stress-provoking event—a reaction based on their fears, insecurities, and needs—the stability of the family is attacked and the role of each member is altered. In some cases the family's very reason for existence may be challenged and the family unit is placed in a situation where it must respond.

In some cases the response demanded and the "risk" encountered are not as threatening to the family unit as in other cases, such as where an elderly member is diagnosed as having a terminal illness, followed later by death.

This is not to say, however, that such situations are not stress provoking. They may indeed be very stressful for all concerned, but they are unlikely to produce disorganization or collapse of the family or its members. When the death of an elderly member occurs, the family loses a bit of its past, but its reason-to-be remains intact. The family still has a future and the members can look to that future with confidence. There is little challenge to the hopes and values of the remaining members and little alteration in life patterns and lifestyles required.

It should be noted that it is important to distinguish here between the depth of threat or stress encountered and the depth of love for the person who is dying or who has died. There may indeed be great love expressed for the elderly member, but his or her passing — because of the expected nature of the event—is unlikely to lead to a major upheaval within the family.

Therefore, because of the way the family defines these events, and with the presence of adequate resources necessary to deal with these kinds of losses, the threat to the family is not of major proportions.

The death of a child or the diagnosis of a fatal disease in a child is a different matter. These events are characterized as highly stressful and crisis precipitating. A child's position within the family is just being formed. A child who dies is pulled from the vital center, the heart, of the family. A family may be so affected by such loss or by the potential for loss that the hopes and aspirations of the members become threatened. Unless the family has an adequate array of personal and internal resources on which to draw, and unless the members can define the event as a "family" problem and not just as an individual one, the hardships produced by the loss will undermine the family's ability to cope.

In many respects, when a child dies the family must face not only the death of that member but also the "psychological death" of the family itself. The life of the family as a viable unit comes under attack.

As noted earlier, the urban family today is often small, consisting of no more than one or two children. In times past, when families were larger, the loss of one child did not adversely affect the functioning of the family system. In earlier times, when infectious diseases often took a heavy toll, child deaths were "expected" and tolerated much as elderly deaths are today. They certainly were less likely to be crisis producing.

Today our children represent our future, and when they are in a terminal condition, our future falls into jeopardy. When they die, often our future "dies" with them. The loss of a child may be so unique that the family unit has no rational or practiced way of responding to the event.[6] Under these circumstances, again unless the family can draw upon sufficient resources to give it strength, it is truly put "at risk," and the death of a child or a fatal illness in a child, as a stressful event, may produce a massive crisis.

Two Predictive Variables

As noted above, there are certain variables or characteristics operative in some families that can be identified and that appear either to intensify or to ease the burden suffered by individual members when confronted by stresssful situations. I have made reference to these variables throughout the previous discussion. What I wish to do here is to make them more explicit by defining these concepts.

For example, to understand the parents' response to child death it is necessary to understand the concept of "family resources," the lack of which can make it extremely hard for individual members to overcome problems of loss and grief. When family resources are available, they can go a long way toward easing the burden experienced by the grieving individual.

In addition we must understand the "meaning" or definition that a family as a unit assigns to the event, which may moderate or enhance the impact of the stressful encounter on the individual. Finally, it becomes necessary to understand the "hardships" of the event, which demand of the family system certain competencies in order to overcome them.[7]

These three characteristics—family resources, the family's definitions, and the hardships of the stress-provoking event—have significance when we consider the family as a unit, as a system. "Resources" and "definitions," as they are defined here, are family or group characteristics; they are distinct from the personalities of individuals. It should be noted that hardships are endured by all varieties of families. How a family or an individual actually responds, however, depends on the resources the particular group can lay claim to, and on the meaning of, or the way the members define, the event.[8]

Thus "resources" and "meanings" become two important variables to be sought out and made operational in developing potential characteristics for classifying the family's and the individual's responses to stress. An analysis of these characteristics is essential to building a more complete understanding of how individual members might cope with the death of children.

RESOURCES OF THE FAMILY

In order to avoid a genuine crisis situation, a family must be able to draw upon sufficient resources to overcome the effects of the stress-provoking event. McCubbin and his colleagues, in a search of the literature over the past decade, have shown four kinds of resources available to a family which, when operative, moderated the personal effects of stressful encounters. These are:

1. family members' personal resources, defined as financial, educational, health, and psychological;
2. the family system's internal resources, defined as integration and adaptability;
3. social support systems available; and
4. coping techniques or mechanisms available and operational.[9]

Family Members' Personal Resources. Personal resources accumulate in a family as a result of the personal characteristics of the individual members. One variety of personal resource is financial. A strong financial resource contributes to the economic security of the family unit as a whole. For example, it is known that financial problems often lie at the basis of family difficulties and create a fertile climate for the development of crises when the family is faced with extreme stress. On the other hand individual family members with steady and well-paying jobs serve to protect the family from the harshness of a stressful event, such as a long-term illness or even a death, that can drain scarce resources away from other vital areas.

A long-term illness, for example, can be very expensive even if the family has otherwise adequate medical insurance. Medical insurance will not pay for living arrangements for a parent to accompany a child to a distant treatment center. It will seldom fully cover the very high cost of outpatient treatment, or special diets, or home-care nursing. Therefore families who are not financially able to afford the high costs of care and treatment may suffer an extra burden.

Fathers, for example, may be required to take a second job to pay the bills; mothers may be forced to work outside the home, sometimes for the first time in their lives, while still being fully responsible for the care of the sick child. These changes in family roles may be disorganizing and disrupting to the point where stress becomes a critical ordeal for the family to deal with.

Also, medical insurance will not cover funeral expenses. And since few families carry life insurance on their children, this could be a major expense the family must face.

Thus families who are not able to afford the high cost of treatment or the high cost of a funeral suffer more stress than those that have this resource available. And the more stress, the more likely a "family" crisis will result.

Another personal resource that can serve to moderate a person's response to stress is education. If the mother and father are "educated," this fact alone should make the stress easier to bear. Education leads to the development of certain cognitive abilities that facilitate a more realistic perception of stress, which in turn could lead to the establishment within the family of certain skills for solving or handling crucial problems as they arise. It would appear, therefore, that a high level of parental education is conducive to easing the burden of any stress-provoking event.

A third personal resource that can help the family and the person deal successfully with a stressful encounter is good health of the members or, in this case, good health of the parents. Parental health can actually facilitate handling the stress of child death or illness. On the other hand parental illness and personal debilitation of various sorts can create fertile ground for the growth of additional family strains. Families in which a parent is suffering from a debilitating illness of some sort and trying to deal with a terminal illness in a child or the death of the child, in many cases present a picture of disaster. It is understandable that families and individuals might find it impossible to cope. This may be particularly true where the family has limited financial resources to deal with the problem. Thus the situation very quickly becomes a crisis.

The fourth personal resource defined by McCubbin is psychological. Personality resources such as good self-esteem on the part of the members, feelings of confidence, and a feeling of mastery over external events can help reduce the stressful consequences of any stress-provoking event. In fact, Pearlin and Schooler claim that what family members *are*, rather than what they *do*, is important in dealing with stress.[10] This implies psychological stability of family members as a personal protective resource for handling any stressful encounter, and certainly seems to be a variable of major importance in the members' ability to resolve stressful issues.

Internal Resources of the Family. In addition to an array of personal resources, families may also have available certain internal resources—that is, characteristics of families as social units. These are represented by the degree of family integration and adaptability.[11]

As noted in Hill, families that are defined as "well integrated" contain the following characteristics:

1. a willingness to sacrifice personal interest to attain family objectives;
2. pride in the family tree and in the ancestral traditions;
3. presence of strong patterns of emotional interdependence and unity;
4. high participation as a family in joint activities; and
5. strong affectional ties between father and mother, father and children, mother and children, and among children.[12]

The other internal resource available to the family is family "adaptability," which, again according to Hill, refers to:

1. previous success in meeting family crises;
2. the predominance of nonmaterial goals;
3. flexibility and willingness to shift traditional roles of husband and wife or of father and mother, if necessary;
4. acceptance of responsibility by all family members in performing family duties; and

5. the presence of equalitarian patterns of family control and decision-making.[13]

These two sets of attributes are defined as characteristics of the family unit and not of individuals. Therefore they carry meaning as group referents and can be considered attributes of certain family types. Families described as well integrated and adaptable tend to respond to stress in a positive way. We can define real families in terms of these characteristics and use these characteristics as predictor variables. Thus if a family can lay claim to a high degree of these internal resources, the members will be better prepared to deal with any stressful event.

Social Support Systems as External Resources. Here I focus on the social networks available to some families and on the support offered by the networks to alleviate stress. There are three kinds of networks available that offer support:

1. neighborhoods
2. family and kinship groups, and
3. mutual self-help organizations.[14]

Cohesive neighborhoods and close-knit family and kinship groups are obvious support networks. Research on the mediating influences of social support for specific stress-provoking events has emphasized the role of these support systems in protecting against the effects of stress as well as promoting recovery from stress or potential crisis.

Although we generally interpret social support as an independent part of the family's external resources, it might also be interpreted as a part of *coping,* as a separate dimension of family resources.[15] This can be seen in regard to mutual self-help organizations, which are sought out by families as a way of coping with or adjusting to the extreme stress of child loss.

Self-help organizations exist in many communities today. These groups have been quite successful in reducing the long-term impact that the death of a member ordinarily has on other members. These organizations have been successful because they often consist of small groups of members of other families in the community who have had similar experiences and who can empathize with those who have recently been bereaved. Although only certain types of families are likely to meet and encounter such groups in the community, these groups are available to all. Any family that avails itself of the services offered by self-help groups should benefit greatly. However, because of the tendency for only certain kinds of families to seek help *beyond* the family unit, these particular family types are likely to know that self-help groups exist, and to use them.

Coping Mechanisms and Strategies. Coping techniques or mechanisms available to a family are also prerequisites to managing stress. The higher the stress level, the more likely that family unity and stability will be threatened by the stress-provoking event. Coping is therefore a strategy for maintaining unity and stability within the family.[16]

There are essentially two varieties of coping strategies available to a family. One has a psychological origin and is called "cognitive coping." It refers to the way members of individual families change their subjective or personal perceptions of stressful situations. The other variety has a sociological origin and emphasizes a broad range of actions "directed at either changing the stressful conditions" or reducing the strain by manipulating the social environment.[17]

For example, cognitive coping may take the form of changing one's perception of the loss by encapsulating it in a dominant and persistent religious perspective. Thus a basic belief in God can be used as a coping strategy; and a strong faith shared by all family members can moderate the impact of the loss on the family and on the members within it. In fact, an acceptance of and a belief in the "will of God" can even remove personal responsibility for a tragedy. A loss can even be interpreted in a "positive" way if one harbors a fertile belief in an afterlife for everyone.[18] We can therefore define a strong religious orientation as a family resource which functions as a coping strategy.

Family members can also cope by manipulating the social environment. In regard to childhood loss or illness as stress-provoking events, the family may attempt to seek support from other families in similar situations and in this way create a climate wherein healing can occur. Also, as noted earlier, some families seek out and make use of mutual self-help organizations in the community. This is not only a way of availing oneself of an important community or external resource, but is also a way of coping by altering the social environment.

Coping behavior is an integral part of the family unit's total array of adaptive behavior. However, such mechanisms and strategies are available or operative only in certain types of families. It appears that adaptive, coping behavior is more likely in families who are cohesive and well integrated, where communication channels are open and where authority and status structures are flexible.[19]

THE MEANING OF THE EVENT

It should be noted that an analysis of coping strategies must also take into account different types of *meaning* a family assigns to a stress-provoking event. This opens another area that is important in trying to identify family types in prospective studies.

As I have noted many times, the event of childhood death in a family often produces an overwhelming amount of stress. This stress has great potential for producing a crisis and overpowering the defensive mechanisms as well as wiping out efforts at maintaining a state of balance. Note that I say that such stress *has the potential* for producing a crisis; but it need not do so. Much depends on how the stress is defined by the family members. A stress-provoking event will have variable "meaning" depending on the particular family and the particular event. The key to whether a family can ride out a stressful event or whether it becomes a crisis has as much to do with the way the members define the event as with the resources they can draw upon or with the severity and hardships of the event itself.[20] Is the event or circumstance defined as a threat to status, to goals, or to future commitments of the family? Is the stressful event defined as a family problem—a family issue—or as a personal problem or an individual experience?

Interaction Between Resources and Definitions. It should be noted that there is an important interactive effect between "resources" and "definitions." How its members define a stress-provoking event is closely tied to the resources a family has available. Thus if the family can claim few personal and internal resources, if it does not have access to mutual self-help organizations and can find no support in the larger kinship system, if it cannot rely on adequate coping and adaptive forms of behavior, then the definitions members will attach to stressful events will be detrimental to their ability to deal with them.

When I talk about defining the meaning of an event, I am talking about the "true" meaning of the situation, not from the point of view of outside observers but from the viewpoint of the family members involved.[21] How individual family members see the situation is important in understanding their response to a stressful situation.

For example, parents who define a child's death as their "fault," or an illness as evidence of their neglect, are more adversely affected than those who consider these events as independent of them.[22] Certain types of families produce members who are more likely to "personalize" events. This appears to be due to their inability to draw on outside support and/or to their lack of access to appropriate personal and internal resources.

The kind of definition attached to an illness or even to a death is, among other things, a function of the educational level of family members. The higher the educational level, the more knowledgeable a family is. Access to important "resources" (such as a higher level of education) might therefore contribute to more "realistic" definitions of the stressful events in which one participates, and hence influence the degree of stress experienced.

As an example, we can sometimes see "different" definitions appearing for certain diseases. "Leukemia," for instance, strikes a horrendous blow to family members. The word itself carries life-threatening connotations.[23] Leukemia, however, is not the disease today that it was even 10 years ago. Much progress has been made in diagnosis and treatment of this illness. However, people often require a relatively high level of education and sophistication to realize this. Therefore, an important interactive effect can be seen in regard to these two predictive variables.

A Definition of Family Types Based on the Interview Results

ISOLATE VS. INTEGRATED FAMILIES

An analysis of the families who were interviewed revealed essentially two basic types. These types have relevance for the problem of stress management and crisis formation. Although the types probably represent "ideal constructs" whose descriptions do not necessarily fit any one family in all respects, they do characterize certain aspects and unique features of the families in the study group.

The two family types are structured in such a way as to have access to different degrees of personal, internal, and external resources. In addition they have different qualities that result in different ways of defining the stress-provoking events as they occur.

For example, as noted earlier, some families in the study did not necessarily support the individual in the face of the severe stress. I have labeled these families "isolates."[24] Isolates are the opposite of the "ideal" family discussed earlier. In this study isolates are families that are internally atomized or separated. They are also closed systems, in that the members do not interact with the larger social environment. Individuals within isolates have minimal social contacts both within and outside the immediate group. Because of the atomized nature of these families they are lacking in closeness and warmth. In addition such families have lost contact with the larger kinship system and cannot draw support from the extended family. Members have virtually no club or organization memberships to draw them out into the wider world. They have little contact with ministers or other representatives of organized community institutions, and for the most part are unknown to their neighbors.

Quite obviously, isolate families do not have access to the array of resources described earlier, and probably define any stress-provoking event as threatening and outside their collective ability to control.

In contrast to isolate types, another variety of family appeared in the study group. These I call "integrated" families.[25] Members of integrated families engage in warm, personal interrelationships with each other and interact freely with the larger social system. Although such families remain closed systems, members do venture out beyond the confines of the family units themselves into the larger community. In fact most of their socializing is done with individuals and groups that lie beyond the individual family. They have confidence in their friends and neighbors, which in turn leads to a sense of confidence in themselves. They seem to trust other people. They also have a supportive kinship system, and in fact have many relationships with the outside community which help strengthen the internal integrity of the family as a unit. The integrated family corresponds closely to the ideal family discussed earlier.

STRESS, CRISIS, AND FAMILY TYPE

In terms of our ability to identify the families in this study on the basis of these attributes, it was discovered that a continuum existed, with most families falling somewhere between the isolate and integrated extremes. The assessment of relative position of actual family types along this continuum was arrived at "after the fact," that is, after assessing how the stressful event was perceived and defined by individual members of each family.

Integrated-type families seemed better prepared and better equipped to handle stress-provoking situations and events. Although all stress is crisis precipitating, actual crises seldom occurred in "integrated" families. In other words these families possessed the resources necessary to avoid crisis situations.

Isolate-type families, on the other hand, were particularly devastated by stress. The stress often developed rapidly into full-blown crises, which in turn shattered the family as a unit. It seemed that their rather meager adjustment capacities were hard-pressed to deal with stressful situations. When an isolate family experienced stress it impacted directly on individual members, who had no cushion to insulate them against the crippling effects, nor could they draw upon anything in the way of a supportive apparatus from the outside community. The family's personal, internal, and external resources appeared to be simply too meager.

Isolate-type families might be referred to as "crisis-prone" families.[26] Crisis-proneness is a function both of family resources and of the definition the family gives to the stressful event. In these families the death of a child produced tensions in other areas of family life which in turn became conflicts in themselves. Loss led to a complete collapse in communication (weakened to begin with), depressive episodes among members (due to a lack of adequate external resources to counteract the effects of isolation), sexual incompatibilities (due to the inability to share and the tendency of one spouse to blame the other), and a breakdown in cooperation. These conflicts in turn created conflicting role expectations, led to accumulation of tension, weakened still further already fragile affectional relationships, crippled what little integration existed, and lessened family stability even more.

Since isolate-type families appeared to have so few resources upon which to draw, and were not well organized to support members or protect them from stress, members of these families were less likely to define the problem as a family problem and, as noted earlier, were more likely to view it as an "individual" problem. This created a strong sense of isolation on the part of family members, and since they had little or no support, the stress of child death or terminal diagnosis took on "crisis" proportions. Isolate families were particularly devastated by any death, but when the loss was a child, it produced an immediate crisis situation of such proportions that it overwhelmed the family's meager support functions.

By contrast, the integrated-type family was more likely to define the stress-provoking event as a "family" problem and to respond to it as a family. Thus integrated families might be called "crisis proof" in the sense that collective "family" goals and needs, rather than individual ones, are emphasized.[27] The family as a unit is structured in such a way as to meet the emotional and physical requirements of the members to a high degree. Individual members draw support and sustenance from the family and therefore meet stressful events *as a unit* rather than as individuals. Integrated families have more personal, internal, and external resources available for counteracting stressful situations. Even situations as stressful as the death of a child are "managed." Such families resolve stressful problems as they arise. And they survive.

Specifically, let us take the loss of a child and try to show how the resulting stress was dealt with in both varieties of families, as these families were defined in the interviews.

In the isolate-type family, when the death of a child occurred the stress experienced by each member in turn seemed to be enhanced by the stress of other members. Each member of an isolate-type family experienced the loss *as an individual*. The family as a unit was deficient in its ability to support members in the aftermath. It simply had few resources to draw upon. Communication channels were essentially closed. The individual stood apart and alone. However, because the member was still hooked into a network of others, there was a laying-on or overlaying of the elements of stress experienced by all members which intensified the stress experienced by any one member. Under these circumstances stress became so severe that individual members collapsed under the impact, and the family as a unit ceased to function as a viable entity. That is, the compounding effects of stress damaged individual members due to the fact that the family, as a potential support system, failed.

In the integrated-type family, however, another process was at work which tended to counteract the effects of this compounding or interaction effect. In integrated-type families members sensed a responsibility to protect other members. Members felt a need to buffer others from the full impact of the stress-provoking event. Family members tended to develop an altruistic outlook—that is, each took into account other members. Each member made a conscious effort to share or to relieve some of the burden from the shoulders of others. This was possible because channels of communication and cooperation remained open. These families acted as true support systems, and seemed to have an abundance of resources available to assist members and help counteract the effects of stress.

Therefore in the isolate-type family stress was compounded for the individual by the stress of others and, paradoxically, by the isolation imposed by the lack of a family support mechanism. Integrated-type families, on the other hand, were structured as true support systems where stress was shared by all. In integrated families, stress evoked a family response and was a family affair.

Conclusions

To draw this chapter to a close, let me conclude by making a few remarks about childrearing in general in today's world.

You know, there is a myth circulating today, and that is that childrearing is easier than in earlier times because of modern medicine, child psychology, modern appliances, etc. Actually the opposite is true. These modern "conveniences" make the matter worse. For example, the improvements is medicine in recent decades have increased the undercurrent of anxiety surrounding childrearing practices within most families. In the past, children often got sick. In the past, they often died. This was to be expected. There was nothing to be done about it; it was a part of the reality of life.[28]

Today, however, we as parents have entered into a paradoxical situation. Even though we may be more aware of all the terrible things that can happen to children, we really don't consciously expect them. We don't expect life-threatening illnesses; we certainly don't expect death. Instead, today we believe we are sophisticated and knowledgeable enough to recognize possible symptoms and conditions early and to take proper preventive action.[29] As parents living in today's world we pride ourselves on our rationality and on our *control* of the events around us.

In the past, children died. It was part of the nature of things. No one held parents responsible. Today when a child develops a disease and dies, or even when death occurs suddenly and unexpectedly, it impacts on the family with such intensity that unless the family can lay claim to an array of self-protecting resources, the onslaught is devastating. Many parents have come to believe that they must accept full responsibility for the safety and welfare of their children far beyond reasonable limits. Even if they are not "blamed" by others for the terrible things that still happen to children, they often blame themselves for not being observant or knowledgeable enough to recognize hostile symptoms, or for somehow not being sufficiently in control, or for not fulfilling the protective role assigned to parents within the family today.

Consequently, because of the *isolation* of the modern family, should something "terrible" happen to children in today's world, family members will experience enormous disorganizing hardships. Unlike the past, illness and death among children are no longer common occurrences. Today for many families and for many individuals they represent major crisis-precipitating events.

In this approach to the problem of childhood loss within the family, I have treated the family as the instrument in the care of *individual survivors*. However, we need to be equally aware that the family as a unit stands alone, and we should perhaps realize that it too needs care and attention.

Perhaps we can set our sights on attempting to build within our own families those resources that seem so vital to the successful mission of the family in the modern world. In fact it would appear that the modern family is the only institution in today's world that has the potential of becoming our personal bulwark against our devastating encounters with child death.

In the next chapter I will begin a discussion of the family and bereavement by looking at the bereavement process as a series of stages with characteristic emotions and response patterns. It will be noted that although grief in response to child death is long and complicated, there is a way out for those willing to put forth the heroic effort required to achieve a resolution.

7

The Family and Bereavement

The pain of grief is just as much a part of life as the joy of love; it is, perhaps, the price we pay for love; it is the cost of commitment.[1]

When a family suffers the loss of a child, the grief experienced and expressed is often long and hard. The fact that grief is intense, however, does not necessarily imply that it is abnormal or morbid. Intense grief can be thought of as normal so long as it can be expressed. Grief becomes morbid only when it is bottled up for prolonged periods and when there is no opportunity for expression.

Enough has been written on the subject of morbid grief responses. It is not my purpose here to repeat this discussion. Instead I will describe in some detail the "normal" grieving patterns in response to the loss of a child as these have been revealed during the interview sessions with the parents.

At the time of the interviews, roughly half the mothers and fathers I talked with were experiencing difficulties in their adjustment to the loss. For example, one out of four appeared in a state of continuing denial, refusing to face, with varying degrees of success, the reality and pain of separation. These parents appeared to be fixated at the *beginning* of the grieving process, unable or unwilling to give up their attachment to the coping mechanism of denial. Another 25 percent or so appeared fixated in the *final* episode of the grieving process—at the stage of loss and loneliness, which gradually overtakes one as the acute bereavement phase ends. These individuals also were unable to move on to the resolution of their grief.

Some might be inclined to refer to these fixations as morbid responses. I prefer to regard them as "normal," given the kinds of losses to which they are a reaction. Child death, as noted earlier, is a violently devastating experience for most parents, who, in dealing with it, have no precedents or past experiences to draw from. They must "play this game by ear," and there are no guarantees concerning the outcome. Therefore almost any response pattern observable at any given point in the after-death phase should probably be considered "normal" for these kinds of losses.

It should be noted that a very few parents agreed to talk with me only after some coaxing on the part of other family members who felt that the interview might help them in some personal way. These few parents seemed totally unable to cope with the aftermath of the loss, were suffering from an array of debilitating physical symptoms, including extreme depression, and were unwilling to allow an outsider into the midst of the personal hell that dominated their existence. In my brief and unfruitful discussions with these families, it was discovered that they were among those who had suffered sudden, unexpected deaths of children—through murder or accident—usually in the late teens or older. It is indeed understandable that those experiencing the most difficulty in handling the loss would be from among this group. And it might be argued that in these few cases we were indeed dealing with a morbid or abnormal reaction.

Certainly not every family suffering a sudden loss responded in this way. However, those few who did apparently could not see the value of open communication and did not wish to expose themselves to further upset and heartache. They simply were not ready at the time of the interview to share their experiences with others.

I might add that it gave me great concern that I was not able to offer these parents a therapeutic response to the apparent turmoil and confusion they were experiencing. However, my intended purpose was to build an understanding of parental responses to child death. It was not my role, by circumstance or training, to assume the yoke of therapist, although it was plainly apparent that, for these few parents, intervention was called for.

This chapter will be devoted to outlining the dynamics of "normal" grief responses as I have defined them and as they were revealed by those parents in the study group who readily agreed to be interviewed. Even though these parents were in various stages of grief at the time of the interview, they were all willing and eager to share their experiences, and were able to provide the kinds of information necessary to build generalizations for developing an understanding of the typical response patterns of those suffering the loss of children. This, then, is the subject of the present chapter.

The Grief Syndrome

It should be noted that normal grief is not a bad thing. Normal grief is in fact a *normal* human emotion. It is an adaptive response to loss, and serves a positive function. Grief, when expressed, has a "convalescent value." As one works through it, ties to the deceased are gradually withdrawn. It allows energies to be reconstituted and new relationships to be formed. The painful, heartrending crying and wailing, disoriented and restless activities accompanying grief serve a useful and therapeutic purpose.[2]

Grief is a process of change and transformation, a passageway if you will, through which one must travel with characteristic points of reference along the way.

During the course of the interviews with the parents it became rather apparent that these mothers and fathers, having suffered their losses anywhere from seven months to 20 years before, appeared to be operating at different stages in the grieving process. In addition, they appeared to move through the intricacies of the grieving process at different rates, i.e., they reached different stages or phases within the process at different times and experienced characteristic emotions at each stage with differing degrees of intensity.

In this chapter I will attempt to identify and characterize the stages or phases associated with the normal range of grief. This discussion should benefit those who may find themselves in the position of "helpers" to grieving individuals. Knowing what stage or phase in the grieving process a given individual is at should assist one in giving the best possible help at the best possible time. It should also benefit parents themselves, in that they will be better able to recognize the character of their own responses following the death of a child.

Six stages are identifiable. Within each stage or phase are typical feelings and distinct reactions as well as definite needs and cries for help. Robert Kavanaugh, in his book *Facing Death*,[3] defines and describes a series of stages or phases in the grieving process that are remarkably similar to the stages that the families actually passed through as they attempted to deal with the aftermath of the death of a child.

Kavanaugh, in discussing his conception of the grieving process, pointed out that the seven stages he envisioned closely paralleled the five stages observed by Dr. Elisabeth Kübler-Ross in her work with dying patients who were aware of their impending death.[4] However, unlike the Kübler-Ross stages (defined as denial, anger, bargaining, depression, and acceptance),[5] the Kavanaugh stages seem more relevant to the grieving experiences of survivors rather than to those who were themselves dying.

The seven Kavanaugh stages (combined into six for the purpose of this discussion) are defined as: (1) shock and denial; (2) disorganization; (3) violent emotions; (4) guilt; (5) loss and loneliness; and (6) the twin stages of relief and reestablishment. I found these stages to be almost a perfect overlap of what was discovered in the interviews. In addition they offered a salient explanation of the experiences of parents and siblings as they ferreted their way through the maze of emotions and feelings in the aftermath of the death of a child.

Before I begin my discussion of the bereavement process and the stages involved, we need to understand that the "stage model" I am using here is simply a reflection of reality and not the definitive approach to understanding parental responses to child death. Also, the "stages" I am about to discuss do not necessarily appear in any kind of order or arrangement. Kavanaugh's description is quite clear. He maintains that the stages of the grieving process are not separate; rather:

> they invariably intertwine and overlap. Nor are they successive in the order listed or in any order. Shock customarily intones the grieving process, while reestablishment, if reached, means grief is over. In between the stages vary in almost every conceivable way. Certain stages can be bypassed altogether, while others may last no more than a few minutes. Highly charged feelings like anger are frequently more like flashes than emotional states, and softer emotions like sadness can remain as permanent features in the post-grief personality. . . .[6]

He goes on to say:

> Only a practiced eye can accurately discern the dominant themes at work and know readily the pressing needs of the griever. . . .[7]

As Kavanaugh implies in the last paragraph of the above quotation, perhaps we all should try to develop a "practiced eye" and become familiar with the stages through which individuals pass as they adjust to significant losses. Important needs appear to be exhibited at each stage. Those of us who are intimately involved with grieving parents need to be sensitized to watch carefully, listen permissively, and respond appropriately.

The Grieving Process

As was pointed out in general terms in an earlier chapter, although each family experienced loss differently, there was nevertheless, paradoxically, a similarity with which each person and family in the present study responded. I believe the differences observed in individual and family grief responses were due to the different stages at which the person or family was functioning. The speed at which a person or family passed through the stages varied greatly from person to person and from family to family. Some moved through the stages rather quickly and "recovered." Others became fixated or delayed at one stage or another and were unable to complete the process in a given amount of time. Various factors entered the situation and helped determine the rate of movement of an individual or family through the grieving process.

For example, different modes of death produced different patterns and movement rates. In the aftermath of sudden, unexpected death, movement through the grieving process was often unsteady, with many points of fixation. Parents experiencing anticipated death, i.e., after a child's long illness, seemed to move at greater speed and with fewer diversions. In addition, personality characteristics either facilitated or hindered the ability of the individual to move from stage to stage. Parents who appeared to be more integrated and secure in their attitude and personality makeup were better able to withstand the emotional battering that such experiences delivered. Individuals who appeared weak, insecure, and unsure of their ability to handle the situation moved unsteadily through the staging process and often became fixated at some point.

Also, certain features of the family itself (as noted in Chapter 6), such as how the family defined the event and the internal and external resources available to deal with the stress of loss, contributed to the speed at which the family moved through the grieving process.

The "similarity" I speak of, then, in regard to the human response to loss was found in the consistency with which the various stages occurred in the grieving process; the "differences" that appeared pertain to the variable rates of movement through the process.

Let us look at the "stages" in the grieving process and try to analyze them from the viewpoint of what the families and parents in the present study actually experienced. There was a sequence—of sorts—that families and parents appeared to follow as they moved through their grieving. That is, as a process, grief seemed to have a beginning, a middle, and for some, an end.

SHOCK AND DENIAL

The beginning of the grieving process almost always entailed the stage of *shock*, and subsequently *denial*. Shock was especially evident in cases of suicide, murder, and sudden death. Where there was an expectation of death (i.e., after a long illness), at the time of death, shock—characterized by an emotional numbness—was generally not evident. Denial, however, regardless of the type of death, usually was present and operative for a considerable period of time. In many cases, shock and denial were the twin stages that served as the precursor of the entire grief episode.

Individuals were generally unable to recognize these stages as they were passing through them. Seldom could the individual sit back and make an objective assessment of his or her feelings and behaviors in the stressful situation. Most parents simply reacted, without considering either the consequences or causes of their actions.

An objective assessment of one's feelings was difficult because of one common feature shared by almost all survivors—an intense preoccupation with thoughts and images of the deceased. Thoughts of the child dominated the parents' minds from the very beginning, and blinded them to an "objective" evaluation of their own behavior and the circumstances surrounding it. This stage became obvious only to others who were present but removed from the trauma of the situation.

How do shock and denial manifest themselves in this initial phase of the grieving process? What kinds of behavior might be viewed as an indication that shock and denial are operating?

First, let us take shock. One important component of shock, as an intense psychological and physical reaction, is emotional *numbness*—the inability to "feel" effectively and respond appropriately. Our common expectations tell us that when the death of a significant person occurs in our lives, we should respond with great emotional outpouring of sorrow.

When a child died, particularly a sudden death, parents often initially responded with bewilderment and shock. The expected emotional outpouring many times did not occur. They often behaved, for the moment at least, as if nothing had happened. They continued with routine patterns, made emotionless mechanical responses, and appeared to be oblivious to the situation. This sometimes led to misunderstandings on the part of others who were prepared for, and expected, a severe emotional reaction.

An individual in shock operates under a condition of total disbelief. It is a time of confusion and bewilderment. The mind is trying to fathom the significance of the event while at the same time attempting to protect the system from the full impact of this harsh reality. Shock carries a physical penalty. When it first occurs, the heart rate tends to speed up, blood pressure falls, the skin turns cold and clammy, and the individual experiences an acute sense of terror.

Shock is usually short-lived; its full impact may last only for minutes, hours at most. However, remnants of shock can last for days. For the majority of parents interviewed who had suffered an unexpected loss, shock was indeed a characteristic first response and tended to be somewhat long-lasting. In fact, as noted earlier, it was found that one of the main differences between survivors of anticipated death (after a long illness) and survivors of sudden, unexpected death was in the length and depth of the shock experienced.

In the case of anticipated death, shock was more characteristic in the immediate aftermath of the *diagnosis* than of the death. It should be noted that during the course of a long illness family members had time to prepare for the eventual death of the child. There was often a form of "anticipatory" grief expressed and experienced as realization of the child's death gradually came into consciousness. The actual death might not have occurred until months after the initial diagnosis. Therefore the "end" was never the traumatic event that it often was in the case of sudden death, or of hearing a terminal diagnosis for the first time. Consequently the actual death generally carried only the "shock" of sudden relief or release, which for many was suggestive of a "positive" experience.

Of course the experience of sudden death was of a different nature. It always produced severe shock, was always a very negative encounter, and always carried with it a set of debilitating physical symptoms. Parents reacting to these losses were unable to think, to feel, or to believe, sometimes for days afterward, a clear indication of the remnants or after-effects of shock.

A mother, whose 8-year-old son drowned in a hotel swimming pool while on vacation, said:

I really could not face it. I guess I didn't want to. It was such a horrifying, unbelievable experience. . . . I would get up in the morning and simply would not—or could not—believe he was gone! I tried not to think about it and yet my mind was totally preoccupied with it. I walked around in a state of total disbelief for over a week.

Another mother, whose 10-year-old daughter died suddenly as a result of an undetected congenital heart defect, said:

She was so healthy. . . . When they told us what she died of, I kept thinking over and over that it was all a big mistake! Someone is perpetrating a cruel hoax on us! Her death made no sense! I could not comprehend it! . . . I know I was in a state of shock for days. . . .

As indicated, shock was usually not of long duration. As the parent-survivor began to recover from its physical effects, he or she almost always entered the next substage, *denial*. Denial is defined here as a psychological defense or coping mechanism that came rapidly into play as shock subsided. It too is a protective device, structured to protect the system psychologically from the trauma that is trying to overtake it. In some cases denial was very long-lasting, extending for months into the postdeath period. Denial can be said to be operating when the individual returns to a somewhat normal, nonaggravated state fairly soon after the loss and with no evidence of grief's continuing to be expressed. The individual begins the process of picking up the threads of his or her previous existence and appears to return to normal functioning.

I was told by a majority of parents that the mere mention of the death, or even the child's name, during this period often triggered intense emotional suffering. Therefore it appeared that parents rejected all discussion of the subject, which led to a tendency on the part of others to avoid them, which in turn tended to perpetuate their denial state. For example, a father, whose 24-year-old son was killed in action in Vietnam in 1974, told me:

When my son was killed, that is, when we first received word of his death, it was as if someone had ripped out my guts! . . . I could not even tolerate the mention of his name for months. . . . I avoided all reminders of him. This seemed to be the only way I could reasonably deal with his loss. . . . I know I drove people away at the very times I needed them most. . . .

Quite frequently outside observers misjudged the situation and actually assumed that the survivor had adjusted to the loss. This was seldom the case, however. In reality it takes years to overcome completely the emotional upheaval caused by the death of a child. When someone appears to be making a rather rapid recovery, we can bet that denial is operating.

Denial is a very "normal" coping mechanism and must be recognized as performing a genuine role in initiating the grieving process. As a protective device, it is designed to buffer the system from the trauma of an event too tragic to deal with all at once. It is important that those in supportive or helping roles recognize the value of this device. While in a state of denial the individual should be tolerated, not berated for his or her apparent unresponsiveness.

No attempt should be made to change or modify the behavior of the griever. We certainly must never attempt to destroy someone's hold on denial. The individual survivor may be consciously, desperately trying to sustain elements of denial as the only possible way of avoiding the overwhelming pain that comes with recognition. It is important that this response run its course, since it is serving a purpose. All that may be needed is our supportive presence. Words may be nonessential and unimportant. As supporters and observers, perhaps our greatest responsibility is to be prepared to "catch" the individual when he or she collapses into the "second stage" of the grieving process.

As I said earlier, denial can be long-lasting; certainly it is more tenacious than shock. Where denial extends into weeks or months, this may be an indication that it is becoming pathological so that perhaps some sort of professional assistance may be required. However, this is a personal and individual decision, to be made only after a full evaluation of all extenuating circumstances.

In regard to the many parents in the present study who displayed shock and denial as initial first reactions, several were still operating in a modified state of denial at the time of the interviews, in some cases years after the loss. In these cases, several parents even recognized that denial was still operating as a part of their response patterns. That is, intellectually they were aware of what they had experienced, but simply found it "easier" (if not healthier) to continue to deny the experience emotionally. If one wishes to refer to these situations as pathological, so be it. To the parents involved, however, they seemed to be getting along fairly well. This was their way of handling this tragedy. They were able to deal with it only in bits and pieces, chipping away at reality a little at a time. Even though this extended their grieving over a very long time, they were surviving. Perhaps we might refer to this response as simple "avoidance," reserving the term "denial" for the more unconscious attempts at escape.

Seldom do friends, neighbors, and relatives understand such long-term reactions, however. This makes it doubly difficult and places a heavy strain on the family and individual survivors, particularly in their relationships with others outside the situation.

DISORGANIZATION

This stage, as it was revealed in the behavior of the parents, represented the actual beginning of the grieving process. As long as denial was operating, no "emotional" recognition of the loss, and therefore no expression of genuine grief, was possible. This stage again was recognizable only from the perspective of others outside the immediate situation.

The line of separation between denial and disorganization was of course not solidly drawn, as might appear from this step-by-step or "stage-by-stage" discussion. The usual case was for survivors to waver in and out of denial during most of the postdeath grieving period. However, at some point, generally not long after the actual death, the individual entered the nebulous period of disorganization or disequilibrium, either after the main thrust of denial had subsided somewhat or even while it was still dominant.

A common characteristic of this stage, as noted by the survivors interviewed, was the heavy outpouring of "confused" emotion due usually (so it was interpreted) to the fact that denial was beginning to lose its grip. Survivors found themselves thrown "out of balance," so to speak, by the event. This was particularly true in the case of sudden death, where disorganization was most noticeable. For these types of sudden death the overwhelming realization of a tragedy came thundering in upon the parents with a vicious intensity. Crying, even wailing, was a common initial symptom, sometimes accompanied by excessive feelings of weakness and fatigue. In fact displays of such physical symptoms as chills, nausea, light-headedness, and dizziness were quite common, and added to the confusion and disorganization the individual was experiencing. From the perspective of the suffering person, life appeared to be in utter chaos and the future seemed out of focus and frightening. A father told me:

My son was 17 when his life was snuffed out by a drunken driver. . . . I can't tell you how difficult it was for me, for weeks afterward, to even put one foot in front of the other! I lost all incentive to live. I couldn't communicate with anyone; I couldn't work; I couldn't sleep; I couldn't stay in the house. I cared about nothing! I was totally confused and disorganized for weeks. My life was in utter chaos. I kept having visions of Tommy lying on that slab in the morgue [this father was called to identify his son and was forced to view his son's bloodied and broken body without any preparation]. I could not get these images out of my mind. I believe these preoccupations contributed to the massive confusion that dominated my life at that time. . . .

This brief excerpt relates a situation that was not too different from what other parents, particularly those suffering a sudden loss, experienced. This of course depicts a situation in the early phases of the grieving process, and we can certainly see the massive confusion and disorganization that is apparent at this time.

It was during this stage that the griever's mind appeared not to be connected to the senses. Individuals often did not correctly see or hear what was happening around them. As revealed in the above quotation, a dominant feature of these early stages was preoccupation with thoughts of the deceased. Such thoughts infiltrated the conscious mind and other thoughts were discarded. Thus the situation became confusing and chaotic, with little consistency in response. The individual walked around as if in a daze, incoherent and confused, trying to do what was right but having little success.

Another characteristic of this phase was the presence of illusory phenomena, which sometimes appeared quite vividly. The individual claimed to hear the child's voice and, particularly, crying. In a very large number of cases survivors actually felt the "presence" of the deceased child. This was experienced during "quiet times," usually in or near the child's favorite place in the home, but also in church, at the cemetery, and in the quiet of one's bed at night. Although confusing, this was by no means a frightening experience. Many parents stated that they wished it could have continued, even though such phenomena did extend well into the later stages of the bereavement process.

It is important for supporters to understand that just about the time survivors entered this "stage of disorganization," important decisions usually had to be made regarding arrangements for memorial services, funerals and burials, what to do with the child's things, how to deal with the child's room, and even whether or not to continue living in the home, which was now filled with painful memories. It is essential that, if possible, decisions be postponed until the person can reestablish his or her grip on reality. If it is not possible to postpone important decisions, they should be made with the help of someone close to the family, someone with a level head who is separated from the emotional trauma of the situation. Certainly the decision of whether or not to change one's place of residence, or what to do with the child's room or his or her personal belongings, or even whether or not to cremate, should be postponed until a later time when a more reasoned situation exists.

In regard to our families, generally none of this was possible. Many problems resulted from decisions made too early, usually during the stage of disorganization, thereby causing burdensome emotional upheavals later when a more objective assessment was possible. A number of these decisions pertained to final disposition, where cremation was recommended and carried through but later parents discovered that a "very wrong" decision had been made. There were also a number of early decisions to move, to change residences, only to discover that, painful as the remembrances were at the time, they were now treasured beyond anything imaginable but now were lost forever. A mother said:

One week after Priscilla's death I was in her room throwing away all her personal possessions. I wish someone then had stopped me! I felt that if I rid my life of her personal belongings, I could go on and finish my grieving in an orderly fashion. I had heard of families creating "monuments" for their children and I was determined not to allow that to happen to us. . . . My God! How stupid can one person be! I literally threw away all my memories! I had no idea how important these little things would become in the months ahead. . . .

We must allow individuals and families the time to pass through this stage and must encourage as few problems as possible along the way.

Survivors in the grip of disorganization and disequilibrium were like paper blowing in the wind. They were tossed about here and there depending on which gusts hit them first. They had no sense of direction, no goals, and could accomplish no tasks. They were completely at the mercy of outside forces and made no attempt to determine their own direction.

It was quite apparent that this again was a time when understanding was required on the part of those involved in, but not directly affected by, the tragedy.

The stage of disorganization, like that of shock and denial preceding it, was generally of short duration. While it was manifesting itself, however, those who were standing by to give support simply needed to be present, providing "protection" for the individual as he or she wandered about aimlessly.

Unfortunately this kind of support was seldom available. Parents were often met with insensitive clichés, unnecessary words, and inappropriate responses at these critical times. Some parents needed quiet times to reflect, but were seldom left alone. Others required continual companionship, but were often avoided. It seemed that so few—and this included close relatives and friends—really knew how to respond to the death of a child and how to truly meet the needs of survivors.

The disorganization phase often became totally debilitating for the parents in our study group. A variety of defensive mechanisms became operative, all designed as protective devices. Denial of course continued to be present while the individual drifted in and out of this coping device as he or she tried to deal with the utter confusion that seemed to dominate the situation. Another kind of escape mechanism which appeared quite prominently among these parents was the tendency to want to sleep constantly. By sleeping, one could "turn off" the world so to speak, at least temporarily, and could escape the pain. There was indeed pain at this stage, not only the pain of confusion but the pain of an increasingly felt sense of loss. And it was searing, excruciating. Sleep of course was one way the body responded to pain, both physical and mental. It was therefore important that survivors be allowed the privilege of escaping pain through sleep, providing that it was not drug induced.

It should be noted that drug therapy serves no important purpose in the treatment of grief. Grief must be "experienced" in order to be resolved. The individual must complete his or her "grief work," as Lindemann refers to it, which implies suffering through the pain of loss and experiencing the emotions of separation.[8] Artificially controlling the emotional reactions through drugs simply delays the healing process. If the individual is kept in a drug-induced tranquilized state, although this is certainly less painful, the body's natural defensive mechanisms become ineffective and the individual falls into a state of "suspended animation" as it were, where all progress or forward movement is halted. Therefore drug therapy, except of the mildest sort, should be discouraged during this and all stages of the grieving process.

There was another symptom of disorganization that appeared quite prominently among our parents. This was the hyperactivity—the agitation, jitteriness, and talkativeness—that seemed to be common when in a wakeful state.

Agitation and jitteriness were probably quite disconcerting to those closest to the situation trying to help. This was often manifested in repeated requests that things be done or that people be notified, even after being told repeatedly that the requests had been taken care of. The reason for this is that the person suffering this symptom was unable to retain information. His or her ears were not connected for hearing nor the eyes for seeing—a sign of the intense confusion of this period.

In addition survivors were unable to relax and busied themselves with meaningless tasks. They seemed to be continually on the go, refusing even to sit through a meal. Preoccupation with thoughts of the deceased again contributed to feelings of agitation and nervousness. It appeared that individuals attempted to rid their minds of this traumatic reality by burying themselves in activity.

Talkativeness can be very nerve-racking for those giving support. Talking was essential at this stage, however. It was not necessary that any sense be made of what was said, nor was a response required. Helpers should be there simply to listen and offer support by their receptiveness of whatever unusual behavior occurs.

VIOLENT EMOTIONS

As realization gradually began to reach inward and achieve control over the person's conscious mind, denial became increasingly difficult to adhere to. As denial began to fade, this propelled the individual forward, as it were, into a new stage in the grieving process. This is the stage of violent emotions, and was typically experienced at some point by all parents in the study. This stage or phase appeared at different times in the life cycle of the bereavement process. For some parents it occurred fairly soon after the loss, usually within days. For others it was delayed, sometimes for weeks. Much depended on the circumstances of the loss and the intensity with which denial impacted. Violent emotions in the grieving process were said to have arrived when anger, resentment, and distrust began to appear at the surface and the survivors lashed out at those around them.

Anger, vindictiveness, and hostility were thrust outward and targeted on anything that moved. This might have been a husband or wife, a son or daughter, a brother or sister, the doctor, paramedics, ambulance attendants, nurses, emergency-room personnel, neighbors, friends—virtually anyone within reach. Even God and the deceased children themselves were not spared from the vindictive outbursts of grief-stricken parents.

Blame was also thrust outward at this stage. Like anger, it too became attached to almost anyone in the near environment. Individual survivors looked for some way to explain what had happened, and in this state of anger they projected responsibility outward onto others. It was only in the later stages of the grieving process that anger and hostility and blame were turned inward, when it became apparent to the sufferer that one is really alone in one's efforts to deal with the reality of death and separation.

Husbands and wives responded differently at this stage. Men seemed to express themselves more in a physical way, in some cases striking outward but seldom beyond the bounds of the family. Sometimes wives, children, and on occasion even the family pet became the target of verbal abuse or physical attack. More often than not, men struck out at inanimate things, i.e., a fist through a wall, a glass door smashed, a door pulled from its hinges, a magazine rack kicked across the room. Many of the men interviewed indicated they had indeed reacted in just these ways.

Women on the other hand tended to turn their anger inward in a less open display. In these cases it often became associated with guilt and self-blame. This was a quieter form of anger. It was also less likely to attract attention, but nevertheless was just as severe and just as debilitating.

As noted earlier, God especially became the object of hostility by both mothers and fathers. We all tend to react with great abhorrence and an inability to comprehend any meaning, particularly in the sudden death of a child: Why? Why did God allow this to happen? How could a loving God condone such a horrendous event? These were questions often asked, especially by those suffering sudden losses, but seldom satisfactorily answered.

The tendency on the part of a parent to question God's loving nature often raised a tumultuous conflict with that person's religious orientation. Many parents "lost faith" at these critical times, and turned away from God and religion because they held Him responsible. For some the rejection of God was of short duration. For others it took considerable time for a "return to the fold" to occur.

For most, the eventual rekindling of one's earlier religious commitments was indeed a rather common occurrence in the later stages of the postgrieving process. It was found that a majority of parents, even those who expressed little religious commitment prior to the loss, eventually turned, or returned, to religion in an attempt to find some peace of mind while living through the blatant loneliness of long-term separation. As noted in Chapter 2, by turning to religion and emphasizing the existence of an afterlife, parents more easily dealt with separation by viewing it as only *temporary*. They came to believe that they had not "lost" the child forever, but only for the length of time that they would live on this earth.

Let me mention another way that anger and hostility manifested themselves at this stage. Perhaps half the parents interviewed indicated (but not without expressions of remorse and guilt) that the deceased *child* became the object of anger and hostile outbursts in the early stages of the grief response. I think it is rather common that grieving parents sometimes attack the object of their grief. Parents reported that they found themselves "shouting" at the child, particularly in the case of an accidental death, "Why weren't you more careful!!!" The reasoning was that if the deceased had paid more attention to what they were doing or where they were, they would still be with us now. It was therefore the child's fault that he or she had died. The child was to blame for the pain that the parents were now suffering. Therefore blaming the deceased for his or her own death and responding in an angry manner with hostile gestures was not at all uncommon. By virtue of the rather large number of parents who admitted these feelings, I would suggest that it was a typical pattern associated with this stage of violent emotions.

This stage of violent emotions served a purpose. It allowed the physical expression of built-up stress and tension. And venting seemed to have a therapeutic affect. One father told me that the way he responded during this phase was to go into the garage, close the door, and scream several times as loudly as he could. Another said that he collected cardboard boxes, kept them in his basement, and on occasion would go there and beat them into confetti with a baseball bat. These harmless outbursts served as a release of tension and perhaps reduced a potentially dangerous situation, at least for those closest to these persons.

The stage of violent outbursts is to be understood as a normal part of the grieving response. It is, however, the most difficult phase for those offering assistance. To be around continual hostility and anger is in itself depressing. We often grow impatient with people who are moody and angry and upset. We become intolerant and angry ourselves, and begin to judge their behavior from the viewpoint of our own moral and psychological framework. This is unfortunate because we miss the opportunity to be of real assistance, and help our friends cope, when they need it the most.

Moreover we need to understand this stage for what it is—the "safety valve" of the grieving process. It allows dangerous pressures, in the form of stress, to escape. This stage, like those before, will also eventually pass into oblivion. And at that time survivors may well apologize profusely for their previously abusive behavior.

GUILT

As one progressed forward through the grieving process, eventually at some point, either sooner or later, the individual reached the phase or stage of guilt. Guilt was the one characteristic that was most commonly associated with the grieving process. It was in fact inescapable. All parents indicated that they felt and experienced guilt at some point during the bereavement period. Why? Why does guilt occur as a response to child death?

One possible answer is that children do not die from old age. There is no such phenomenon as "natural" death in childhood. Therefore, since parents knew that children die from some "cause," this led to an inescapable sense of guilt generated from the survivor's perceived failure to eliminate or recognize that cause beforehand. Parents felt that if they had recognized early symptoms, or if they had been more perceptive in regard to some of the dangers all children face while growing up, or if they had made one decision rather than another, their child might still be alive. These "evaluations of behavior" relative to what they should or should not have done led to the growth of feelings of guilt that tended to persist, sometimes for years afterward.

Of course guilt is very difficult to deal with. There are no clear-cut answers to the question of how to relieve it. It is something every surviving parent must face and something every parent must in some way come to terms with. It can and did reach devastating proportions, even to the point where some parents became incapacitated. Under the impact of severe guilt contemplation of suicide was common, and in a few cases it came to be defined as the only escape. It may be that the "wish to die" (discussed in Chapter 2 as a common pattern shared by most parents in the aftermath of child death) was in part prompted by guilt reactions. Attempted suicide was an extreme response of course, and I do not mean to imply that it was common.

There were many ways that guilt was expressed, and many motivations involved. Sometimes the prospect of achieving pleasure and enjoyment was a source of guilt. Sometimes guilt was generated simply over being alive—surviving, while the child died. This is known as the "survivor syndrome" and is a common response to other kinds of losses as well. Sometimes the loss was defined as a "punishment" for some wrongdoing in one's past life, which in turn generated guilt and self-blame. There were various levels of responsiveness in regard to the way parents ultimately came to handle guilt. Some seemed to handle it better than others. However, there was no easy way out.

Also, guilt was something to contend with on a continuing basis. Although it appeared at a particular point in the grief pattern, once in place it tended to remain firmly entrenched.

Roughly half the parents in the study group indicated at the time of the interview that even though they had worked through most of the stages in the grieving process, they still retained some elements of guilt. This was particularly true of those who had experienced sudden losses. They indicated that they were gradually dealing with their guilt feelings, at the time not as pronounced as they were earlier but still a part of their overall response patterns. Thus even after several years parents were still unable to rid themselves completely of these now-subdued feelings.

From the viewpoint of supporters, it does no good to admonish individuals for feeling the way they do. Survivors will be more receptive of advice if our response is one of understanding and support rather than judgmental in tone. As supporters, we must simply recognize that guilt is a part of the grieving process. Parents are required to bear the weight. There is nothing anyone can, or perhaps should, do to try to remove it. Mothers and fathers must learn to live with it, with the hope that "time and patience" will heal the wounds and encapsulate the guilt.

One thing others can do is to encourage parents to deal openly with their guilt. It should not be buried or pushed out of conscious existence. However, many parents dealt with it in just this way. When this occurred, it plagued them in an insidious way and was far more destructive than if they had faced it and dealt with it directly. Allowing guilt to slip beneath the surface of conscious awareness tended to produce a highly destructive impact and greatly complicated other problems. Guilt is difficult enough to deal with without being compounded by other unconscious psychological difficulties. By keeping it conscious and current in our minds, we can consciously work to reduce its intensity.

LOSS AND LONELINESS

Somewhere in the grieving process, after the stage of disorganization and after the individual has passed through the acute stage of emotional expression, and most likely after guilt has made its appearance, the individual survivor will enter the most personally devastating period of the entire bereavement episode. This is also the stage of longest duration, lasting anywhere from a year to a lifetime. Although this stage is called by various names, I prefer to refer to it as Kavanaugh does and call it the stage of loss and loneliness.

It is at this stage that our survivors "fall off the edge of the world," so to speak, into a darkened, bottomless abyss. Every single parent I interviewed indicated this to be the most gripping and lonely and frightening time of the entire postdeath period. Feelings ran deep, characterized by remorse, sadness, emptiness, hopelessness, and above all, depression. This stage usually crept in insidiously without warning. No preparation was possible.

Often this stage was postponed until late in the grieving process, after the upheaval of the acute phase of grief had passed. When the family began to settle down to a fairly normal routine, when it appeared that active grieving had passed, it was at this point that the sickening and bone-chilling sense of loss began its assault.

Parents seemed to come to a realization that they had to face this loss *alone*, without help from other relatives, friends, or community. In a sense others had put the loss behind them and had taken the attitude that life must now return to the state that existed prior to the loss. These associates, who at one time might have been called "helpers," now stepped out of their supportive and helping roles, returned to the status of ordinary "friends" and "family," and expected the survivors to cease their grieving and return to the "swing of things" which was defined as "normal" family routine. There seemed no longer to be a willingness to share, to give tolerant support, or to even talk about the loss. Most others now considered the topic to be morbid belaboring of an event that they preferred simply to forget.

The intimate family, however, whose body and soul had been assaulted by the tragedy of child death, could not "simply forget." They still harbored the burning need to remember, to experience, and to talk. But now there was no one willing to listen or to share. Consequently, rejection by those meaningful other people, who no longer felt compelled even to recognize that a loss had occurred, propelled the survivors into this new stage characterized by intense feelings of loss and loneliness.

As noted in Chapter 2, parents vowed *never to forget*. And the hurt was intensified because now others had indeed forgotten. Guilt often filtered into this phase, which increased its intensity. Parents felt guilty that they too might again come to enjoy life, that they might achieve some degree of normality in their life patterns. Many actually feared their eventual recovery, since it would mean—so they thought—that the death of their child didn't matter! Thus when on occasion they felt some sense of joy in living again, when they were able to laugh again, they simultaneously experienced a searing sense of guilt. It was as if they were intentionally hanging on to these negative feelings as insurance that their child was important.

During the weeks and months of this stage grief often reached delusional states, and in some cases temporary morbid reactions were encountered. Although grief can reach this level of intensity at any stage in the beareavement process, severe reactions are more likely to be experienced during this stage of loss and loneliness. Since the survivor is now shut off from the rest of the world, as is characteristic during this stage, grief became physical and debilitating because it could no longer be expressed openly. It seemed that as long as feelings could be expressed to others, the crises that continued to build tended to lose their cutting edges. However, when survivors were forced to bottle up these feelings and expressions of guilt and pain, as was characteristic of this stage, the guilt and pain tended to become internalized and gave rise to a myriad of physical symptoms. Common physical responses, some of which appeared in the study group, included chronic headaches, insomnia, stomach and digestive problems, and in more severe cases, ulcerative colitis, respiratory distress, and evidence of certain neurotic and antisocial behaviors.

Four out of ten of the parents interviewed experienced an array of such symptoms as they moved through this stage of loss and loneliness.

Again I do not mean to imply that this was the only time in the grieving process when these types of severe grief responses occurred. However, this was indeed a fertile period. The parents were cut off from meaningful participation, so the pain and hurt reached a high degree of intensity which often triggered such reactions.

When grief begins to manifest itself with this kind of physical intensity, this may be an indication that it is overtaking the individual's adjustment capacity, that he or she cannot adequately resolve the problem. Grief of this kind might be defined as "abnormal," and professional help might be required to deal with it. The individuals in the study group seldom sought professional help, however. In the usual case where these kinds of reactions developed, they were simply allowed to run their course, and in most cases the individual survived—not without the emotional scars that such experiences inflict, however. These parents can look back on their experiences during this phase of their grief and know they have been through a major battle; they carry the wounds to prove it. The war still is not won but they are surviving, and they are making some progress.

Of course severe or morbid grief reactions of the type noted above were generally *not* the rule at this stage for the majority of parents in the study group. The usual scenario was that as parents began to pass through this phase, active or acute grief simply "changed" into a form of "chronic" grief. Chronic grief is not morbid, nor is it even necessarily defined as severe; however, it is often more difficult to deal with. Chronic grief was experienced as a dull ache felt deep inside the person. The individual was unable to find continuing satisfaction or happiness in life. Preoccupation with thoughts of the deceased child continued at this stage. Nothing one did seemed to help the ache or the preoccupation. The loss became very vivid and real. All details of the events leading up to, and including, the death as well as the aftermath now came into clear focus. Even the facial features and other personal characteristics of the deceased child, which previously seemed out of focus and far away, became crystal clear and very near. Such images were what created the intense feelings of loneliness for most parents. Quiet crying by oneself was common at this stage. Parents came to believe that they were the only ones in the world who still cared and the only ones who were still suffering. They searched desperately for relief, but could find no real peace.

I talk about "parents" suffering, but it should be noted that this was an individual hell, containing only *one* person. Even one's spouse became "out of reach" during this stage. If the mother remained in the home and had no outside job that could pull her away from the sights and sounds of a homelife that no longer contained the deceased child, she suffered severely and alone. She tended to lose touch emotionally with her husband, whose work took him away from the home for most of the day. The father had contacts outside the home in the form of work associates and friends. He also had a consistent time-consuming activity which took his mind away from morbid thoughts. The father was perhaps even able to find a number of individuals among his outside associates who were still willing to listen and who themselves were willing to give support. In short, the father's outside contacts and outside activities tended to make his period of loss and loneliness less intense and of shorter duration. A wide gulf often opened between husband and wife during this stage, leading to a breakdown in the communication that is the cornerstone of a successful family life.

I spoke about this earlier in my discussion of the strains on the marriage produced by violent deaths. However, I think it is safe to say that in any case of childhood death the gradual curtailment of communication between husband and wife that often occurred during this stage of loss and loneliness had a disastrous effect on the integrity of the family organization. As the gap widened, the husband generally came to the point where he no longer understood his wife's continued unhappiness and remorse, and even began to question her mental state. Nor did the wife understand the husband's apparent lack of interest in the event and his "coldness" toward her and what she was struggling with. She often accused him of no longer having any feelings for the dead child. He often accused her of trying to live in the past, of trying to hang on to the child.

Various writers have indicated, depending on which study is quoted, that from 30 to 70 percent of the marriages of parents who suffer the death of a child end in divorce. And these dissolutions usually come during the stage of loss and loneliness. Thus divorce is seen not as a cause of marital dissolution but as a symptom of the family's inability to deal realistically with this very painful phase in the grieving process.

Less than one in ten families in the study group had actually experienced a family breakdown, but many knew of other families that had in fact dissolved under the impact of these events. A very large number of our families had indeed experienced many of the symptoms that lead to collapse, but somehow had managed to hold the family unit together. This is not to say that they will not experience problems in the future. In fact several families, perhaps as many as a third, were experiencing significant problems at the time of the interview, to the point where they were contemplating a split. Perhaps the reason I did not encounter a rate of dissolution comparable to that reported in the literature was due to the voluntary nature of the interviewing process. Broken families were probably more reluctant to volunteer to be interviewed. Therefore my study group was probably biased in favor of families which had somehow managed to hold themselves together.

It should be noted that this represents the *final* stage in the grieving process. The intensity of feelings associated with this stage, although very great for a time, gradually subsided as the weeks and months passed. I might add, however, that remnants of the primary symptoms of this phase often tended to remain in subdued form for a very long time, perhaps for the majority of the parent's life. Such remnants of feelings are not blatant, but often come to lie just below the conscious surface. They consist of feelings of a mild sense of anxiety and a general dissatisfaction with life. Anniversaries and various other times during the year—birthdays, death days, holidays of various kinds—become particularly difficult for the individual. These are important times for family members. They are also troublesome times. These are the times that tend to keep the subdued expressions of grief alive.

We might refer to this tendency to hang on to the past as a form of "shadow grief."[9] Although the concept originally applied to the long-term grief experiences of mothers in regard to infant death, in many respects it also applies to child death. It may be that shadow grief is a particular and unique aspect of the long-term response to infant *and* child death in our society.

RELIEF AND REESTABLISHMENT

For those few, more fortunate individuals who made all the right decisions and who could count on continued support from family, friends, and community in dealing with all phases of grieving, the end of the grieving process was reached. The "end" was not really a stage at all but the termination and resolution of grief. When this occurred, the person reached "relief" and was in the process of "reestablishing" himself or herself in the world of the living.

This "end," however, never arrived all at once. The line between the stage of loss and loneliness and this end zone of relief and reestablishment was not solidly drawn. There was a huge "gray area" between the two phases in which a significant amount of rebuilding took place. As the intensity of the feelings of loss and loneliness gradually subsided, the individual began the slow ordeal of picking up the pieces of his or her past life and painstakingly fitting them back together. This was a time all grieving individuals strived for, but I must admit that only a few of the parents interviewed had made it.

However, if all "goes right" for the individual as he or she moves through the latter part of this stage, the person might successfully experience a sense of genuine "relief." However, I stress that all must "go right." All did not always "go right" for many families. Some lost their base of external support too early. Relatives and friends withdrew their help and assistance, or communication became disrupted within the family, with the result that external and internal support for each person was curtailed. Consequently these families were unable to reach the final phase and instead remained fixated in the throes of shadow grief, sometimes for years.

Perhaps I should note that one means of achieving success in the grieving process, and eventually resolving even the remnants of grief in shadow form, is to seek out *support groups* in the community. These are special, organized groups, noted earlier, consisting of other families who have had similar experiences. They are designed to form strong bonds of friendship and love between parents and families.

As members of such groups, the parents in this study were working their way through the maze of the grieving experience, and with the help and unfailing support of other parents, were achieving some success in resolving the remnants of grief. Perhaps one might never come to the point of truly *accepting* the loss, but with help provided by an active, interested support group, one might learn to live with it. In many ways this could be the greatest gift of all.

One might spend a very long time functioning within the protective cocoon of a support group. And individual parents found this to be a very worthwhile and satisfying experience in that they were not only helping themselves but also helping others.

For those who were able to achieve this end zone of relief and reestablishment, happiness was no longer out of reach. Rather it was eagerly sought out. Satisfaction in life and living returned. Parents found that now they could "remember" and at the same time be happy and content. Memories took on a new existence. They became pleasant—no longer morbid, no longer anxiety producing.

A great leap forward was made. Oh, one might still cry. One might still feel sad on occasion. Reminders of the deceased child, such as photographs, cherished things, favorite songs, might still bring pangs of sadness, but in a new way. In reality the hurt never altogether disappeared. However, one could now experience remembrances, and the emotions that accompany them, as normal. One might even come to cherish them without feeling guilty or anxiety-ridden.

This, incidentally, was the point when guilt vanished. Guilt had served its purpose. It was no longer useful. And with the disappearance of guilt, the individual was now surely on the road to recovery.

The road was long, not without potholes, but much better paved than the rocky road of the past. One could sail along at one's own pace, remembering fondly but no longer tied to the past, reaching for distant horizons, filled with hope and an appreciation of life.

Actually, such feelings and experiences of relief and reestablishment may not arrive for years, particularly in the case of sudden, unexpected death. However, such relief, once achieved, is well worth the trek. There is indeed a light at the end of the tunnel to be reached by those who have the courage to make the journey.

Grief Patterning

Observing how grief unfolds within individual families, we see some differences in the patterning depending on the type of loss experienced.

Considering the three types of losses that are of concern to us in this book—anticipated death, sudden death, and murder—we can observe three rather distinct patterns in terms of the adjustments parents experience in the aftermath of these losses.

Figures 1, 2, and 3 represent typical adjustment patterns of parents in response to the three types of losses. These are summary patterns and do not reveal the uniqueness of individual differences. On the average, however, each pattern of responses is representative of the way a "typical" family or individual parent might initially respond and subsequently adjust to the loss of a child after a long-term illness, from a sudden catastrophe, or in response to murder.

Figure 1 represents the typical parental response in the months following the diagnosis of disease and subsequent death of a child where there is anticipation of loss.

Figure 2 represents the parental response to sudden, unanticipated death. One can see a different pattern emerging here, particularly in terms of the "chronic grief" phase and the eventual inability to resolve the grief.

Figure 3 represents the typical parental response pattern to murder. An altogether different pattern appears here which depicts, most notably, the absence of a chronic stage.

The stage of chronic grief, initiated by the onset of feelings of

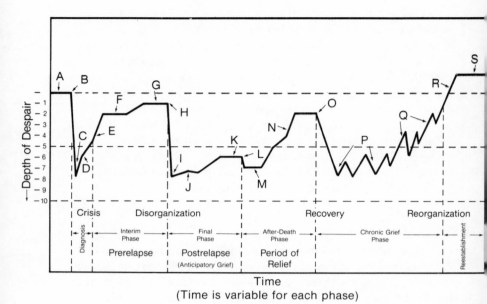

Figure 1. Course of Adjustment: Parental Response to the Diagnosis and Death of a Child After a Long Illness. (*A*) Prior level of functioning or level of marital adjustment *before* death. (*B*) The *crisis*—the diagnosis of a terminal condition. (*C*) Parents plunged into turmoil, confusion, and despair. (*D*) Rapid recovery as hope for survival increases following explanation of treatment protocols. (*E*) Hope continues to rise as "remission" becomes a certainty. (*F*) *Remission* confirmed. (*G*) Return almost to the level of prior functioning. This level will be retained as long as remission lasts. (*H*) *Relapse.* (*I*) Feelings of impending doom and despair overwhelming. (*J*) Slight improvement in mood as secondary treatment protocols are put into place. (*K*) Leveling-off of mood rise. Death now expected. Despair intense. (*L*) *Death* of the child. (*M*) After-death depression in mood slight. (*N*) Feelings of relief and release lead to improved outlook. (*O*) Onset of the period of "loss and loneliness." Beginning of intensive chronic grief response. (*P*) Loss and loneliness strike hard! Plunged into depths of despair. Intense feelings of isolation. Length of time variable. (*Q*) Unstable recovery expected. Ups and downs in most cases. (*R*) Reestablishment progresses. (*S*) Subsequent reorganization at a higher level of functioning than before the diagnosis due to the fact that long-range adjustment usually carries with it the connotation of a positive result from such a loss.

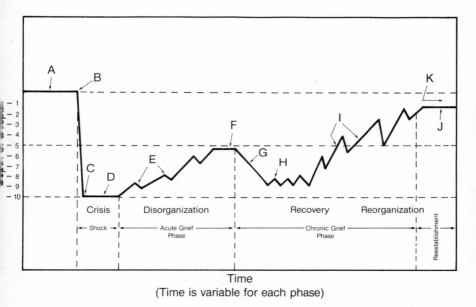

Figure 2.   Course of Adjustment: Parental Response to Sudden, Unexpected Death of a Child. (A) Prior level of functioning or level of marital adjustment *before* death. (B) The *crisis*—an unexpected death. (C) Parents plunged into extreme despair. (D) Period of shock, extreme confusion, and disorganization. (E) After a period of time (variable for each family), small hesitating gains in mood begin to occur. (F) At the end of the postshock "acute grief" phase, a leveling-off occurs, but still at a relatively low level of functioning. A plateau of moderate depression is reached. (G) Onset of the period of "loss and loneliness." Chronic grief phase begins. (H) Plunged into the pit of intense despair. Intense feelings of isolation. Variable length of time. (I) Hesitant and halting recovery. Ups and downs characteristic. Chronic grieving continues. (J) Subsequent level of reorganization and reestablishment eventually reached. (K) Gap created by "shadow grief." Many unable to completely close and return to prior level of functioning.

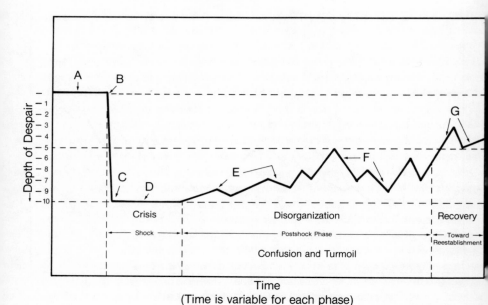

Figure 3. Course of Adjustment: Parental Response to the Murder of a Child. (*A*) Prior level of functioning or level of marital adjustment *before* death. (*B*) The *crisis*—death by murder. (*C*) Plunged into despair. Reaches the lowest level possible. (*D*) Shock and numbness apparent first responses. (*E*) Confusion and disorganization apparent in attempts to deal with the reality of what they are experiencing. (*F*) Progress slow and fitful. Many problems encountered with the criminal justice system. Unable to grieve appropriately. Many ups and downs. (*G*) Inability to work through feelings evident by up-and-down movement in mood. Still unable to grieve appropriately. This condition may extend indefinitely into the future. Many families eventually require some assistance in handling their responses.

loss and loneliness, is evident in only the first two of these postdeath patterns. In the case of death by murder, except for the shock, numbness, and extreme despair coupled with feelings of confusion and disorganization that usually accompany an acute grief response, there is little that might be characterized as a long-term chronic grief reaction. The families of murder victims become so caught up in the complexities of the criminal justice system and the search for the guilty party that they really do not "have the time" to grieve appropriately. There are so many intrusions into their lives by the media, by attorneys and prosecutors, and by the judicial system that they are forced to postpone the chronic phase of their grief response until later. The "activity" that seems to fill their lives in the aftermath of these deaths leads to active grief which then becomes suspended. The feelings of loss and loneliness, and the "work" that is implied to deal with it, become postponed, sometimes for months or even years.

Observing these "typical" patterns relative to different types of losses helps us understand more thoroughly the way parents adjust to the loss of a child. It is quite apparent that the response patterns are different for different types of losses, which might imply different modes of assistance and support at different phases in the after-death period.

This should be useful not only to helpers, who can redefine their support of parents at different stages, but also to parents themselves, as a way of predicting adjustment patterns they most likely will experience as they begin the journey forward in the aftermath of child death.

The next chapter will deal with some of the special problems experienced by mothers and fathers as survivors of the death of a child. These include: the lack of community support, common in regard to child death; some of the experiences of parents in regard to the hospitalization and treatment of children with terminal illness; some of the problems encountered between doctors and parents; the unique problems associated with autopsies, funerals, burials, and grave visits; the child's room and personal belongings, as well as the family home, which often become associated with pain and sorrow; and days or times during the year that carry special significance. This chapter will be both descriptive and analytic, and an attempt will be made to offer some ways of handling these concerns.

8

Some Special Problems

As parents encountered the reality of the death of their children there emerged a whole array of unique problems that tended to create obstacles to the resolution of the emotional stress that the death created in their lives.

I want to devote some time to a discussion of some of these "special problems" in this chapter. I think it is important that parents and others be made aware of the pitfalls that lie in the wake of the death of children and in the aftermath of the diagnosis of a fatal illness.

Each of the concerns I am about to discuss was defined as a significant trouble spot for which many at the time of the interview had no legitimate response. Parents indicated that they *did not know* how to handle the problems as they arose, and often used up considerable time seeking appropriate solutions to them.

If recognized early, these special problems can be alleviated, if not avoided, by parents and others through learning ways of identifying them and of dealing with their primary symptoms.

I will discuss *eight* such problem areas: lack of community support, the hospital experience, the physician and the sick child, the autopsy, the funeral, grave visits, the empty room, and special days. We need to keep in mind, however, that these eight problems do not represent the gamut of what was mentioned as being of concern to parents, but were simply among those mentioned most often.

I might add that some of the problems were of the type the parent personally could do nothing about. Their solutions could come only from others, such as family, friends, physicians, or funeral directors.

Lack of Community Support

One area of concern—a problem I heard expressed most often by virtually all parents—was the lack of community support in the aftermath of the death and also during the various stages of care in a terminal illness. Parents indicated that of all problems encountered, this was the most serious from their personal point of view.

I have mentioned this before, and in the next chapter (on coping) I will discuss it again in more detail, emphasizing the necessity of talking and the willingness of others to allow freedom of expression.

At this point let me simply make a few points about this concern as it appeared in the study group. As I have said earlier, those of us who have never experienced the death of one of our own children cannot fathom the torment and emotional pain that such an event produces. Even when we allow our imaginations full rein, we still cannot get deep enough into the experience to truly feel its full impact. Therefore most of us tend to respond to child death—i.e., the death of *other* people's children— as we would to any death. We offer sympathy to the parents, and in some cases active help and support— for a time. However, we always withdraw that support too soon. After a month or two we leave them alone, assuming that they should be getting over it and back into the normal routine of living.

This neglect was quite noticeable with regard to parents in the study group. Such neglect during the most active phase of the bereavement process left them isolated and alienated. Unable to draw support from others, parents turned inward, away from friends and relatives, and became dependent on their own meager abilities to handle the continuing pain.

This tendency to withdraw from others (and others from them) often intensified the grief response and lengthened it beyond normal limits, causing grief to be bottled up in "shadow" form for what sometimes amounted to a lifetime.

The tendency of others to withdraw was also noted during the months of care for a terminally ill child. Initially everyone outside the family seemed concerned and offered help. However, as the weeks and months passed there seemed to come a point when others grew oblivious to the increasing attention parents continued to bestow upon the sick child.

Terminally ill children, particularly those receiving the majority of their care at home, required increasing amounts of time, and families changed their usual routines to adapt to these requirements. All conversation became centered on the child, and as long as there was hope for recovery or even improvement, all effort and attention were devoted to achieving this goal.

This tendency in itself served to drive a wedge between the family and others in the community, and led the family to a more and more isolated existence. Thus in time those once thought to be "good" friends simply stopped coming around. When a family member needed to cry or needed to express frustration, "friends" simply could not be found. Consequently family members became resigned to this general lack of support and no longer reached out for help when they needed it. They came to rely on their own internal family structure for support and guidance.

Those of us closest to the bereaved parent or to the parent caring for a terminally ill child, whether family or friend, need to be aware of this withdrawal tendency and should make every effort to break into this vicious circle by becoming *active* supporters. We must realize that there really is no end to the grieving of parents who have lost children, and no greater concern expressed than by those caring for terminally ill children. Our greatest gift to these parents can be our understanding and support for *as long as there is a need.*

In the next chapter, on coping, I have offered some suggestions on how friends and even acquaintances can remain active helpers throughout the grieving and anticipatory grieving process. It is up to those of us who may occupy these roles to take heed of these suggestions so that we do not become extra burdens for bereaved parents to contend with.

The Hospital Experience

In the case of long-term illness parents have indicated that special concerns emerged in regard to care and support of children in hospitals. Every parent who cared for a child with a potentially fatal disease eventually had to face problems encountered in hospitalization.

The hospital can be a strange and sometimes terrible place for a child. Even for an adult, a stay in the hospital can be a stressful and frightening experience. For a healthy child the experience may be tolerable, but for a sick child it can be absolutely overwhelming and the hospital stay filled with anxiety and stress.

Certainly for children, particularly younger children, who were victims of debilitating and incapacitating illnesses where hospitalization was required for rather long periods of time, many needs arose—important emotional needs that could be satisfied only by the diligent guidance of parents.

However, the majority of the study parents complained that hospitalization of their child was as confusing and traumatic for them as for the child, and many often did not know how to respond to the unique demands placed on them at these critical times.

A mother said:

It's hard to be fully responsive to the needs of your child in the hospital. We were terrified at the prospects of Timmy's hospitalization, yet we were also comforted because we felt he could be helped there. We just didn't know what would be expected from us. . . .

A father said:

When your child is in the hospital, you lose control of him. . . . He belongs to the system! Other people direct his life and yours! What is one supposed to do? How is one supposed to act? The impersonal atmosphere was hard to take. . . . We were so embroiled in regulations and routine, we missed the emotional side. . . .

Another father:

When your child is put in the hospital, you know he is really sick! We were scared to death! We had all we could do to keep ourselves from coming apart. I know John was scared too, but I really couldn't help him the way he needed to be helped!

Hospitalization for the purpose of diagnosis and initial treatment in the early stages of an illness was bad enough; however, the more serious problems arose when hospitalization was required in the final stages of a terminal illness, when the child was dying.

At these times parents of course must be allowed to maintain an element of *hope*, and the physician and other hospital staff usually did whatever was required to make sure that hope remained intact. However, parents also had to deal with reality. And one aspect of this reality was that the child was dying.

The parents in this study generally realized this all too well, which in part is what created problems at these times.

During the final days of the child's illness, parents became preoccupied with death to the point where they were able to think of nothing else. The preoccupation centered on avoiding it, which led to a frantic search for one last treatment protocol. They would leave no medical stone unturned! A father expressed this preoccupation quite well. He said:

Yes, we thought about her death constantly, but not in a morbid way. We became preoccupied with a search for specialists, for new combinations of drugs, for experimental procedures—for *anything* that might work and help us effect a cure! I know my wife would not give up. . . . She was consumed with hope and continually communicated this to our daughter. We would not allow her to even think of any other possibility! . . . I think she died in this state of unrelenting hope!

This overemphasis on death and the frantic effort to avoid it even to the very end was unfortunate in that parents often missed vital opportunities to satisfy important emotional needs of their children. They also missed the unique chance to "enjoy" the experience of sharing deep and intimate personal concerns with their children as they approached death.

Of course the prospect of an approaching death was terribly frightening to parents. When they weren't searching desperately for a cure, they simply avoided the topic. Many parents lived in a "closed-awareness context" with regard to their dying children. They refrained from mentioning the seriousness of the illness and did not allow themselves to even think of death while in the presence of the child. Nor did they allow the child to express thoughts of death and dying. Many felt that they had to maintain a positive attitude. To do otherwise would be tantamount to giving up hope.

Thus many became ineffective in offering the kind of personal guidance terminally ill children desperately needed. Parents were often simply not available; they were ill-prepared for the final days or hours before death.

A very typical response was noted by a young mother whose 7-year-old daughter died of leukemia. She said:

We of course knew Susan was dying—we had known for about three months prior to her death that there was no hope. But we never told her! However, I think she knew! . . . I could tell by the things she would say. . . . I just couldn't confront it! . . . She died without revealing her thoughts to us. . . . I find this difficult—very difficult—to live with now!

Another mother, responding to the death of her 14-year-old son:

I did not learn till later that Mark shared his innermost feelings about his death with his basketball coach, who came to see him occasionally. He never once opened up to me or to his father. I can understand this now because I don't believe we ever gave him the opportunity. As a result I believe we missed something very special!

As the child begins the slow, progressive slide toward death in the terminal stage of the illness, parents need to reorient themselves to the *changing needs* of the child. In this respect children are not unlike adults who approach death. They must be given time to prepare.

Excessive concern with finding "one more effective treatment" may no longer be the relevant issue. What becomes even more important is offering emotional support and guidance, and sharing personal and intimate concerns with the dying child.

It may indeed to be too painful to tell a child that he or she is dying, but there are some ways of responding that will lighten that burden while accomplishing the same goal.

As parents we need to spend a great amount of time in the presence of our children, constantly assuring them that it is alright to feel the way they do. This will particularly be the case during their hospitalization. We need to tell them that we understand the turmoil and confusion they are experiencing, tell them that we will not abandon them, that we will always be there no matter what happens, and that we will help them deal with their fears and anxieties.

Parents should try to build and maintain a support system for their children; they should try to live within an "open-awareness context" and allow their children the experience of encountering the unknown of death, unencumbered by unrealistic demands placed on them by parents who refuse to surrender.

Certainly some of the parents in the study group were able to adjust to the pain of separation and impending loss earlier than others and were able to share intimate feelings and experiences with their children as death approached. In Chapter 3 I have discussed in some detail the relationship between parents and the dying child that illustrates this response pattern.

Typical among these parents was a father who related to me the final days with his 11-year-old son. I think you will agree that this experience leaves little to be desired in building the kind of relationship that will leave a lasting positive impression on the parent. He said:

We were with Dan to the very end. He died in our arms unencumbered by medical technology. We had ceased treatment of his condition the week before. All he was receiving was a medication for pain. He was lucid and clear-headed until the very last. He knew he was dying and we allowed him to talk freely about it . . . and he talked constantly! We learned more from this lad the last week of his life than in all the previous eleven years. . . . I will never forget the serene look on his face when he closed his eyes for the last time. . . . It was as if he had made his peace with himself and with us!

A mother communicated how she was able to meet her 9-year-old daughter and journey with her to the end:

I was able to communicate—really communicate—with Sharon for only a few short days before she died, but it was a time I would not trade for the world! She said she had known for the past six months that she was dying, but knew it would be very upsetting to me if she tried to say anything. . . . We both cried a lot, but we also talked. I told her that soon she would be out of her pain. I told her not to be frightened, that dying was going to be, for her, without pain. I told her that she didn't have to worry about me, that I would be able to live without her and that I would see her again someday. I told her that she would live in heaven while waiting for me. The more I talked, the easier it became for me and, I believe, for her.

Another mother:

I think I prepared Bryan by talking to him about heaven, about meeting his grandfather, whom he was very close to, and about the beauty of living with Jesus. He was very open with me and we shared many intimate moments just before he died. I am so happy I had this time with him. I cannot tell you what this has meant to me in overcoming the emptiness in my life since his death.

We can share these kinds of feelings and concerns with children regardless of their ages.

Children who are dying often know it without asking and without being told. Even very young children tend to develop a sixth sense about these things. Of course, should they ask—most do at some point and in some way—they should always be told the truth. However, there is a way of telling that does not destroy hope. Parents should explore their own relationships with their children, consider the unique attributes of each child, and find the best way to do this.

Children tend to mature very rapidly under the conditions of a sentence of death. They grow up fast as they are dying. The parent may not know how to respond to this "new" child, capable of thinking and talking about his or her condition and other aspects of life in a very "adult" manner. The changes may be so great that they may startle parents!

Parents need to be prepared to recognize these changes in their children and to respond to them appropriately by learning to change their own attitudes and alter their own perceptions in order to meet the child at whatever level of maturity emerges. Without this preparation parents will not know what to expect or how to interpret what they meet; consequently they may withdraw, turning their attention to the medical aspects of the disease, leaving their children to fend for themselves at the critical moments before death.

Of course, being there, being available day-in and day-out, is very stressful for parents. But later the greatest stress will come if they look back and realize that they failed to give their children every ounce of love and support and caring that was within them at the time![1]

Woodson talks of the "social pain" that comes when a person reaches a point where death is imminent and then realizes that there is so much unfinished business remaining![2]

When we are faced with death, we need to put some kind of closure on our relationships with family and friends. When we are denied the opportunity to do "last-minute" things, the quality of our relationships and our interactions with others around us greatly deteriorates.

Parents need to bear this point in mind when dealing with young children. Children too can suffer social pain. Children too have unfinished business, and if they are prohibited from completing it by others who do not recognize that even the young can contemplate their own death, and even plan for it, they will suffer emotional distress.

Dying children, just like their parents, need the support and patience of others. They certainly need the understanding of parents willing to give them the time and opportunity to say their good-byes, to distribute their worldly goods, and to deal openly with their fears.

I think the greatest gift I could give my only son if he were approaching a certain death is the freedom to allow him to seek his fate with a sense of dignity, unfettered by unnecessary restrictions placed on him by me, and enough understanding on my part to let him go!

The Need for Discipline. As parents, however, we strive to maintain control of the situation. Certainly as much normalcy as possible should be maintained in the care and discipline of children. Yes, I said discipline! Discipline is vital. It is in fact probably more important during these critical times than at any other time in the child's life. In the hospital, children are away from the routine of homelife and it is easy for parents to become lax in their effort to maintain control over their behavior. It is easy for parents to respond with pity.

We see children suffering from a terminal condition. We see them struggling against perhaps unbelievable odds. We see them in pain. We see them fighting as valiantly as any adult to survive. We reach for them; we want to comfort them. How can a child do wrong while struggling to survive?

In our effort to be sympathetic and understanding, we stroke them and comfort them and treat them in an excessively lenient manner. We become unrestrictive in our demands on them.

This is by far the worst thing we can do for these children. We fail to understand that there is a large difference between what *we* feel, what *we* need, and what *they* need.

Children under the threat of death should be treated as normally as possible—without pity, without overindulgence—and with discipline!

Children who are overindulged and pitied fall into a destructive form of behavior where they let go, physically and mentally. They take the view that "If Mom and Dad place no restriction on my behavior, if they allow me to do what I please, if no one really cares what I do, then I don't care either!"

A child allowed to have free rein in the hospital will quite quickly get the impression that things are really worse than they are because now "no one cares whether I misbehave or not." Therefore, so goes the reasoning, "It must be true—I am dying!"

The parenting system must not become dysfunctional just because the child is out of the home. This does not remove him or her from the protective custody and authority jurisdiction of the parents. A code of proper conduct must be maintained and adhered to here just as in the home, if for no other reason than to maintain a condition of normalcy for the benefit of the child.

Thus by treating the child in a normal, consistent manner, by placing restrictions on behavior, you demonstrate consistency in your concern and support for the child, which in turn helps him or her deal more realistically with the situation.

The primary responsibility for maintaining the discipline of children should fall on the parents. However, the hospital staff also has a duty and should share some of the responsibility for maintaining discipline and meeting the emotional needs of the child.

The hospital staff must also find ways of improving the competency and helpfulness of parents in the wake of this overwhelming medical crisis.[3]

Thus when parents and staff work together, ways can be found to alleviate some of the serious problems encountered in the final days of the hospitalization of dying children.

The Physician and the Sick Child

Although many parents reported good rapport with the primary physicians during the course of treatment and continued to feel a sense of trust even after the death of the child, there were nevertheless certain aspects of the doctor–parent and doctor–child relationship that deserved some comment, if for no other reason than to ward off potential problems that might arise in other cases. In discussing with the parents their relationships with their physicians, it was possible to piece together a picture of the vital role that the physician played in this drama.

Without doubt, the physician usually came off badly in the case of a child dying from a dreaded disease. Physicians experienced great distress as children under their care slowly slipped away. They were given the medical responsibility for the care of the sick child and now, as their remedies failed, they had to face their own inability to conquer the disease while continuing to be supportive and reassuring to parents and the child. A sense of great failure and remorse gripped doctors as they struggled with this dilemma.

For the majority of parents, no episode in life came even close to the one they were experiencing in terms of the stress it produced. They were confused, upset, and fearful. Their needs were monumental, and extended beyond the medical support they were receiving. They quite naturally turned to their doctors for help and advice in meeting these needs, which forced physicians into the roles of counselor and consoler in addition to their medical responsibilities.

Parents needed help in dealing with the physical and emotional changes occurring in their children; they needed advice on how to handle other siblings, grandparents, and other relatives; they needed advice on hospital procedures and routines, on insurance and expenses; they needed help in dealing with their own physical and emotional problems that resulted from the stress and turmoil of the situation.

The physician was there, a part of the situation, and was therefore called upon to respond to these needs. This placed a very heavy additional burden on doctors and increased the points of friction between doctors and parents.

Physicians found themselves in untenable positions. They were required to be the stable players in this drama. They had to be strong and communicate an element of hope to all parties, even though they were grieving and were well aware of the hopelessness of it all. They had to support parents who were crumbling under the weight of what was happening, and at the same time had to deal with their own sense of failure.

Doctors essentially had to be all things to all people, not only to the parents but also to the children under their care, who came to rely on them for confidence, strength, and truth. Physicians had to meet a whole array of responsibilities over and above their prime task of keeping the child alive.

It was common for parents to depend heavily on their doctors to stabilize the situation, particularly in the early stages of the illness. However, as their children continued to deteriorate and it became obvious that medicine no longer had remedies to offer, parents turned away—they lost faith in the doctor's ability to conquer the disease. This was not as traumatic a development as it may seem. Parents often understood that medicine had its limitations. They knew that the illness was terminal, i.e., there were no known cures. Therefore as the child approached death, parents seemed to perceive the doctor as simply a practitioner who had reached the *limits* of what could be done. Only in a very few instances were physicians perceived as "miracle workers" and expected to perform heroic feats and effect miraculous cures. For the most part parents were quite realistic in their perceptions of the physician's ability to conquer and cure. In fact I think that parents were often more realistic than the doctors themselves, many of whom refused to surrender.

As time passed and death approached, parents often insisted that all further treatment cease and that they be allowed to take the child home. It was more difficult many times for the physician to admit that there was nothing more that could be done and to release the child under his or her care.

There is really nothing in the medical training of doctors that prepared them for the proper ways of responding to these "impossible" situations. Different physicians tended to respond differently. Much depended on personal characteristics and unique qualities that allowed them to be flexible enough to admit defeat.

Of course many physicians, particularly oncologists, who had ample experience in treating the more dreaded fatal illnesses that strike children, were quite prepared for the reactions of parents and children as they attempted to deal with the reality of impending death. These doctors gravitated into this field of medicine not only because of their specialized training but also because they had personal attributes that allowed them to deal with the trauma that such illnesses generated.

Certainly if the disease responded to treatment and the child began to make progress toward recovery, there were few problems that were likely to develop in the doctor–parent or doctor–child relationship. It was only when medicine failed that difficulties arose. Under these circumstances strains began to surface, which in turn produced an impact on the quality of the relationship between *parent* and *child*. This became a potential problem because, at this critical point in time, this relationship could not afford to be tarnished.

The Autopsy

Whether or not to have or to request an autopsy was a difficult and heartrending decision faced by parents in the immediate aftermath of the death of the child.

Autopsies are always required with certain types of death and always recommended when there are questions about the cause of death. A child who perhaps died from complications due to leukemia, cystic fibrosis, or hemophilia was almost always autopsied to find out the immediate cause of death and thereby provide information that might be useful in the treatment of other children with the same conditions. Similarly, children who died suddenly or were killed in accidents were autopsied, again to determine the immediate causal agents responsible for death.

In many cases the autopsy was performed more or less as a routine procedure with no effort made to share results with parents. This caused some consternation for many parents.

Thus the autopsy was defined as a problem area by parents in this study. Many parents were not given the opportunity to share in the results, and many had very negative feelings about the procedure itself. The solution to this problem, like many others noted, does not lie in the hands of the parents but in the hands of the physician, who can do much to relieve the trauma of these procedures.

Through the physician's efforts much guilt and failure that parents experience can be released, particularly in regard to certain types of death. In the case of murder, sudden death, or death under mysterious circumstances, the physician should recommend that an autopsy be performed. The doctor should then indicate to the parents that the information will be available and that he or she will discuss the results with them as soon as these are received. This will go a long way to soothing parental fears where causes of death are clouded or unknown.

Autopsy results can be confusing and should never be given to parents without some explanation by the attending physician. It is perfectly alright for parents to obtain copies of autopsy results, of course, but they should always be thoroughly explained in layman's terms by a physician at the time they are received.

It is important for parents to know that their child will not be disfigured during the autopsy procedure. This was a fear that lingered in the backs of the minds of many parents in the study group, although many were unable to express it at the time. They often carried a rather gruesome picture of the autopsy procedure, even when they willingly agreed to it, and therefore suffered guilt and resentment over their decision.

Again, the doctor can be responsive to these deeply buried fears and can contribute much to removing them by being as candid as possible about the procedure. I think it is acceptable, for instance, to tell the parents that the child will be treated with respect and dignity at all times, and that an open-casket funeral is possible, if so desired.

As noted, most of the parents in the study group defined the autopsy as somewhat threatening, though in most cases they realized the necessity of it. Their biggest complaint was the lack of responsive-ness on the part of the doctor in explaining the results to them.

The problems many parents experienced with the autopsy can be easily relieved through the concern of sensitive physicians who take the time and make the effort to search out, and respond to, the vital needs of parents in the aftermath of child death.

The Funeral

Funerals for children were an extremely stress-provoking experience for most parents. There were so many questions that parents had to struggle with as they began to make plans for the funeral of their child. Should they have a simple family affair or a more elaborate ceremony? Should the casket be open or closed? Should they cremate or choose ground burial? In fact some kind of decision relative to funerals and burial was usually required just as parents were finding their way through the initial state of disorganization, when confusion abounded and circumstances were fuzzy and unclear.

Some parents were not sure what they wanted. But they went ahead anyway, under the impression that they could not wait, mak-ing decisions on the basis of scant information or on the advice of others.

Nothing quite compared to the stress and remorse suffered by parents who later found that they had made *wrong* decisions at these critical times!

ADVICE FOR THE FUNERAL DIRECTOR

Parents often told me that they became extremely sensitive at the time of the child's death about how the child's body was treated by those assuming responsibility.

My remarks here are directed to funeral directors, who were often placed in immediate contact with parents at the time of the child's death. Responsibility for care of the child was shifted at death from the doctor and medical setting to the funeral director and the funeral home. The funeral director took on the role of counselor and consoler. He suddenly became the main source of comfort and sup-port for the family. How he performed in this role greatly affected the family's continuing ability to cope.

For example, funeral directors should be particularly careful in how they approach a family, especially when the child has died at home. Oftentimes there was a hesitancy on the part of the parents to surrender their child to the funeral home representative, if the child had been under the personal care of the parents prior to death.

Parents in the study group told of rather "insensitive" and "uncaring" approaches made by those who were called to the family home after the child had died. Stories of wheeling in a bare steel stretcher, briskly placing the child's body on the cart, and covering it was a blanket—all under the gaze of grief-stricken parents—were common! Even very young children were often treated with "indifference" by some funeral directors, who seemed to consider the task to be somewhat routine, displaying little concern for the feelings of the parents. The death of a child is anything but routine, and families tend to resent funeral directors' treating it as such.

From the viewpoint of the funeral director, a very sensitive and gratifying way to approach a family whose child has just died is to simply arrive and wait, patiently, until the family is ready to surrender their son or daughter. If the mother or father is holding the child at the time, you, as the funeral director, might gently approach the parents with the request that, *when they are ready*, you are there to receive the child. Make it a request, not a demand! Allow the parents to give up the child to you. Do not take the child from them. This may require a bit more time than you have allowed, but the reward will be great for both you and the parents.

If the child is young enough to be personally carried to the hearse, do so! Do not put a very young child on a empty gurney in the parents' presence. At the moment, this is too abrupt—too final for them to bear. It is a scene they will remember, initially with pain, later with anger and resentment.

Receiving the child from the arms of the mother or father, gently covering the child's body with a blanket, and carrying the child in your arms to the waiting hearse will be remembered with great fondness and appreciation for a long time to come.

As you do this, tell the parents that you will treat the child with dignity and respect. Use the child's name often in your exchanges with the parents. Tell them that they are welcome to come to the funeral home and help prepare their child for burial, such as by dressing or fixing the hair. In fact these tasks can be shared by all members of the family, even siblings.

If parents respond to this invitation, while they are at the funeral home allow them to touch and hold the child as much as they have a desire to.

It is important to remember that as a funeral director you are also in the business of grief management, and anything you can do to make the transition parents are experiencing easier to bear, it is your responsibility to do.

These permitted activities, particularly those surrounding care and preparation of the child in the funeral home, may especially be needed in the case of sudden death, where there is much disorientation, bewilderment, and denial. Involving the parents in the final disposition process will go a long way toward removing some of the debilitating effects of denial and allow them to begin the grieving experience sooner than might ordinarily be the case.

As the time approaches for the actual funeral services, talk with the parents and explain to them some of the alternatives available. Explain to them that the family can have the privilege of seeing and stroking the child, even though they may prefer a closed casket for others. This should be an option freely chosen.

Sometimes, if the child is young, the parents may not know where they want the burial to take place. Some cemeteries allow burial of a small child on top of an already-occupied grave such as that of a grandparent. This may or may not be an option that appeals to parents, but at least they should be made aware of it.

If cremation is selected as the preferred method of final disposition, as the funeral director you should attempt to make very sure that the parents have arrived at this decision without being pressured and with full knowledge of the significance of the choice and the alternatives available.

Making the proper decisions regarding the final disposition of a son or daughter is important since the choice the parents make will predispose them to a particular type of after-death grieving experience. If ground burial is selected, there will always be a "place" that contains the child, and this place—this grave—might exert a powerful pressure on parents to make regular grave visits and to keep it presentable. This could extend into years, making significant demands on their behavior, and in some cases keeping the wounds open.

If cremation is selected, there usually will be no such "place." Cremation of the body carries a different connotation for most people, which may predispose them to a different form of grieving and bereavement behavior.

These choices must be selected freely with full knowledge of the consequences of each. But decisions should *not* be made during times of confusion and disorientation. Parents need to be aware that some of the critical decisions regarding final disposition of their child can wait. The preservation afforded by embalming does not require immediate interment or cremation. Funeral directors who are sensitive to the needs of parents at these times should be prepared to make appropriate alternatives available—temporarily, of course—until a more reasoned time arrives.

The funeral need not be a tragic time for parents. The entire family should be involved. Funeral directors must be prepared to share their performance of tasks with survivors so that family members can fully participate in, and understand the meaning and significance of, what they are experiencing.

It is important to involve not only the parents in active participation in the funeral, but *siblings* as well. If the parents are too distraught to involve other children, as the funeral director you can see to it that brothers and sisters are kept fully informed and given active roles.

It is important to be truthful with other children, explaining to them what has happened as well as what is about to happen. Allow them, just as you do the parents, to see and to touch their deceased brother or sister if they so desire. Children have many questions and the funeral director should attempt to answer all of the them. You should explain what you do in simple, uncomplicated language.

If the children are old enough (usually, at least 6) and if the opportunity presents itself, show them the facilities, allow them the privilege of exploring the funeral home, allow them to look behind the doors and in all the closets. Demonstrate to them by your nonsecretive attitude and straightforward explanations that there is nothing sinister about death.

If the deceased child is young and the casket small, ask if the mother or father wishes to hold it on the lap during the drive to the cemetery. In this way parents can maintain a sense of closeness that will be remembered always.

If ground burial has been selected, at the cemetery the grave should be open with no ground cover. Parents and siblings should be allowed to participate in lowering the casket into the grave.

These simple suggestions, although they may seem stark and out of place in today's world, nevertheless will pay great dividends in the long run, particularly in their ability to remove some of the sinister characteristics of death.

Parents and siblings must eventually come to deal with the reality of death. By allowing them some freedom of choice in regard to the funeral and by being open and truthful with them at all times, you will be removing some of the stresses that usually accompany it.

Grave Visits

Grave visits were a mixed blessing for most families. Many are drawn to the grave but often find the visit an agonizing ordeal, almost too painful to endure. This is why a choice regarding final disposition is so important!

If ground burial is selected, as noted earlier, there will always be a "place" where the child exists. Whether they wish it or not, parents will be predisposed to a particular type of mourning behavior. Thus they should prepare themselves to face a possible difficult time in the bereavement period, and perhaps even for a longer time.

As to the parents in this study group, an array of different types of responses were noted. Some parents told me that they intentionally *never* visited the grave, indicating a type of denial or escape. They felt that they could not deal with it at that point in their lives— it was just too painful. Some parents suffered extreme guilt over this avoidance; however, guilt was more tolerable than a possible feared severe reaction that a visit might trigger. A mother, whose 17-year-old son was killed in an auto accident, expressed a typical sentiment about not visiting the grave:

I have not been to Roy's grave since the funeral, three years ago. I want to go—I really do! I have even tried on several occasions, but always back out or find excuses not to go at the last minute. It has become more and more easy, as the years pass, for me not to go—the pain has softened somewhat. I don't think about it so often these days. . . .

I think I know why I didn't go earlier when the compulsion was so strong: I was afraid of how I would react! . . . I could envision myself literally coming apart at the seams, and I just could not go through that again! I suffered so much after his death and was getting to the point where I could hold myself together. I could not allow that fragile balance to be disrupted! So I didn't go. It was a conscious decision. I just did not go! . . .

Maybe someday I'll feel differently, but as of right now, I still don't think I could go! I just cannot open up those old wounds again! Maybe I will never find peace with this, but I know I cannot go through it again, and that cemetery—that grave—would bring it all back!

Other parents did not make grave visits for other reasons. Some said they did not go because the grave carried no real meaning for them. Some of these parents based their rejection of the grave on articles of faith, i.e., their reasons for not visiting were religious in nature. Others based their rejection on mystical or philosophical grounds. A mother, whose 14-year-old son died of cancer, talked about why, for her, the grave had no "pulling power":

Dan really isn't there. His body is, but *he* is not! So I don't go! I did in the beginning, but I got nothing from it. . . . I have talked to others who have suffered through similar losses and they tell me the grave acts as a magnet, drawing them there. I never felt this way! . . . I can feel close to Dan without going to the cemetery. . . .

Another mother, who lost a 9-year-old son:

No, I really haven't been back since the funeral. I don't need to go. His soul is in heaven now, so I have no need to return. If I want to talk to Billy, I go to church!

Still another mother, whose 6-year-old daughter died suddenly:

I have never thought much about going on a regular basis. We still go on her birthday and will put flowers on the grave, but it's no big deal! I mean, it doesn't really affect me in any way. I guess I know she is not really there. There is just a body in that grave. I know it's not really Helen!

Make no mistake, the grave did exert a powerful force on some parents. The reasons and responses differed from family to family; however, there was little doubt that the choice of ground burial did subject some parents to a particular type of bereavement behavior. A number of parents I talked with claimed that the grave acted as a powerful "magnet" drawing them to the cemetery, sometimes even against their will. One mother said she goes to the grave every day, and has been doing so since her 15-year-old son was buried eight months before:

I guess I can't help myself. I feel bad and upset if I don't go every day! . . . My husband has even requested a transfer to another city hoping that this will break the habit. . . . I wish I could stop, but I can't. . . .

This same mother revealed that on rainy days she stands over the grave with an umbrella, in a meager effort to protect it!

A father told me about visits to the grave of his 18-year-old son:

I have been to the grave every day (at least every work day) since his death in August [this statement was made the following February]. I stop on my way home from work. Sometimes I just drive by—he is buried near the roadway. Other times I will stop and get out for a few minutes. . . . I guess I feel compelled to do this! It's my way of keeping close to him. I generally feel good about doing this. . . .

Another father, whose 6-year-old son was killed instantly in an auto accident in which the father was driving:

Jerry's death was so painful for me! . . . I still go to the grave several times a week. Sometimes I'll pull weeds and work around it; other times I'll just sit and think "Why? . . . Why? . . . Why? . . ." I should be in that grave, not my son! . . . I suppose his grave will always be a special place for me. It is a place where I can always feel the pain. I guess I need this.

Some parents make grave visits a family affair. They become an outing and are experienced as very satisfying occasions, almost with a sense of happiness and joy. A father said:

We make it something the whole family can do. Usually on Sundays we take a picnic lunch and go to the grave with the other children and let them explore and play. It's comforting to me, personally, to do this. It's like we're keeping the memory of John alive by involving the whole family. . . .

A mother said:

Our entire family—my husband and the two boys—go quite often throughout the year, especially on Christmas, Easter, his birthday—these are special times for us. We actually enjoy it. I know the boys do. They have never once objected to going. . . .

Thus different families have different conceptions of the grave and grave visits. No parent indicated that grave visits were not painful experiences in the beginning. Where the pain was too overwhelming, as noted, they simply stopped going. Others continue to go in spite of the pain, or perhaps because of it, as one father, who lost a 16-year-old daughter, noted:

I could not cry anywhere else, nor at any other time except while at her grave. Needless to say, I spent a lot of time there! In the weeks following her death I needed to feel the hurt, I needed to cry and mourn, and her grave gave me that! . . .

Parents need to be aware of some of the many diverse problems they will experience with the grave. Each parent will have to contend with it in his or her own way. Listening to parents express themselves, I have come to the conclusion that there is no single answer—there is no "right" or "wrong" way of dealing with the grave. For some it is a gift used to allay guilt and relieve the emptiness of loss. For others it is a burden filled with anguish and heartache. Some find joy in visits; others find pain. The point is that every family must find its *own way* through the maze of possible responses generated by the presence of a grave.

The Empty Room

When a child died, the void left behind in the hearts of parents was gaping. The feelings of emptiness engendered were intensified by a constant flow of reminders of what once was but no longer is. These "reminders," found virtually everywhere, were usually in the form of personal belongings of the child with which parents had to contend: the child's clothes, a wristwatch, a wallet, perhaps a bicycle, a favorite cap, a football, a favorite doll, a stuffed animal—the list was long! These things carried enormously painful but cherished memories.

Parents often experienced tremendous difficulties searching through and cleaning out personal belongings left behind. Sometimes this task was delayed for weeks or months until some of the pain and anguish had subsided.

The parents in the study group indicated that of all the things children leave behind, what proved to be the most troublesome and heartrending was the empty room!

We can all imagine the enormous difficulty that would arise in the lives of grief-stricken parents over having to face the now-empty room of the child. The empty, made-up bed never to be rumpled and messed up again; the dresser and closet still containing the child's clothes; the array of personal belongings scattered about—confronting these things stretched the limits of human endurance.

Of course different parents responded differently, but facing the child's room was always a problem. The same questions recurred: "How am I going to face it?" "What am I going to do?"

Some avoided it completely, refusing even to enter the room or to change it in any way. They simply closed the door and literally walked away from it! They removed it from their conscious presence. Such physical avoidance was similar to emotional denial and served the same purpose—it insulated the individual from further pain.

Avoidance seemed to work, at least for a time. Parents often reported that this was the only way they could handle it.

This particular method of responding was especially effective where violent death had occurred in the room. One family, whose 19-year-old son committed suicide in his room by shooting himself with a high-powered rifle, said that they never passed by the room without conjuring up images of their son lying in a pool of blood! The same image appeared to both the mother and father. The mother said:

I can't get it out of my mind! It's all around us in that house! His room is a death place for us. Everytime I pass the door [which is always kept closed] I see him lying there . . . the bloodstains are still in the rug! It's horrible! . . . I try desperately to think of other things! . . .

This family is contemplating changing their place of residence— permanently avoiding—in the hope the images and nightmare will fade.

It is obvious that a bizarre death, particularly if it occurs in the home, can affect the attitude of the parents toward the entire house. Not only a room but an entire house can become a "death place" in the minds of the survivors, and it may become an extremely painful experience to live there.

Sometimes the empty room was a source of comfort and support to parents. If a child was cared for at home during the final days of a terminal illness and died in the home, the place in the home where death occurred—the child's room, or even a living room or den—may become filled with good memories and good feelings for the parents.

Parents sometimes savored these "special" places and wished never to change them in any way.

I might add that this kind of special attachment to a place in the home might also be defined as a form of avoidance or denial of the reality of the loss. For some parents these places actually took on a "sacred" quality. Even though a room was entered often and even integrated into the remainder of the home, it might be left just as it was at the time of death, with nothing changed. In these cases the parent or parents may wish to surround themselves with as many "memories" as possible. This might be their way of clinging to remnants of the child that they find comforting. Thus this could be a way of denying death, or at least avoiding its reality.

In the first case avoidance takes the form of avoiding all memories and all places defined as too painful. In the second case avoidance takes the form of avoiding the "necessity of letting go," as one parent put it. That is, grief and grief work are delayed until the parent learns to face reality and deal with painful memories, or until he or she can effectively "let go" of the son or daughter.

Letting go or facing painful memories may be related in a very meaningful way to the kind of adjustment one is able to make in regard to the empty room.

Sometimes time itself is all that is required to deal with the heartache and abnormal attachment to, or rejection of, the child's room. One mother told me that it was 18 months before she could enter her child's room! For a year and a half nothing was touched. The door was always closed. For a year and a half she could not mourn. She felt great sadness, but could not express it. She eventually came to believe that her inability to express her grief was tied to her refusal to enter her son's room.

It has now been four years since this mother lost her 7-year-old son. She is now entering his room more and more frequently, and is able to cry. She still identifies it as his "place" and becomes upset with other family members who wish to use the room for other purposes. But she believes that she is beginning to release her hold on it. And as she does so, she is finally beginning to grieve openly.

The empty room is something from which one cannot escape. It is a part of the home but, at death, it becomes apart from it. Learning to experience the pain associated with it in a realistic manner is essential in order to complete one's grief work.

Moving from the residence, or psychologically closing off the room or immersing oneself in it, thereby creating a shrine for the child, are all very inappropriate ways of dealing with the matter. A father indicated that after their 15-year-old daughter was killed the family moved from their home of 18 years because they simply could not tolerate living there without her. This father said:

She was born in that house! It was *her* home, and after she was gone it just no longer seemed like home to us. . . . My wife and I decided to move! . . . We decided that it would be better to leave our memories behind and start fresh elsewhere. . . .

However, the same father goes on to say:

We did not realize at the time that this was impossible! You cannot discard your memories like an old shoe! They are always a part of you, but now we have no place to store them! . . . We sold the only place we had that was intimately a part of our daughter's life—our home!

These parents were regretful of their decision, and their story should warn others to proceed cautiously in arriving at decisions to change the place of residence after the death of a child because of the painful remembrances contained therein.

The memories will be painful regardless of where one lives or what one does with the empty room. Realizing this may help in arriving at a realistic response to the ordeal of living with the empty room in the aftermath of the death of a child.

There are some ways—some suggestions—that come from the parents themselves that might be useful for others contemplating what to do about the empty room.

Certainly there is no hurry! The room can be left intact for a period of time. It may indeed be too painful to deal with immediately after the death. As noted earlier, time itself will make facing it easier. However, totally avoiding it may simply extend the grieving process far beyond reasonable limits. Therefore, painful as this may be in the beginning, I believe that parents should make every effort not to avoid the room or to cut it out of their lives. Nor should they turn it into a living memorial. Instead, they should make an attempt to use the room as a place to grieve and cry, a place to experience and express the pain and anguish of loss. A mother said:

Cindy's room became my wailing wall! I would go there and sit sometimes for an hour or two several times a week and cry and cry! My psychiatrist told me later that this was the best thing I could have done at that time!

A father:

Tom's empty room was at first hard to take! I found myself avoiding it completely. However, later, I was drawn there as a place where I could truly grieve. It is now an integral part of our home. I wouldn't trade it for anything!

The suggestion was also made that the room be redecorated or remodeled and turned into something else, such as a den, reading room, or TV room. In this way the room will be kept as an intimate part of the family home. In fact a number of families indicated that this became their solution to the problem of the empty room. One mother gave a rather typical description of this kind of transformation:

About eight months after Jeff's death, I decided it was time we did something with his room. So one day I moved the bed and dresser out and put them in the basement. I packed up his things and sealed them in boxes and put them in the basement also. I then painted his room a nice bright color, bought two lounger chairs, moved in the TV from the family room, and now my husband and I spend our evenings there. It's still a little bare looking—I need to pick up a few more pieces of furniture . . . but I'm glad I did it. Of course I cried all the while I was doing it! But it gives me a good feeling now—a kind of closeness to Jeff—when I'm in that room. . . . It also has been very good for my husband. He says he likes the feeling of intimacy he gets from being in Jeff's room!

This way of dealing with the empty room may not be for everyone. But relying on the imagination can conjure up other ways of responding to what was often described as a very painful situation.

Special Days

Time did not move forward in a smooth continuous flow in the days and weeks and months following the death of a child for parents in the study group, but was interrupted by periods—days—that came to have special meaning for the bereaved parent. These "special" days, as I call them, often carried enormous pain and heartache for parents as they tried to survive in the aftermath of child death.

Special days may be birthdays, death days, Thanksgiving,

Christmas, Easter—any holiday that carried special significance for the family as a time for getting together and sharing.

Birthdays were particularly difficult. Christmas was often impossible to deal with. Thanksgiving, when the family gathered for the turkey dinner, became overpowering for parents in revitalizing their sense of loss.

As these days approached, parents, particularly mothers, experienced increased anxiety and depression. This was usually a conscious process, the mother being well aware of her difficulty. Anger, sometimes hostility, erupted as the days neared. Irritability was common. All the old feelings that usually remained beneath the surface for most of the year came bubbling to the surface, causing great distress and pain.

There is no easy solution to this kind of problem. It is something parents must simply learn to live with. They must come to accept the changes in their mood and behavior that will occur as these days approach.

The one day that carries a special significance for families is of course Christmas. The old cliché "Christmas is for kids" is no less true for families suffering losses. How does a family deal with this holiday when one of the main participants is missing?

The families in the study group provided some suggestions on how to make Christmas without a child bearable and less painful.

They suggested, for instance, that the family might change the usual routine that had become established in the home. If the family usually opened gifts on Christmas morning, try opening them on Christmas eve. Do something different on Christmas day, such as going out to eat if you had always had your big meal at home. Or visit relatives or friends if it was usual for you to stay at home.

And don't be afraid to just get away for the holidays. This can sometimes prove extremely beneficial. Spend Christmas, or any special day that is difficult to deal with, elsewhere. Some might call this escaping, but so what! If it helps the parents get through these special days with the least amount of pain, they should do it.

One mother gave this account of how the family—her younger son and older daughter—spent their first Christmas after the death of her 25-year-old son from leukemia:

We agonized over what we would do on Christmas! It was the first one after my son died. My older daughter finally suggested we all go to

Florida for the Christmas holiday! This is something we had never done before. At first I thought it was out of the question, but the more I thought about it the better it sounded. I just couldn't bear the thought of spending Christmas without Dan! . . . We made reservations in early December and left on December 23rd. . . . Spent Christmas in Miami. We came home on New Year's Day—and it was wonderful! It took our minds off our troubles and allowed us to sneak through the holidays without many painful thoughts about Dan. . . . We have done this for the last three Christmases. Call it escape if you want to. . . . All I know is that it saved our lives!

This family found their answer. This approach may not be for everyone, but it is something worth thinking about.

Perhaps an even greater problem that appeared at Christmas was how to arrange one's life to make the necessary preparations, such as decorating the tree and doing the Christmas shopping that must be done. This often became an impossible task for many parents. They just could not bring themselves to spend the time roaming through stores and completing their shopping with one very important person missing from their list.

Again, the families I interviewed suggested that one way around this is to shop with another person—a friend or other family member who can assist in the process. Or sometimes simply wait until the parents have a "good" day and then try to complete most of it at that time. At any rate, when the parents are forced into this activity, they can try to incorporate it with some other more pleasant task, such as having lunch with a friend or visiting a museum or seeing a movie—breaking up holiday shopping activity with other things.

In preparing for the holidays, other children can be allowed to help. Give them a greater role to play. Let them trim the tree, bake the cookies, decorate the house. Give them a greater responsibility for completing some of the more painful tasks that must be completed at Christmas.

An interesting note appeared in *The Compassionate Friends Newsletter* of the St. Louis Chapter on "Getting Through the Holidays." I would like to quote a portion of this article here because I think it gives other helpful ways to cope with these stressful times. The article, originally written by the Fox Valley Chapter of Aurora, Illinois, says in part:

We must realize that grieving persons have definite limitations: we do not function at normal capacity; therefore we must reevaluate our priorities and decide what is really meaningful for ourselves and our families.

We must decide what we can handle comfortably—and let these needs be known to family, friends, and relatives:

- whether or not to talk about our child openly.
- whether we can handle the responsibility of the family dinner, holiday parties, etc., or if we wish someone else to take over some of these traditional tasks.
- whether we will stay at home for the holidays, or choose to "run away" to a totally different holiday environment this year. . . .

Our greatest comfort may come in doing something for others; some parents feel they can acknowledge their loss more meaningfully by:

- giving a gift in memory of our child.
- donating the money we would have spent on our child's gifts to a particular charity.
- adopting a needy family for the holidays.
- inviting a guest (foreign student, senior citizen, etc.) to share our festivities.

Whether it's greeting cards, holiday baking, putting up the tree, decorating outside, or having a big family dinner, ask these questions before making any decisions:

- have I involved or considered my other children?
- do I *really enjoy* doing this? Do other family members really enjoy doing this?
- is this a task that can be shared by other family members?
- would Christmas be Christmas without it?

How many stockings shall we hang? We may decide to:

- put them all up.
- hang no stockings at all.
- put thoughts and feelings about our child on notes and put them in that special stocking. Family members are free to read them. This gives a special opportunity for young children to express feelings.[4]

These few suggestions are important and can serve the needs of parents quite well as they contemplate their behavior during the holiday season. As suggested above, changing the routine on holidays can be a way of handling the heartache that usually accompanies a loss for the first year or two. This can work with any holiday or special day. The parents should ask themselves "What can I do that will be different from what I ordinarily do?" Then do it!

It may be rather hard to change a routine that one has lived with for a number of years; however, this may be the only way to lessen the pain.

On the other hand, perhaps it may serve a useful purpose in the parents' life to actually experience the pain of holidays and other special days throughout the year. This may be the only way that they can truly deal with their grief. Holidays and other special occasions may serve this function in that they allow parents the time and place to carry through with their grief work.

Each parent needs to assess his or her own situation and contemplate whether holidays or other special occasions might not be serving this important function of allowing the expression of emotion.

I have talked about a number of problems that seemed to trouble some of the parents in the study group. Not every parent reacted with the same degree of concern over these issues. However, concern was noted in enough instances to warrant my treatment of them in this chapter as special problems.

None of the problems discussed is unsolvable. However, it will take some initiative and dedication on the part of the array of different individuals that the family has contact with during the long months of a terminal illness and in the aftermath of a death, to recognize the problems as being important and worthy of confrontation and action.

The family generally stands alone in its encounter with death. It does not know where to turn or how to deal with many of the issues with which it is confronted at these critical times. As I have noted earlier, it is often up to others to solve and attempt to relieve many of the problems facing the family in its encounter with death.

Where there is a will and a determination to assist in these endeavors, equitable solutions to all problems are possible.

In the next two chapters I will take up the problem of adjusting to loss and will offer some suggestions on how to cope. I will also deal exclusively with the problem of the depression that inevitably surfaces in the aftermath of loss. I will discuss some of the common characteristics of depression and will offer some suggestions on how to deal with it, both from the point of view of the bereaved person and from that of friends and relatives.

9

Coping

What I want to know is where are the exits?! How do you find your way out of this? You can't live with it forever! There's got to be a way of resolving the pain, of relieving the guilt! But how? . . . It's been three years for me and I haven't found it yet! . . .

These words were spoken to me during a conversation with a 36-year-old mother whose 11-year-old son was killed while riding his bike home from school. How often I have heard similar expressions during the months of interviewing! Mothers and fathers, searching desperately for some relief from the hell that was created for them when their sons or daughters died, asked these same kinds of questions over and over: "Where are the exits? How do I find my way out of this?"

The young mother quoted above came to the interview perhaps hoping to find some answers, some way of resolving the turmoil and pain caused by the death of her son.

How does one respond to such pleas?

The grief suffered by parents after the death of a child, as I have said many times before, is a very different kind of grief from that experienced in response to the death of an elderly person. It is of a different quality, a different nature. There are no standard or conventional ways with which to cope with it. Most parents had never before experienced anything like it. Consequently they were often totally ill-prepared to deal with it. They had no perspective within which to place the experience and make sense of it. They had no backlog of ready-made responses. Even those who had suffered through the loss of an older loved person—a parent or brother or sister—indicated that even this compared in no way to the death of their child.

In my interviews over the last several years with more than 300 parents who survived the death of an infant or an older child, I have come to believe this to be true—relatively few experiences can compare to that of losing a child.

The dictionary defines "coping" as "struggling or contending with some success," and as an obsolete meaning, "striking back or fighting." For our purposes we can still rely on the obsolete meaning of the word. To cope means to strike back or fight. In fact this is what "mourning" is all about. To mourn—actively and willingly to work one's way through the grief—is to cope. To mourn is to fight back. Mourning is the process of purging ourselves of the grief of loss. We must work or fight to rid ourselves of the bitterness, the anger, the guilt, the sorrow of grief. *Coping means allowing ourselves to mourn a loss actively.*

We may not win all the fights and battles involved in mourning, but those who are able and willing to make the effort will eventually be successful in finding peace. But how do we find our way through the many battles without losing ourselves in the clusters of entrapments along the way?

One such entrapment is that parents often do not realize that they must work—and work *hard*—at mourning or coping with grief in order to finally resolve it. Some think that all they need to overcome their heartache is for someone to hold them or hug them as a favorite parent used to do when they were young, and in this way make the hurt and pain go away. Many seem unwilling or unable to understand that the only way the pain will be moderated is if they themselves work to make it so. This takes dedication and an acceptance of further suffering in an effort to heal themselves. It is as if one must undergo the pain of loss again and again in order to live once more.

Also, as noted, the grief of child death is felt very differently. Parents have no experience with this kind of loss, no knowledge against which to judge their progress. Grief manifestations can lie hidden beneath the surface for months, even years, unrecognizable as such. In addition, as parents move through the grieving process, the pain and hurt never really stay the same. Their impact on the individual is always changing. This creates confusion in the person because one never seems to know, or to be able to predict, what one is going to be experiencing from one day to the next. One day anger overwhelms one; the next day guilt penetrates to the core of one's existence. Then bitterness, then despair, then depression, then anger again. And on top of this come all the physical symptoms that are defined as frightening and upsetting: insomnia, loss of appetite, headaches, stomach upsets, etc. These compound the emotional problems and increase confusion and distress.

For some, the feelings generated by the grieving experience change into compassion and caring and loving, sometimes extended to others who have suffered similar kinds of losses. These individuals become "helpers" themselves, moving out into the community and seeking out other grieving individuals to offer them the understanding that they themselves often sought but seldom received. Such individuals can often cope with their own pain in this fashion, temporarily compensating for their own losses and postponing their own grief work.

For others, grief turns to anger and resentment which consumes their existence. They reject God and their religion. They reject anyone attempting to offer comfort. Their anger isolates them and eats at them. They cannot rid themselves of these hostile, aggressive feelings. This reaction is in fact very typical among parents whose children were murdered. Their anger may become hatred that tends to grow in magnitude, dominating their life experiences, again leading to the postponement of their grief work.

So there are indeed many pitfalls along the way that trap the bereaved parent and hinder his or her forward movement in the grieving process. Parents need to be aware of these dangers and must seek to overcome them as they continue the uphill battle for survival in the aftermath of child death.

The Road to Survival

It is a fact that one can *learn* to survive, even under the most barbaric living conditions imaginable! In the 1930s and 1940s, millions of European Jews were incarcerated in Hitler's concentration camps. But not all those who died did so in the gas chambers. Many died simply because they refused to face what was happening to them. They surrendered to the overwhelming hardships encountered.

On the other hand many of those who escaped the gas chambers lived only because they learned what behaviors and attitudes were necessary for survival. They were able to carve out an existence for themselves in spite of the barbaric conditions because they faced the reality of what was happening.

It is my contention that just as individuals can learn to live under inhumane physical conditions, they can also learn to live under inhumane emotional conditions. Parents can indeed "carve out" an existence for themselves under the conditions caused by the death of a child. However, like the concentration camp prisoners, they must accept the reality of the situation and make a concerted effort to survive. And many parents have done just that!

Parents do not hurt by choice. They in fact become weary of the hurt and the pain. They would like nothing better than to put it behind them and get on with life as they knew it in the past. But this is not possible. The hurt and pain are there, a part of their daily life experiences.

Many of the parents in the study group came to recognize this quite early in their bereavement experience. They came to recognize the agony and pain as being there, a part of their daily existence, a reality in their lives. And they also realized quite early in their journey that the road ahead was rocky and they had a very long way to go. More important, they came to realize that they had to make the journey *alone*! There were no shortcuts, no easy ways out, no magic solutions.

These parents, however, were able to see the light at the end, to catch glimpses of the final end to pain, and were at least willing to make the personal effort to achieve it. Life in that dark tunnel remained undesirable and foreboding, but it did finally become bearable for those who made the effort. These were the true survivors of the "concentration camps" of grief.

Other parents in the study group, perhaps as many as a third, did not see the situation in this way. They tended to remain, like the young mother quoted earlier, transfixed in time, suffering the pain, the guilt, the physical symptoms that unexpressed grief produces, sometimes for years. They were unable or unwilling to move forward because of the excruciating pain encountered as they attempted to face the reality of the death of their child. They lost not only hope but also faith in their own ability to survive. So they groped about with no sense of proper direction.

For these parents, time became their worst enemy. Instead of using it as a way of soothing the intensity of their responses, they fought it, and tried to hold it still by refusing to face the pain and sorrow that come with its passage.

Remnants of shadow grief dominated and often remained a part of their existence, sometimes for years.

We are often taught that grief has a beginning, a middle, and an end. We are also taught that, given enough time, we all should be able to find our way through to the end. However, it became apparent that this was simply not true for everyone. For some there seemed only to be a "middle," within which they were caught, unable to move forward. So when these parents turned to me and asked "How do we find relief from the despair and anguish we are suffering?" they were asking—searching—for help!

How do I respond to this? Can I help? Can you help? Can anyone help? Is there a light or a goal to be reached at the end of that long, dark passageway? Is there a way out for those parents who seem unable to help themselves?

I think the answer to these questions is "yes," but with qualifications. For these parents it will take a change of attitude, a change of orientation, and development of a willingness to make the journey, a willingness to suffer the continuing pain of "working through" their bereavement. But these changes and the willingness to make them can be *learned*!

Eric Lindemann, in his classic study of the survivors of the 1944 Coconut Grove fire in Boston, pointed out that one grieves until one completes his or her "grief work."[1] Grief work cannot be hurried. Each person has a built-in time frame for completing it. However, one must make a determined effort to meet it—to face it—head-on, and to *accept* the pain that realization of the loss will bring.

Of course it is easier to do this if one has help and support from the community of friends who surround the individual. This tends to remove feelings of isolation and leaves parents with the impression that the death of their child was an event that mattered in the eyes of others as well.

However, this kind of support, particularly in response to child death, is often terminated too quickly. Family supporters and friends often treat the death of a child as they would any other type of death. They give support and assistance for a few weeks and then expect the grieving to end and the survivors to get on with living as usual. Thus support and understanding are curtailed too soon and the survivors are left on their own to fend for themselves in the wilderness of their intense emotions. This produces a double hardship for parents, and under these circumstances only the strongest are likely to progress.

The others will remain fixated at some point in the bereavement process.

How can this situation be alleviated? I think it is important to understand that many people who are a part of the community of friends, neighbors, and relatives that surrounds a person, but who are not a part of the trauma of the situation, can be of assistance in helping families and parents understand the changing nature of their responses. These individuals can serve as sounding boards against which parents can "bounce" their feelings and reactions, and in this way see and understand them for what they really are.

Therefore it is important that individuals who might be called upon—either by the families themselves or by the person's own sense of duty and empathy—to offer support and assistance to grieving parents be aware of the kinds of help that are most useful.

Outside help and support are necessary, and make the transition through the grieving process a reality for more than just a few.

Thus this chapter is being written from two points of view: first, from the viewpoint of the parents themselves. What can they do to help lessen the impact or soften the blow of this tragedy on their families and on themselves? There are indeed some things that parents can learn which should help them find their way out of the long, dark tunnel of grief. But they cannot do it alone.

Therefore I am also writing from the viewpoint of "helpers," "supporters"—friends, neighbors, relatives—anyone who cares. A "true" helper or supporter can simply be a friend who has never experienced a tragedy of this magnitude but who is willing to be available to give assistance and support to those who have, and who understands the importance of the role he or she is about to assume. Such a friend is someone who is there when needed, someone who does not have to be asked to help. They are perceptive of the needs of grieving parents. They are not sympathizers but empathizers. They make a determined effort to understand the impact such tragedies produce even though they cannot feel the emotion themselves. They do not stand over, but next to, the griever in the struggle for survival.

Let us first consider what kinds of help friends can offer, and then I will make some suggestions as to what the parents themselves might do, on their own, to deal with the problems of surviving the death of a child.

Friends as Supporters

First of all, we need to be aware that as supporters we have no real answers to the kinds of questions parents may ask in the aftermath of child death. I don't really know that parents are looking for answers in the first place. Perhaps as supporters—i.e., as "true" helpers—we need to be aware of this.

When a mother or father asks the question "Why? Why did this happen to us?" as they inevitably will, we may feel obliged to try to give an answer. However, I do not think parents expect an answer. What they are really seeking is our approval or recognition that the question is legitimate. Grieving parents are not stupid. They recognize that we have no answer to that question, just as they have no answer, but they want us to recognize their right to ask it.

Similarly, if parents tell us that they have been unable to fathom what has happened to them, that they do not understand, they are not asking us for a response, but simply for some recognition that *we* understand and that it is alright to be confused, angry, and upset.

Parents seldom are looking for, nor do they need, "words of wisdom," which few of us have anyway, but simply permission or approval from us that it is alright to feel the way they do.

Also, in my discussion with parents I have come to know that so many really do not know how to grieve. They find it hard to cry, hard to give way to emotion because of the mixed signals they receive from their community environment. They often try to escape the pain by keeping busy or keeping active. They try all sorts of ways to keep from thinking about it. Some even take drugs to deaden the pain. Others turn to alcohol to take the edge off. They develop all sorts of defensive mechanisms and hang on to them long after these defenses have done their jobs. Friends and acquaintances need to be aware of these ways of responding and should recognize that their greatest help comes from their simple presence and their willingness to accept the grieving parent at whatever point he or she is.

Before we fit ourselves into a particular kind of helping role relative to the bereaved, we first need to ask ourselves what kind of relationship we have with the bereaved. Would you define yourself as a close, intimate friend, a "significant other" to the bereaved, or are you simply a "close" acquaintance who wishes to offer help? How personally you become involved in the grieving process will probably depend on how you answer that question. When the friendship is not very close (casual in nature), although you may still feel great compassion it would be best if you refrained from any overt action excepting an expression of sympathy. Many times "outsiders" can intrude into a very personal situation. You may not like the term "outsider" applied to you in this situation; however, you need to assess your relationship from the viewpoint of the family and ask seriously where you fit in the friendship pattern that surrounds the griever.

We know that friendships extend outward and surround a person like a series of concentric circles. In the first, or closest, circle are the intimate associates of the family, sometimes other family members, relatives, or very intimate, close friends of long duration. In the next circle, extending outward from the center, may be neighbors, or perhaps new-found friends, whom the family knows well but less intimately. In the next circle might be more casual acquaintances, such as workmates, people known in only one role. And so on. Therefore as a potential helper you must properly place yourself in one of these concentric circles and offer only the kind of assistance that might be appropriate.

It should be apparent that only those in the immediate, intimate circle of friends can offer a family solace and support during the initial, critical stages of the grieving process. Only later, after the person has passed through the acute phases of grief, can other, more distant acquaintances fill the role of helper by offering assistance in bringing the person back into the realm of the living—by assisting in his or her transfer back to reality.

(Parenthetically, a few parents have indicated to me that their "close, intimate friends" turned away. It was their "acquaintances" who were really there for them and who provided support when they needed it the most! So there are always exceptions to this general assumption.)

Where do you fit in this pattern? If you are in the innermost circle, there are important ways to help. First, you need to be aware that in the immediate aftermath of child death parents can do *nothing* for themselves. They have enormous difficulty taking care of their own needs, let alone those of other family members. They are of course grief-stricken, which in the early stages means confusion, disorganization, and preoccupation. Many of us are likely to approach a family in this turmoil with the statement "Please call me if I can be of some help." If you are in the position of being an intimate friend and you wish to make your presence known through a support function, don't wait to be asked! Jump into the midst of things and *do* something! Do some of the practical things that will be necessary to keep the family together and functioning. It is important to remember that since we are talking about the death of a child, the parents, as the mainstays of the family, will be the most debilitated. Friends and supporters should therefore be available to assist with other family members and with some of the tasks of normal family functioning.

Do some of the grocery shopping; bring in hot meals; clean up the dirty dishes; take care of the laundry; keep the house clean; chauffeur the kids to school if necessary; take over the care of the younger siblings and be prepared to help them work through their feelings regarding the death of their brother or sister. Try to keep other siblings occupied by taking them to Cub Scouts or Brownies, or roller-skating, or to the movies. In other words, get them out of the home for periods of time. Parents need *time* for themselves, particularly during the early phases. They need time to recover from the shock of loss. They need time to be alone without having to assume the responsibilities of keeping the family running.

Such help and assistance may be required for only a short period in the immediate aftermath of the death. However, this is the most valuable help you can offer at this particular time, for without it the family may founder under the burden of having to assume responsibility for its own care at a time when it is least able to handle it.

A question that may be asked is why the family can't draw support from within its own structure at these critical times. After all, at least two people are involved—the mother and the father. Both may feel the weight of the loss equally. Both can sympathize with each other and offer support that cannot possibly be gained from someone removed from the situation. Does not the cliché "grief shared is grief diminished" apply here? The answer is no! This cliché takes on meaning only when that someone with whom one "shares" grief has none to begin with. We cannot expect one crippled person to pick up and carry another! The "sharing" of grief means just that— sharing—*unloading one's burden,* partially at least, onto the shoulders of another who is essentially unburdened.

Grieving individuals need support from others *outside* the immediate situation, from those who are not so intimately involved in the loss. These "others"—close friends—can offer a refuge, some safe port in the storm of outrage and intense sorrow.

The sharing of grief with other human beings who are there, willingly giving of themselves, has enormous therapeutic value. The simple physical presence of another individual who can feel the depth of what a grieving person may be experiencing tends to remove the sense of isolation that often crushes grieving individuals.

"Participatory" grievers—those who can feel compassion as they empathize with a friend who has suffered a loss—must be flexible and resilient. They must be prepared to meet the grieving individual on his or her own turf.

It is a simple fact that grieving individuals often experience enormous difficulties in finding others in their immediate environments who will allow them the privilege of *continued* expression of emotion and feeling. When they can find no willing helpers who remain interested longer than a few weeks, they turn inward and away from all others and their grief remains essentially unresolved, manifested in shadow form throughout their future existence.

Shadow grief then exists because the grieving individual is ultimately forced to confront his or her emotions and feelings *alone*—without the support of the community, without the support of helping friends.

As participatory grievers we can enter this arrangement, take charge, and give of ourselves. As friends in this role, we must be prepared to break down the walls of resistance that many families throw up to protect themselves from the insensitivities of others. We must seek out and relate to husband and wife, treating each as an individual, offering each a shoulder to cry on and a hand of support. Allow each the full range of human emotion without passing judgment or admonishing them for their expressions. As true helpers, we should be there as their safe havens. And most important, we should be there for *as long as it takes,* as long as there are needs to be met. However, only the most intimate friends can accept this role and take on this function. Others must be prepared to wait for a more positive time, when the bereaved has entered the later stages of the grieving process and is ready for assistance in returning to the world of the living.

A Few Words of Caution. Parents who are grieving often misinterpret the separation of friends and relatives from them at the time of their loss as a lack of caring, a lack of interest, or even selfishness on their part.

I think it is important to realize that the neighbor or friend who appears to "turn away" during these times of need is the same person now that he or she was before the death. What we observe now, however, are inhibitions, fear of rejection, and unfamiliarity with what to do and how to do it.

Many good and, under other circumstances, helpful people simply lack experience. Probably they have never had a friend suffer the death of a child before. They may desperately want to help and may truly empathize, but are fearful of intruding in a very personal situation. Many friends who say "Please call if I can help" really mean it!

Also, grieving parents need to understand that *no one person* can even begin to fill the void left in their lives. Their needs are so extraordinarily great, particularly in the period immediately following the loss, that no one can meet them. So when others fail them, it may not be because others do not care. Sometimes lack of understanding or caring or compassion is the reason for inactivity. But just as often these elements are present but are not given because others simply don't know how!

In order to sensitize friends and potential supporters to the needs of parents as they pass through the various phases of the bereavement process, listen to what the parents themselves have indicated are their most prominent needs. These "expressions of need" come directly from the parents; they are taken out of context, but are stated in their own words. These needs were expressed not only to me, but to the various support groups to which the parents belonged. We as helpers and supporters should find this list useful in formulating strategies for offering assistance:

I need to be with others who know what I'm feeling.

I need help in accepting the loss I have experienced.

I need strength to deal with my present situation.

I need to share how I feel about why God called my child.

I need help to get over my hurt.

I need someone to care about me so that I realize I'm not alone.

I need help to preserve our marriage.

I need others who know what I'm feeling and who are willing to communicate with me.

I need to discuss and set new values for my life.

I need to learn how to express my true feelings to people who are close to me.

I need emotional support.

I need to deal with the loneliness.

I need to improve communication with my family.

I need to learn more constructive ways of living with my sorrow.

I need to understand some of my feelings of helplessness and loss.

I need support as I attempt to deal with the emotional impact of death.

I need to understand *me*.

I need a place to share thoughts about my child.

I need a place to just talk about everything.

I need someone who will listen.

Each of these expressions represents a cry for help. We should all listen and respond.

By being aware of some of the needs of parents, supporters should be in a better position to offer the kind of help required. For example, in regard to the last three needs expressed above—the need to share, the need to talk, and the need for someone to listen—how can supporters respond?

Regardless of the length of time that has elapsed since the death of the child, the family—the parents—will still have a strong need to talk about and share what they can remember about their deceased child as well as the events surrounding his or her death. For these needs to be to be realized, "listeners" are required! *Anyone* can function as a listener. These are needs that can be met by anyone, intimate friends as well as acquaintances.

It may be that parents find that talking about it is hard to engage in discussion, particularly after months of silence on the subject. Family members may in fact find it more "comfortable" simply to say nothing since they usually find that talking about it is upsetting to others. Eventually so much time passes that it seems useless, or burdensome, to talk about it anymore. One mother told me:

Sure I want to talk about Billy, but what good does it do? No one really wants to hear about it, nor even cares anymore. . . .

Another mother:

Of course I'd like to talk about it, but it's been so long. I'd probably be accused of dredging up all the hurt again. I know my friends and even my husband and daughter really don't want to hear about it anymore. . . .

Still another:

I really have no one to talk to anymore. Perhaps it's good because I often wonder if it's healthy to keep dredging up old memories; at least, so many have told me it's not! . . .

And another:

My greatest joy comes when someone asks me about my daughter! This gives me an opening and I spill out everything I've bottled up for so long. . . . I need this! I need to talk. . . .

These statements were typical of so many parents. It seemed that open communication about the deceased child and the circumstances surrounding the death was relatively short-lived. Parents often indicated that they really had few outlets. Even in the immediate aftermath of the death there appeared to be few individuals who really cared to hear about all the details in the way the parents needed, and were prepared, to discuss them.

This is truly unfortunate, because what makes all of us human is our verbal exchanges and interactions. Expressions of concern, expressions of feelings, to others are how we define our humanness.

It should be noted that just *talking* can be extremely therapeutic. Whenever we experience an event that has such a devastating impact on our lives, we must verbalize it, if only to feel the reality of it. By talking about it we make the event *real,* and therefore it should lose some of its inherent fear-generating qualities. We can get it "out in the open" only by talking about it. And in the process we should be better able to deal with our feelings and attitudes surrounding it.

Therefore it is important for helpers and supporters to realize the importance of open and effective communication with bereaved parents. It is important that we encourage parents to talk about their loss and express their feelings. Indeed, "dredging up old memories" is good and should be supported as a sound basis of operation. Reliving the past through talk and discussion is *not* emotionally damaging, as some uninformed observers would have us believe.

Parents have a genuine need to keep memories alive. They have a need to rehash all the events surrounding the death of their child. They have a need to remember as many of the details of their child's past life as they possibly can. And they need opportunities to express these remembrances to others.

As helpers and supporters we also need to encourage others to listen as well, and to encourage the families themselves to talk with us about their experiences.

Nothing can quite compare to the feelings of gratefulness and relief experienced when parents sense a willingness on the part of others to listen with no effort being made to give advice, no effort at forming platitudes or responding with clichés. Simply listening with a genuine sense of sincerity is really all that is required.

A good feeling will accrue to us from these parents as a result of our willingness to spend time with them, allowing them to air their feelings, to vent their emotions, to relive memories. This can be the greatest therapy of all. And it can be our greatest gift to our friends who have suffered such tragedies.

Here are a few additional hints that friends may find helpful in their attempt to offer support to grieving parents:

1. Don't be afraid to take the initiative in introducing the subject of this tragedy to the individual family members, i.e., don't be afraid to mention the "unmentionable," but don't force the issue. This includes mentioning the child's name. You should have no fear of reminding the parents of their loss; they haven't forgotten it! However, always use common sense and good judgment.

2. Don't say "You can always have another child" or "You're so lucky to have other children!" These are the last things parents want to hear! Their child can *never* be replaced by "another" child or "other" children. Such clichés and platitudes are insensitive and cruel.

3. Don't be afraid to cry with them. This is a mark of true empathy and is often understood and appreciated by family members. However, be mindful of "public" displays, and also note that the mourners may feel compelled to become the consolers, which might add another burden to their already heavy load. There are a time and place for shedding tears; choose them wisely.

4. Don't be afraid to touch. Touching communicates a gentleness and sensitivity that family members, even men, understand and identify with at these critical times. Gently holding a hand or putting an arm around the person will be remembered as a gesture of genuine concern and friendship.

5. Give special attention to other children. They too are hurt,

confused, and in need of help. In the immediate aftermath of the loss the parents are often too preoccupied to offer much support to other children. Friends can often fill this need if they are aware of it. Be there, take charge, turn some attention to the siblings who are often the forgotten survivors of child death.

6. Don't judge. Accept the family as it is. Don't tell parents how they should feel or how they should behave or where they should be in their grieving process. Support them wherever they are. In fact, words are unnecessary. Your simple presence is what will be remembered.

7. Don't get impatient with their slow progress. The grief process cannot be hurried. Even no progress may be "normal" for a time. However, be mindful of pathological grieving and be prepared to stick by the mourners regardless how long it takes. Don't desert them in midstream!

8. Don't expect *complete* recovery. There will always be elements of shadow grief present, and we can never expect parents to return to where they were before the tragedy. This is the one certainty in regard to child death, particularly for mothers. However much we believe remains to be done in the grieving process, we must accept them at whatever point they emerge without insisting that they "finish" it. For some, there will be no end!

Adherence to these simple suggestions will pay great dividends for friends and supporters. Knowing that you, as a friend, have given freely of your time and offered genuine help and assistance to families at the time of their greatest need can enhance your own feelings of self-esteem. You can feel satisfied that you were not a burden to the family, but met the human criterion of concern for others.

Support from Within

The major battles to be fought in this war with grief must be fought by the families themselves. As I have said earlier, the main sources of support for the family caught in the stress of child death must come from the members themselves, who must make a determined effort to overcome the obstacles to the successful resolution of grief by engaging in the work—the "grief work"—necessary to accomplish this.

To cope with loss is to mourn actively. Since mourning is such a painful experience to undergo, it seems understandable that the parents would rather escape—run away—than continue to face the reality of loss every day, day in and day out! And it seems that there would be a strong temptation to do just that. Therefore, what can I possibly say to parents that would have any real meaning for them? What can I propose that would allow them to say "Ah, here is sound advice. Here is something I can use. Here is information that will help me deal with this—that will help me face and accept the reality of this burden"?

Parents in the throes of grief are receptive not to *words,* but simply to silent *presence.* So how can I write words that will be meaningfully accepted by parents, words that will be useful for them?

I think that initially, in the early stages when grief is fresh and raw, I cannot. But in the later stages of grief words do become important again, when parents themselves begin the active search for understanding, for reasons, for causes, for consequences of their experiences. And in retrospect, words can be comforting and supportive of one's past efforts and past "accomplishments" relative to coping with the grief of child death.

So here are some words that parents may find useful at some point in their grieving, words that may help move them through the heartache of grief work. It is hoped that these words—in the form of suggestions—can eventually become moored in meaning and anchored in attitude as parents begin their precipitous journey.

1. *Recognize the loss!* Accept the grief. *Believe* that it is happening to you. It is real. Recognize the shock and numbness you feel. Don't fight it; roll with it; go wherever it takes you. Recognize that you will attempt to deny its existence. But also recognize that you are strong enough to overcome. Recognize that you *will* survive!

2. *Understand that it will be painful!* In fact it will be the most painful experience of your life. It will also be enormously frightening and confusing. Let yourself feel it. Don't run away. Don't cover up. Allow yourself time to hurt. Know, also, that you can handle it. Know that the pain is not forever!

3. *Realize that guilt is real!* It cannot be avoided. We teach our children to be responsible and to accept blame whenever anything goes wrong in life. This is a lesson we have all learned too well. We blame ourselves and feel responsible for the untimely deaths of our children. There is no way to escape it. Therefore recognize it as a part of the grief complex and keep it visible—in the open. Gradually try to

reduce your dependence on thoughts that begin "If only. . . ." Remember, you are good. You are complete. You are worthwhile!

4. *Be aware that you are not alone!* Loss is an integral part of life. Everyone experiences it. You have comrades. Join a group of others like yourself, parents who have suffered the loss of a child. Other bereaved parents, who can truly empathize with your experience, can be your best support in the long run. Such support groups may even be defined as the *only* salvation for some. Seek them out!

5. *Give yourself time!* Healing is time-consuming. The more significant the loss, the more time it takes. Time will *not* heal, but it will make the loss more bearable. Time will help you "let go" of your child, which you must do first in order to get him or her back again in a way that will allow you to resolve your grief. "Letting go" is the final step in the grieving process and occurs during the stage of relief and reestablishment. And time is essential to achieving this. So give yourself time—you deserve it. Relief will come!

6. *Keep active*—even when you don't want to be! It may be painful at first, but the rewards will be great. But don't allow yourself to become hyperactive. This can be as damaging as inactivity. Set a regular pace and stick to it. Try to accomplish something constructive each day.

7. *Cry!* Give yourself permission. Put yourself in a position where it's okay to cry. Crying is the most therapeutic activity a bereaved person can do. It is a form of release and greatly reduces stress. This suggestion equally applies to men. Strong men can and do cry. One father told me that the only way he can cry is to listen to the taped funeral service of his daughter, which he does often. Use other techniques and devices to bring tears. The rewards and satisfaction that accrue to those able to cry are enormous. Do it!

8. *Know that tomorrow will come!* Each day will pass, and with it, the pain experienced on that day. It will get easier. You may doubt this at first, but don't surrender—don't give up! Fight this battle—and:

9. *You will survive!* No doubt about it! In grieving, as in life, if you work at it there is a beginning, a middle, and an *end*. However, having reached the end, you will not be the same as before, nor would you want to be. But you will be complete. And you will find joy and happiness once more.

So here you have a few simple suggestions that should reap benefits for those who try to live by them.

As I said earlier, however, perhaps these are just *words* that carry little meaning for those pining for a dead child. If this is true for you, I urge you to have patience. The time will come, as it does for all, when you will begin an active search for written material that will help answer some of the questions that will become significant issues in your life in the months and years ahead. Perhaps at this time you will be able to find some comfort and support in this discussion.

Something of Value

The death of a loved child is one of those experiences in life that (if you're successful in achieving some resolution to the intense grief accompanying it) can result in something of value.

It may seem strange to say this, given the terrible price parents must pay as they attempt to work their way through the ravages of the grieving experience. But I believe this to be a valid conclusion. Those parents who have *worked* to overcome, who have managed to recover to the point where life once more begins to take on some meaning, tend to develop a sense of omnipotence and invulnerability relative to life's other hardships. They come to feel that there are simply no obstacles that they cannot overcome. They believe that they have met the ultimate challenge to their own survival and they have conquered it!

Granted, this feeling of omnipotence does not come all at once, and for some it does not come at all. It is slower to achieve in the case of sudden loss where the shock, disorganization, and guilt are longer lasting. Considerable time is required for some sort of adjustment to, and acceptance of, these losses to occur. But this eventual change in attitude did appear to be a *universal* phenomenon among the parents in the study group who had survived long enough to have resolved most aspects of acute grief. The time to accomplish this was different for different persons. These parents, however, had met the "test of fire," had survived, and had become stronger because of it.

It of course appears paradoxical to speak of anything of value coming from such a tragic and personally devastating event. And of course such a result would not appear for months, perhaps even years. However, once parents progress to the point in their grieving experience where they can begin to look beyond their own personal frame of reference, a shift in orientation is likely to occur. As parents begin to pull out of the mire of remorse, out of the confines of the personal hell into which they have been plunged, only then is it possible to begin the process of rebuilding or reconstructing one's life. And in this process of rebuilding, it tends to become obvious that the survivor has indeed encountered the ultimate tragedy and *has survived*. What could life possibly deal them now that would surpass the previous event in terms of the devastation it has wrought in their lives? Even another death could be no worse than what the parent has already passed through!

Thus a feeling of power and control tends to descend upon the individual, which leads to significant and sweeping alterations in the value orientations of the person. These changes are often experienced by both parents and affect the organization and functioning of the family from that point forward.

Things that were once considered important lose their importance or become less important to the family. For example, families who were once very materialistic, where parents were wedded to their careers and devoted to accumulating the various symbols of status and achievement, no longer seemed interested in pursuing these activities and seeking these types of goals.

The home became redefined. Relationships were redefined. One's entire orientation to people, places, and things seemed to undergo a significant alteration.

Time also took on new meaning. These families found themselves reoriented to the present and present circumstances, and away from anticipations of the future. It seemed that what they had *now*, today, became more important than what they might be able to achieve in the future! They wished to cultivate and develop what was presently within their grasp and not reach for what was beyond it.

This tendency to define the present as primary affected the career patterns of many parents. Some said they were locked into certain career patterns prior to their losses. They were oriented to the future, never satisfied with where they were at any given time, always striving to move ahead and keep ahead. As these same parents began the slow and painful process of recovering from their loses, their orientations changed. Career patterns lost their importance. Fathers and mothers became less concerned with career development and more concerned with savoring what they now had.

Family relationships took on a new meaning, a new significance.

Life seemed larger, more vital, more brilliant, more precious than before. Living for tomorrow at the expense of today simply could no longer be tolerated.

Perhaps these parents came to realize that tomorrow might never come. It never came for their child, so it might not come for them! Thus *today* took on a new importance in a way that perhaps can be understood only by those who have experienced the "ultimate" tragedy.

It is too bad that we cannot all live by this philosophy. Elisabeth Kübler-Ross, in her seminal book *On Death and Dying*,[2] puts forth this same message. She points out that so many of us are ruled by what the future might hold. We are all oriented to the future. This seems to be characteristic of our way of life today. We tend to forget that the present is all anyone really has. Yet we tend to let it slip away without ever enjoying the moment at hand. We don't really miss it until we are given our sentence of death—only then do we come to the glaring realization that we have no future after all!

Kübler-Ross's message is simple: Do your best to enjoy the moment—enjoy and relish *today*, for tomorrow may never come! This message, seldom heard by the rest of us, however, comes in loud and clear for bereaved parents!

I am defining this as a valuable after-effect of the devastation of loss. And one that many of the study families have come to experience.

This new philosophy might be defined as the good that comes from these events. It is unfortunate that such a devastating event in the lives of so many is required in order to come to this realization!

Attitudes Toward Death

Another related result of child death in the family that produces a long-range positive effect is the change that occurs in the parents' attitude toward death and their own dying. Of all the parents who participated in this study, the vast majority—over 90 percent—indicated that they had lost their fears of death as a result of having experienced the dying process in their children. This was true for both mothers and fathers.

The very fact that a child *can* die, and in many cases even find some sense of peace in the process, produced a profound impact on those observing these events.

Such fearlessness of death was most pronounced in parents who had followed their children through a long-term illness, but was no less evident among those whose children who had died suddenly as a result of accident, suicide, or murder. However, in the case where the dying trajectory was drawn out, the parents had a greater opportunity to assess their own feelings toward death and were better able to verbalize and relate the meaning that death had taken on in their own lives.

These parents eventually came to the point where they no longer viewed death as the enemy. Many saw that death could be a friend! This was particularly true for those whose sons and daughters had reached a complete deterioration toward the end. For these parents death was a relief—a release—a blessing! This "new" view of death impacted on the family in a significant way, leading to an altered, more accepting attitude toward it.

With overt fear of death removed as a result of the development of a more positive attitude toward it, parents felt that they could deal more effectively with the subsequent deaths of others as well. They also felt more understanding and tolerance of what others go through as they face death. In addition these parents felt that they could now approach their *own* deaths more with a sense of awe and curiosity than with remorse, anxiety, or fear.

Arriving at this stage seemed to follow a rather standard pattern. For example, rather than avoiding thoughts of death, as is the more common response of most individuals, these parents were often, at least initially, preoccupied with such thoughts. These thoughts tended to revolve around the death experiences of their children, and in the beginning were often accompanied by sadness, sorrow, emptiness, and yearning. As time progressed, however, and parents watched the process of dying overtake their children, they came to the point where their attitudes and thoughts about death began to take on a more positive character. Thus as they continued to be a part of the dying experiences of their children, they began to think about death—even their own death—with little or no fear or anxiety.

Thus for many parents in the study group death simply lost its emotional overtones. It was something they had come face to face with in the death of their children—and survived!

However, since it was something their children experienced, they felt that they could too. "If my child could face it and meet it with such courage and resolve, I certainly can" was the argument often heard. This kind of reasoning created a sense of acceptance of this harsh reality in the minds of many parents. Consequently many even said—with a sense of conviction—that although they were not willing to rush into it, they *looked forward* to their own death in the future, since this would mean a reuniting with their child.

Perhaps we might define this too as a positive effect that has some relevance for the ability to cope with these types of losses.

Turning to Religion

Another way parents in the study group seemed to cope with the death of their child was by turning to a religious interpretation of what had happened. Often this was not possible until several months had passed after the death, since the initial response to their child's death was a *loss* of faith, with anger at, and sometimes even hatred for, a God who "allowed this terrible thing to happen."

Parents often ask: "Why did God do this to us?" "How could He permit this to happen?" These questions occur to parents whether they are suffering through a long-term illness, an accidental death, a suicide, or a murder. Parents cannot fathom a "benevolent" God's allowing something terrible to happen to children. Consequently child death, from any cause, often gives rise to a lot of questions, a lot of resentment, and a lot of anger. In a way this can be somewhat therapeutic in that when something bad happens to a child there is *always* the tendency to assign blame or responsibility. And I suppose blaming God is "better" in the long run than blaming oneself or one's spouse.

Many parents who had in fact blamed God and held Him responsible indicated later that they did not really feel any shame for doing so, and that at the time it was "good" to be able to hold *someone* responsible. They came to realize that God was indeed "big enough" to take it.

This question—"Why?"—is probably one of the most persistent ones the parents must deal with. They cannot rid their minds of it regardless of how hard they try. And the inability to find answers to it leads to a kind of preoccupation that is difficult to control.

Preoccupation is the way the mind attempts to comprehend some aspect of reality. Losing a child is a sword-thrust through the heart! It is often unbelievable. The stages of shock, denial, and disorganization linger. Preoccupation enters this state and one becomes consumed with the details surrounding the event, unable to shake these thoughts and always muttering "Why? Why? Why?" Preoccupation reveals itself in the inability to concentrate, the inability to feel or express emotion, the inability to assign meaning. The individual tries desperately to "understand" this event, to fit it into some comprehensive framework where he or she can see some reason behind what has happened.

A state of preoccupation will continue until the individual begins to find some meaning in it all. In some cases the intense sense of loss and preoccupation will last only weeks. In other cases it will be months—and in some extreme cases, years—before the individual is finally able to find some sense of relief from the nagging feelings of emptiness and hopelessness that accompany the inability to find meaning.

One way out of the turmoil encountered during these heartrending days of "meaningless" existence is to reach beyond this life for explanations.

Religion and faith were eventually rekindled in the minds of the majority of parents in the study group as the only logical and satisfactory explanation of what happened.

When one comes to the point in one's struggle for survival where one asks "Why me?" but can counter that with the question "Why *not* me?" one is beginning to press for a "religious" interpretation. This became the solution for many of the parents in this group—their answer, their way out, their exit from the heartache of "meaningless" grief.

Thus a vast majority of these parents simply turned or returned to their faith, to God, for an answer to this ultimate question, and dealt with their preoccupation from this point of view. Many times simply *saying* "It was a part of God's plan" was an effective panacea for dealing with the loss and resolving the grief. One accepts the belief that the Almighty knows what He is doing, and whatever "reasons" exist (the search for these may have dominated one's existence for months) are now seen as His reasons.

As one comes to accept a religious explanation, one can be successful in counteracting the effects of preoccupation and can seek some meaning that is responsive to the resolution of grief.

Listen to how individual parents eventually came to express themselves on this issue, how they came to accept an explanation and meaning in terms of a strong religious commitment (both mothers and fathers are speaking):

I really don't know why this happened to us, but I've stopped looking for the answer! I just have to put my faith in the Lord's hands. . . . Only He knows—only He has the answers!

The Lord works in many strange ways. At first I simply could not fathom this, but then I accepted the Lord. . . . He must have had His reasons, and these—whatever they are—are good enough for me. . . .

At first I was confused and bewildered and angry. Why did this happen to us? Why did God permit this to happen? . . . Then I began to realize that it was the will of God. . . . Who am I to question further?

Nothing pacified me after Tommy's death. I couldn't understand how a loving God could allow such a thing. . . . However, I eventually came to realize that God was my greatest salvation; whatever His reasons are for taking Tommy, I can now accept them! I think of Him as holding Tommy in His arms until the day I can join him. . . .

"The Lord giveth and the Lord taketh away"—that is a quote from the Bible! I never knew exactly what it meant until this thing happened. . . . You're damned right, I questioned! I was angry and filled with hate over the loss of our son. . . . However, the anger and hate softened as I accepted the Lord. I put myself in His hands and immediately felt a sense of peace overtake me. . . .

For some, turning to the Lord was *not* the answer. For others, however, a belief in the wisdom of God, accepting one's faith at face value, was an effective way of dealing with loss and allowing one to move forward to the resolution of the bereavement process.

This way of coping requires time to work through the initial sense of anger and hatred, but eventually the majority of parents in the study group were able to achieve some relief from the trauma of the situation by redefining their religious commitment. In reality, the Bible has a great deal to say about sorrow and pain. Many parents were able to achieve some sense of satisfaction simply by reading passages from the Bible, and as time passed they began to see the larger picture and found that they were not so mad at God after all. They came to believe that here is where the answers lie to the riddles that plagued them for so many months.

As noted in Chapter 2, this rekindling of religious commitment even took place among those who were not particularly religiously oriented prior to the loss. The loss of a child is such a monumental ordeal for most families to deal with that reaching beyond the scope of the rational world seems the only sensible way of coping.

A Living Reincarnation

Before I end this chapter I want to say something to those parents who are reading this book and who have *recently* suffered the loss of a child. I know you are searching for some resolution to your grief, some way of finding some meaning in what you have experienced.

One thing you can actively do now to make the situation perhaps a "little more bearable" is to think of yourself as the living reincarnation of your deceased son or daughter. In a certain respect, after your child died you were really all that was left of your child's genetic endowment. Whatever your child had to pass on to the future can now be accomplished only by you acting in his or her behalf.

Therefore if you as a bereaved parent can think of yourself as an actual extension of your deceased son or daughter, this may help you to come to terms with the loss in a way that may not be as devastating. In many ways your son or daughter is still alive—alive in you, in your thoughts and memories of a life you have experienced together—and can influence the future only through your own behavior.

Think of yourself as having an obligation not to allow your life to wither away. By giving up, by selecting the first "alternative" (as noted in Chapter 1) which is within your options to choose, you will be surrendering not only your life but also, in a very real sense, the only available way your son or daughter has to "live."

Therefore, painful as this will be in the beginning, you should try to live the best life you are capable of. This is something you must reach for and work for. But, believe me, the price you pay will be well worth it in the end! Even though the remnants of grief will remain in shadow form perhaps for a lifetime, there is a way out of the darkest depths of defeat and the agony of loss.

When you have accomplished this, your thoughts will be alive and fresh with good memories of your son or daughter. In this way you will be serving your deceased offspring well.

I know what you are saying at this point: "These are just so many words. What does it all mean?" "It's one thing to say live the best life possible for the sake of your son or daughter, but how does one really accomplish this?" "How does one keep alive memories of deceased sons and daughters when everyone surrounding you wants you to forget?"

One way of actually living within the framework of this model is to begin doing things for others and doing them in the *name of* your son or daughter. Your child's school or club would probably have any number of projects that need to be completed which you could undertake to finish. Sometimes setting up a scholarship in the name of your son or daughter can reap benefits for others and satisfying results for you. Donating books to a library or a work of art to a school or museum in the name of your son or daughter is another way of "doing something" that will allow your child to live on in your own thoughts and in the memories of others.

Still another way of creating lasting and meaningful memorials for your child would be to buy needed equipment for a school or club and present it in the name of your child. Sometimes space will be made available on the school grounds or elsewhere for the planting of a tree, truly a living memorial. Sometimes spending a certain portion of your time, such as on weekends or evenings, working with sick or dying children can be a way of making a contribution in the name of your son or daughter and keeping the memories alive.

Let your imagination go. Think of other projects that will occupy your time and give you the satisfaction of knowing that you are keeping alive the memories of your child and creating a reason for your own continued survival as well.

As you carry out these activities, keep a written record of what you do and a journal of your thoughts and feelings as you do them. These written accounts will come to be valued treasures in the years to come. You will return to them often as a way of retrieving and cultivating memories.

You never *want* to forget. You never *will* forget. Because all you have are your memories. It should be your task to make them good and give them substance so that others too will never forget.

Letting Go

In a recent issue of *The Compassionate Friends Newsletter* of the St. Louis Chapter, there appeared a letter by a mother whose 6-year-old son was killed in 1971. In it, she talks about "letting go"—releasing her emotional hold on her son—and what this has meant for her. I want to close this chapter with the concluding paragraphs from this letter because I think that what she says, in a very poignant and beautiful way, has some relevance for all parents who somehow feel that there will be no end to the heartache and turmoil they are now experiencing.

It seems that there is one ingredient that is important in achieving release from the bondage to a deceased son or daughter, and that is *time*. Although I have said earlier on many occasions that *time alone does not heal,* it does contribute something to the healing process. Perhaps all bereaved parents can learn to use time to their advantage to help them resolve their grief and achieve a state where they can "let go." This appears to be a paradox. How can you let something go and yet at the same time get the same thing back?

Read how this particular mother was finally able to "let her son go" and yet get him back in a way that few who have not been through the pain can understand. Every parent who has suffered the death of a child will in time be able to achieve what this mother has achieved. It will take longer for some than for others, but I am convinced of the outcome.

She concludes her letter with these words:

My intense grief was long and hard. I knew nothing about how to grieve and there was no help for grieving parents in 1971 when Arthur was killed. I didn't allow myself to cry as much as I needed or to give vent to my emotions. I tried to keep busy with frantic activities in order not to think about my son. My doctor, who looked at my grief reactions as "sick," gave me drugs that masked much of my pain. I continued this way for five years! I hurt as badly at [the end of that time] as I did that first day. It wasn't until I looked at my grief with a clear head [that] I was able to begin to work through it. I not only had to *start* my grieving five years after he died, but I had developed destructive coping mechanisms which took additional time and energy to change. . . .

It takes different lengths of time for each parent. And you should not be concerned if this hasn't happened in your life yet. It took me almost ten years! As a matter of fact, I realized only recently that I had "let Arthur go." I know that after a couple of years [of active grieving] I began to feel better and find meaning and joy in life again. Eventually I began to be able to have happy memories of Arthur without pain or sadness. I realized that I was talking about him in conversation just as I would any of my other children. At family get-togethers I could say things like "Arthur would be getting his driver's license this year," or "I'll bet he would have been broad-shouldered like Ed, Jr." I could say [these things] as statements of fact without the usual stab of pain that was formerly a part of every thought of Arthur. In the retelling of things the other kids did when they were younger, I could retell things about him without that "different" feeling. I can look at his picture and think "My little grandson has hair just like Arthur had," without hurting. There is just a warm feeling at the thought of how many times I ruffled my hands through his hair. I can say "He has been dead for ten years" and not have the pang of regret and emptiness that usually accompanies that thought. . . .

I now have him back in a more beautiful way. Arthur is a part of my life as none of my other seven children will ever be. He is deep in my heart and no one can ever take him away from me. Arthur will always be my six-year-old "baby boy." The other kids will grow up and change, but he never will. The other ones will have their own lives to live, their own interests, and their own families that will pull them farther away from me. Arthur will never leave me.

Arthur is as much a part of my life today as he was in his six short years, only in a different way. And really, isn't this true of our other living children as well? Relationships with our families are constantly changing. We have to "let them go" too.

No longer am I plagued by guilt if I don't think of Arthur for a few days. No longer do I feel I have to punish myself by hurting because Arthur isn't physically with me, or that I am betraying my love for him by being happy again. When I think of him it is of the twinkling brown-eyed boy, not the still, dead one. I can think of Arthur with joy and gladness and of the six years I had him, not the sad ones since he was killed.

It feels so good not to hurt anymore, not to feel guilt, or anger. I loved him when he was alive without all those complicating emotions, and I can do that again now.

Silly as it may sound, I have this mental picture of Arthur, free now to run and play and be happy in heaven. No longer does he have to worry about taking care of me. I can visualize him running off to play, glancing over his shoulder and saying in an offhand way, "Thanks, Mom, see ya!"[3]

The next chapter tackles the problem of depression as a natural by-product of grief, and lays out some of the ways of coping with this often-debilitating condition. Some suggestions are offered that might be useful for the depressed person in dealing with depression in his or her own life, as well as for supporters outside the immediate situation in their attempt to modify the impact of depression on the lives of others.

10

Coping with Depression

What Is Depression?

Depression is often thought to be a bad thing, something to be avoided at all costs. Yet it is a very common form of emotional disorder, experienced by virtually all people at one time or another. In fact, "depression is so ubiquitous that it is often called the common cold of the mental disorders."[1] Some 75 percent of all psychiatric hospitalizations are for depression. And in any given year, 15 percent of the population will suffer significant depressive symptoms.[2]

David Peretz maintains that depression may occur as the dominant feature of the bereavement state. It can occur in the immediate period after the loss, or develop gradually during the weeks and months following the loss, or even after apparent recovery.[3] Depression and grief go hand in hand. Although depression can be experienced without grief, grief cannot be experienced without depression.

As to the parents in this study, I did not talk to a single parent who said that depression was not a reaction to his or her loss. Although depression occurred throughout the grieving process, it was most pronounced during the stage of loss and loneliness, after the acute phase of grief had passed, as the individual began to experience a revival of feelings of isolation and loneliness.

Depression among these parents was at times very severe, taking the form of depressive illness. At other times and in other cases it tended to be of the milder variety, experienced more as a "normal" depressive mood. In the latter case, time was all that was required to resolve it. In other, more isolated cases, symptoms were severe enough to require professional intervention.

Depression can best be understood when viewed on a continuum. At one end is normal depression, of which a reaction to grief is the best example. If you lose a loved one, it is entirely appropriate to have depressive thoughts, to suffer a loss of interest in things, and to hold a pessimistic view of the future. You may feel empty and be convinced that life will never be the same without that person. This type of reaction is temporary and expected.

At the other end is depressive illness, of either the neurotic or the psychotic variety. This has a tendency to be much longer lasting with more severe symptoms. Depressive illness too can be the result of a reaction to significant loss. For example, when grief deepens and goes on for more than several weeks, the individual may begin suffering from an array of exaggerated feelings that are both frightening and difficult to control. Thus the normal depression that one might naturally experience having undergone a significant loss might in time become a depressive illness. We know that "any depressive reaction that is mild can become moderate and go on to severe."[4]

In fact the psychiatric profession cannot agree that there are any *significant* differences between "clinical" types of depression (depressive illnesses) and simple depressive moods.[5] In the final analysis we really do not know whether normal depression and depressive illness are "two separate entities or whether they represent two extremes on a continuum of symptoms. . . ."[6]

Therefore I do not think it is appropriate to refer to depression in response to child death—even the extreme variety—as "abnormal" in any sense other than to say that it is "unusual." Brown and Harris have said:

> In some instances we believe that it is as normal to develop depression [in response to a loss] as it is to develop a blister when a hand has been burnt by a hot stove, although it is *unusual* to have a burnt hand in a random selection of hands.[7]

They go on to say:

> We are only willing to see clinical depression in general as abnormal in the sense of "unusual." And, of course, the unusualness is significant because of the associated distress and handicap.[8]

Thus both normal depressive moods and depressive illnesses are associated with important losses.

Symptoms of clinical depression or depressive illness can sometimes last from several months to over a year or two.[9] In fact it may take up to 18 months to work through the type of depression associated with extreme grief.[10]

The Effects of Depression

The effects of depression are experienced physically, emotionally, and mentally.

The parents in the study group often displayed an array of physical and emotional symptoms that could define a depressive syndrome. Not every parent showed every symptom, but they occurred enough times in enough individuals to form a pattern.

PHYSICAL EFFECTS OF DEPRESSION

These symptoms, taken individually, might just as well be defined as a nuisance and nothing more. They become symptomatic of depression, however, when we consider them as occurring together. These symptoms include:

1. *Erratic sleep patterns or insomnia.* Waking in the middle of the night and inability to go back to sleep, the inability to rest properly, or the inability to fall asleep at all, even though you may be very tired, are all signs of depression.

2. *Lethargy or agitation*—either one! Lethargy refers to the inability to accomplish tasks because of a lack of energy or stamina, or to feelings of being unmotivated. Agitation refers to restless activity and jitteriness. That is, you feel either like you're carrying a knapsack filled with rocks, weighing you down, or like you're on pins and needles or barefoot on hot pavement—you can't stand still!

3. *Loss of appetite or the tendency to eat constantly.* Food either loses its appeal or you can't get enough of it. The more severely depressed you are, the more these symptoms manifest themselves. In many cases, over the long run they eventually come to be associated with weight loss or weight gain.

4. *Loss of sex drive.* This may particularly strike women. Men who are mildly depressed may actually experience an increase in their sex drive as a compensation for a threatened ego. However, for the severely depressed, both women *and* men are likely to suffer a reduced drive. In women it can also mean irregularity or stoppage of the menstrual function.

5. *Unkempt appearance.* This generally results from a poor self-image. It is usually a reflection of the way people see and evaluate themselves. When individuals dress sloppily, or when they appear

unclean or disheveled when neatness is called for, it may be an indication that they have given up on themselves.

6. *Many physical complaints.* The depressed suffer an array of physical maladies—fatigue, weakness, shortness of breath, heart palpitations, headaches, constipation, heartburn, sweating, etc. These physical symptoms can be so disconcerting that they can actually perpetuate the depressive episode. They can also "mask" the depression, in that the individual may become so preoccupied with these complaints that they come to be the center of attention.

EMOTIONAL EFFECTS OF DEPRESSION

Physical symptoms represent only one part of the depressive syndrome. Emotional symptoms also occur as a part of the pattern. When enough of these symptoms occur in conjunction with an array of physical symptoms, it is a good indication that depression is being experienced. Emotional symptoms include:

1. *Loss of affection,* or the tendency to withdraw from others. Declining love for a spouse or other children is often an associated symptom. This can be quite serious and will hinder one's ability to overcome. This can also produce a reaction of resentment on the part of others who feel that the individual no longer appreciates them, which in turn intensifies the withdrawal tendencies of the depressed individual.

2. *Sadness and gloom* become a way of life for the depressed. One loses the ability to respond to humor and may actually resent the joy expressed by others. In fact we often misinterpret sadness as depression itself. And in a way the two terms are interchangeable. However, depression is not just sadness, but an *exaggerated* form of sadness in that the person will recognize himself or herself as being sad but with the impression that the sadness will persist indefinitely, regardless of what one does about it. This is what distinguishes sadness, as a mood, from depression. Depression *is* sadness, but sadness coupled with extreme pessimism.

3. *A sense of emptiness.* In fact this symptom may even overshadow and circumvent feelings of sadness. It is characterized by a general lack of feeling. The individual feels nothing at all! He or she may show little or no emotion, little or no response to people, places, or things. This symptom implies a turning inward, away from the

external environment and away from the hurt and pain that exist there. And the more severe the depression, the greater this unresponsiveness becomes. In some cases the individual will simply "sit huddled and downcast in gloom."[11]

4. *The "weeps"—involuntary crying—or the inability to cry.* Either characteristic can accompany depression. The individual may suddenly be struck with a crying jag brought on by the most unlikely occurrences at the strangest times and in the strangest places. Or he or she will simply be unable to bring on tears, no matter what he does or how hard he tries. Individuals unable to cry may resent it, feeling that if they could cry they would feel better. The inability to cry is probably the more serious symptom because it means that the individual is unable to experience any relief from the stress building up inside. The individual becomes like a pressure cooker with the lid tightly closed and steam building inside to the explosion point.

5. *Hostility.* This is generally a component of anger, where the individual lashes out at everyone with angry gestures. At first hostility may be directed at the deceased child, later at anyone in the vicinity, and still later, turned inward. This component can sometimes become highly destructive. It is usually during depressive episodes that the individual may entertain thoughts of suicide. Turned inward, hostility can sometimes trigger self-destructive acts. In other cases self-destructive thoughts may come from the generated anxiety associated with the prospect of facing life once more.

6. *Irritability.* The person may be in a constant state of irritation. He or she may come to resent others for feeling good and enjoying themselves. He or she may become irritated at the energy and vitality displayed by others. This symptom also creates unneeded barriers between the individual and friends and family because of the impatience that others will display when encountering individuals who seem constantly upset and irritable. No one likes to be around irritable persons for long, and as friends and relatives make their departures, this contributes to feelings of isolation and intensifies the depression.

7. *Anxiety, fear, worry.* Feelings of loneliness and despair lower the fear threshold. Everything seems to become an excuse to worry. There is also a strong apprehension of death and other morbid thoughts. The individual may fear that he or she is becoming seriously ill or may even come to believe and fear that death is approaching. Anxiety may also lead to increased agitation and jitteriness

which may mask the depressive reaction. There is a danger here of misinterpreting and using the wrong approach in dealing with these symptom patterns, such as prescribing tranquilizers when antidepressants would be the proper medication.

8. *Inability to feel pleasure.* This is the hallmark of depression. The individual loses all interest in things that once gave him or her pleasure. Practically everything the person once thoroughly enjoyed doing now becomes a boring, unstimulating, time-consuming activity which the person does not feel he or she has the energy to complete. A depressed person would feel like it's just not worth it.[12]

9. *Loss of self-esteem.* All the preceding emotional symptoms may be combined and experienced as a loss of self-esteem. This is a vital characteristic displayed by the depressed person. As all previous feelings and symptoms unfold, individuals gradually come to think of themselves as worthless, as having no substance. As parents, they sense that they are failures: they failed to perform in the vital role of protector of their child and can find no way of justifying continued existence of their own lives. Associated with, or perhaps because of, a lack of self-esteem, the primary symptom of hopelessness appears, tipping the individual into a depressive state. Hopelessness serves as the final emotional characteristic of depression.

10. *Hopelessness.* The individual may be literally overcome by this feeling. The person feels trapped by circumstances; he or she can find no way out. What's the use of even trying? Why even bother to get up in the morning? The past is filled with grief; the present is a hotbed of anguish; the future is seen as gloomy and uninviting. There are no solutions. There is no hope in sight![13] This too can sometimes contribute to morbid thoughts and ideas of suicide. Feelings of hopelessness can be so pervasive that the individual may lose the ability to function on a day-to-day basis, and may withdraw from physical contact with others, thereby closing off avenues of potential help and support.

It should be noted that depression does not always follow the death of a child. Brown and Harris, as noted earlier, have zeroed in on the symptom of hopelessness as being a key factor in *generating* depression. They point out that "loss is less important in producing depression than feelings of profound hopelessness which may not stem from loss."[14] This may explain the rather deep depressive reactions that often occur among parents caring for a terminally ill child:

"Hopelessness may occur in response to thoughts about a possible loss."[15] Feelings of hopelessness can overtake the parent in the final phases of the child's terminal illness, stemming from the parent's extreme pessimism about the future. Hopelessness may be triggered as a result of dwelling on a time when death will likely occur.[16] Under these conditions, depression is an understandable response.

Hidden Depression

It should be noted that at times depression is hard to detect and can go unnoticed although the depressive process is still there, causing turmoil and distress to the sufferer and disrupting the lives of family and friends.

For example, sometimes when people become depressed the depression itself releases so much anxiety that the original depressive symptoms are lost—"masked" by the release of anxiety. Such agitated and anxious individuals are depressed, however, and will usually respond well to antidepressive drugs.[17]

In other cases the depression is converted into bodily functions that are expressed in somatic distress. Thus the aches and pains that so many often compain about in the aftermath of a significant loss may be a form of masked depression, but unrecognized as such.

Still others might simply deny—turn away from—it and essentially treat it as if it does not exist. Such individuals, using *denial* as an escape mechanism, sometimes intentionally try to look happy and content. This is called "smiling" depression, and can be a serious and crippling form of unrecognized depression because it involves the coping mechanism of denial, which has a tendency to be tenaciously adhered to.[18]

It usually will require professional assistance to deal effectively with symptoms of masked depression.

Causes of Depression

Depression does not just happen. It always has a cause. In the present circumstances we might wish to think of "the death of a child" as the cause. However, this "cause" may be interpreted as the "excuse" for depression—the "gun" that fires the emotional bullets that cause depression. Brussel and Irwin state that the death of a loved one "is only the triggering mechanism. . . . The cause is a repressed past painful emotional trauma stirred out of its deep grave by a re-creation—more often symbolic than parallel—of that depressing event."[19] The experience of death is simply a precipitating mechanism.

In the final analysis there is no comprehensive agreement on the causes of depression. What we do know is that there are probably many contributing factors—psychological, emotional, and social. Perhaps what are important are not so much the causes as the consequences and what we can do to deal with these.

Depression as Protection

As to our ability to cope with depression, it is important to note that depression as an experience can serve the important function of "protecting" the individual, of insulating him or her from permanent damage by a reality too harsh to digest all at once.

Ross Mitchell describes four ways that depression can fulfill this "self-protective" function:

> [1.] Depression can *lower responsiveness* so that a depressed person does not respond too violently to the stress around him. As the stress increases, the resulting depression acts as a reciprocal protective screen.
>
> [2.] If the external stress becomes too great, the depression can act as a *cut-out:* the person stops responding altogether. This has its drawbacks, because it also stops any adaptive responses taking place but, presumably, the cut-out is activated when basic survival is threatened—adaptation can come later.
>
> [3.] With its associated grief and weeping, depression has a *cathartic effect*—pent-up emotions are expressed, the cork is blown out of the bottle, and adaptation—which otherwise might be inhibited by the unexpressed feelings—can then begin.
>
> [4.] Finally, depression can be thought of as a period of time during which the individual diverts his energies inward while he is making an adaptation to external events. He is pulling up the drawbridge—not just to keep the enemy out, but so that he can spend time getting his defensive guns ready.[20]

So perhaps we ought not to be so quick to jump in and do something about our depressive moods. They can perform a protective function for the individual and can serve a positive purpose.

Dealing with Depression

We all know that depression is a common response to child death. Even severe depression may be "unusual" but "normal" for many individuals.

Without doubt, however, in spite of the apparent protective function it performs for the individual, depression is something we would all prefer to be without! In many respects it is like the common cold—we can learn to live with it if we have to; but it is certainly a nuisance and is energy-depleting and time-consuming to deal with. Therefore we would prefer to rid ourselves of it and get on with life as we would like it to be.

How can one accomplish this? We should be aware that sometimes professional intervention may be called for when symptom patterns are complex, severe, and long lasting. In other cases, where the condition is manifested in less severe form, perhaps all that is required is support and understanding from important people in the immediate environment.

In any case we need to be cognizant of symptom patterns and recognize them as being *triggered* by significant losses, but *caused* by a series of unknown variables or circumstances. Therefore we should refrain from taking any condition of depression too lightly! We must look at the total reaction pattern of the individual, make some assessment of the personality and background of the individual, then couple our observations with common sense before we launch upon a "therapeutic" program to help the individual through the episode.

WHAT THE PARENT-SURVIVOR CAN DO

Within the normal range of responses there are some things the depressed person can do for himself or herself in attempting to counteract the symptoms of depression. Equally, there are things that others—friends and supporters—can do to help a depressed person to get through the depression and to live a more fruitful life.

Here are some suggestions that might be successful in dealing with depression from within. These are rather simple suggestions that, if followed, could prove beneficial in removing the devastating emotional anguish that one experiences in a depressed state. Of course, the person can do nothing and simply rely on various medications to help deal with his or her feelings. There are a great variety of antidepressant drugs on the market through prescription that are designed to counteract the symptoms. However, antidepressants treat symptoms only and do nothing to get at the cause, nor do they lead to a change in living patterns and attitudes, which in the long run may be much more effective as a permanent "cure." In addition, sometimes one does not have access to drug therapy, or perhaps one may prefer to rely on a self-help regimen.

Here, then, are some simple suggestions that might help (my thanks to Carl Lancaster of the Greenville Mental Health Center for his contributions to the following discussion):[21]

1. *Be sure you are getting enough rest.* Insomnia, or sleep disturbance, is one set of symptoms that the person can do something about. It is true that we have no active control over insomnia; however, this is a symptom that feeds upon itself; i.e., the more you are unable to sleep, the more sleep you need; the more sleep you need, the more difficult it is to fall into a regular pattern for obtaining it. It is therefore important that you attempt to reestablish a sleep pattern by setting regular hours for going to bed and rising. We often try to compensate for insomnia by staying up late so as to be sure we are really tired, or by engaging in strenuous activity to wear the body down so that sleep will overtake us. This is a wrong approach. We are all programmed to need a given number of hours of sleep each night. Going to bed at a regular and reasonable hour, even if one does not feel tired, will gradually return *routine* to one's life. This may be ineffective at first, but don't give up. After several tries, restful sleep will again be possible.

It is easy when in a state of depression, in an effort to escape the emotional hurt that accompanies it, to sleep excessively—to escape into sleep! Too much sleep is as ill-advised as too little. How much sleep you need depends on you. What is important is not really how much, but establishing a regular pattern for sleep and then making sure you stick to it.

Adjusting to this pattern may require frequent short naps in the afternoon. The point is, when you feel tired, *rest.* Eventually the body will come to respond to the pattern you are trying to set.

This simple suggestion should go a long way in helping you deal with depression. Fatigue is often one cause of depression. You must learn to control it!

2. *Eat—at least five meals a day.* Eat no more than you would

ordinarily eat at three meals, but eat more often. The logic behind this suggestion is that numerous smaller meals will keep your blood sugar at a constant level. Since level of blood sugar is related to mood, by keeping this under control the mood-swing into depression can be controlled. Even if you are not hungry, even if you prefer not to eat, do it anyway. It will have a positive effect.

3. *Spend some time alone every day.* This may seem counter-productive since isolation is a common by-product of depression. However, everyone needs some time to be alone, particularly if you live in a household with small children or if you work in a place that keeps you constantly in contact with others. You need to get away from the hustle and bustle of everyday existence. It need not be a lengthy time—an hour or two at most. But it should be a time when you are least likely to be interrupted. During this time, do whatever you wish. Even if this is your "crying time," set some aside and do not feel guilty about taking it. This must be your time to do your thing—*whatever* that may be!

Now it may be that part of your problem is that you are spending *too much* time alone! You need to examine this from all sides. The problem may be only partially self-imposed and may be due primarily to circumstances beyond your control, such as the imposed community isolation that often accompanies child death. However, this type of isolation probably does not include complete solitude. And this is what you must strive to achieve, to spend some time completely alone, in complete solitude. This should be a sought-after goal and may be very helpful in counteracting the effects of depression.

4. *Do something for fun each day.* This may seem enormously hard to accomplish, since when you are depressed the last thing you will think of is having *fun!* This may indeed take some effort to accomplish. However, having fun can be a rather simple activity. In fact, the simpler the activity, the more fun it is likely to be. Activities such as reading a light humorous novel can be "fun," and if done during your free time, can essentially be killing two birds with one stone! Repot some houseplants; do some gardening or light repairs; lie in the sun for a while; go shopping—spend a little money on yourself. This can be great fun! Whatever you once defined as an enjoyable activity, do it! Even though you don't feel like doing it—and you most likely will not—and even though you may no longer define the activity as enjoyable, do it anyway! Force yourself, if you must.

Associated with this is a related suggestion, and that is:

5. *Accomplish some task every day.* Concentrate on finishing something. Complete some project that you have been putting off, or start something new, but finish it! Even if it is some small thing that has no great significance in your life, it is important that you prove to yourself that you can complete a job. Clean out a closet, or the garage, or the basement. Wash the car, cut the grass, paint or wallpaper a room, anything—regardless how small the task—as long as you complete it. This will help you regain your self-esteem by proving that you can do something well. If the task you select requires physical exertion, you will also be meeting the requirements of a sixth suggestion, and that is:

6. *Do something physically strenuous each day.* One of the important contributing factors to depression is stress: the stress of the experience of the loss itself; the stress encountered in simple survival after the loss; the stress in adjusting to a world without your precious child. Stress can be devastating! The only effective way to relieve stress is by working it out through physical activity. Therefore each day set aside some time for dealing with stress. If you live near a country club, play a round of golf, go swimming, play a set of tennis or handball. If you don't care for physical sports, jogging or vigorous walking is ideal. The activity must be strenuous, however. You must breathe hard and work up a good sweat. You will be amazed at how much better you feel after a good workout. Cutting the grass, chopping wood, punching a bag, pounding a pillow are other ways of releasing stress. In fact, a simple exercise routine of a strenuous nature, on a daily basis, will accomplish the same thing in a more organized manner.

One other suggestion for dealing with depression may well be a fantasy rather than a practical suggestion. However, if this can be accomplished in some fashion, the dividends it pays will be great. Therefore even though you may not be successful at first, do not dismiss this suggestion as being impossible. Hang on to it for future use; the suggestion is:

7. *Do something social each day.* In other words, meet people! Interact! Socialize, even if this is a painful experience at first. You may be deeply depressed but you are not dead—even though you may wish to be! Therefore it is essential that you maintain some contact with the *living* world. Every day you should make an effort—

a powerful effort—to do something that has some social significance. This could be as simple as going next door to have a cup of coffee with your neighbor, or inviting a workmate to lunch. Telephone a friend and just talk for a while. In fact, a tennis game with a friend or a twosome for golf will fulfill your desire for physical activity as well as your need for social interaction. Even shopping or dinner out with a friend can be both fun *and* social in nature.

Let me mention one last suggestion that may help when all others fail:

8. *Get away for a while.* Take a vacation! Get away from the office, the home, the children—even if only for a few days. A change of scenery can sometimes pay great dividends by diverting your attention to something new and fresh. Again this will be difficult to do, especially when you are depressed and don't really care about getting out of bed in the morning, let alone leaving your home. However, certain places can often become associated with depressive feelings. If your home contains memories of the deceased child, this may be a particularly depressing place for you, even though you may cherish these memories. Getting away, even for a short time, can be very helpful in breaking the link between your home and your depressive reaction. Getting away means not only new places, but also new things to do, new faces to see, and it can also be fun. Do it!

Adhering to these simple suggestions for relieving depression will pay great dividends in the long run. Some, as I have noted, will be difficult to undertake and you will need to be motivated to make them work. Perhaps it is well to remember that ridding yourself of depression is a sure way of dealing with grief, and this realization should provide all the motivation you need.

WHAT OTHERS CAN DO

Since we live in a social environment, surrounded by other people, the depressed person's behavior will be highly scrutinized by family, friends, and neighbors. Interrelationships between the depressed person and others will usually be disrupted, causing hardships and strains in all social encounters.

These disruptions and strains often cause more concern for others than for the depressed persons. Friends and supporters develop strong needs and desires to offer help and assistance to the depressed person. Often, however, they do not know what to do. They do not know the points of entry into the life of a depressed person and therefore are usually forced to remain *outside*, observing but offering little in the way of significant help designed to bring about change.

What can others do? What suggestions can I give that might make nonprofessional supporters more effective in their mission?

Actually, the suggestions I have to offer are of a very general nature and are in the form of encouragements or reassurances that can be offered a depressed person. I am not saying that they will always work. However, by adhering to these simple suggestions, supporters can at least be assured that they will not become extra burdens to bereaved and depressed parents by responding to their grief and depression in meaningless and ill-advised ways. Depressed and grief-stricken individuals have enough problems taking care of their own needs without having to deal with the insensitive clichés and platitudes of others put forth in the guise of support!

Perhaps my suggestions might be better stated in terms of some "don'ts"—things *not* to do, *not* to say—when encountering depressed and grief-stricken individuals. Here then are five "don'ts." Take them for what they're worth.

1. *Don't tell the person that things are not that bad!*[22] Your credibility will be lost if you approach a depressed person with that platitude. A depressed person sees the world through dark glasses, and to him or her things *are* that bad! Nothing you can say will change this perspective. On the other hand, *don't sympathize with the person.* Don't help him or her justify feelings of self-pity. A better approach would be to indicate that you understand how he or she could feel that way, while reassuring the parent that the depression will end. They may not believe you, but they need to hear this over and over.

2. *Don't push the person into situations he or she can't handle.*[23] Doing this will likely drive the individual deeper into the depression. Depressed people have very low opinions of themselves and really cannot handle the usual kinds of social situations. You may encourage participation, but don't push. Also, do not insist that they make important decisions. They are confused and upset and will eventually come to resent your insistence. In fact, depressed individuals should be given only the simplest tasks to perform, and should never be called upon to make critical decisions. Even at work, less arduous duties should be assigned, and if they are in key posi-

tions where critical decisions are called for, they should be temporarily relieved of that responsibility. They need time to repair their damaged self-esteem and should be tolerated, not berated for their lack of social involvement.

3. *Don't push the person into festive events.*[24] Fun and games are definitely not what depressed parents need or want. This can be disastrous and the individual may respond with irritation and hostility at the prospect of even contemplating festive events, let alone participating.

4. *Don't run away—get the person to talk!*[25] Ventilation of feelings in your presence can be very therapeutic. By gently encouraging the person to talk, you are providing him or her with an escape valve, which many depressed parents greatly need but are too subdued by others to reach for actively. Don't be afraid to encourage the individual to let off steam. This suggestion implies, however, that you must be present and become the receptive listener!

Don't push for a discussion of the loss or the depression. Let the person select the topic. By enjoying this freedom of expression on topics of his or her choice the depressed person may eventually come to the realization that the depression is masking other feelings that the individual is resisting expressing. Herein lies the real value of this suggestion.

5. *Never admonish, but try to lighten the guilt!* Rather than preach to the grievers, try to relieve some of their feelings of self-blame that often surround childhood death and that contribute to the onset of depression, by helping them *search* for answers! As helpers, we need to assist parents in finding reports or explanations when there is an answer. We tend to say "You shouldn't feel that way" and believe we are relieving the self-blame by such a comment. However, the parents need to search out answers and process them over and over.

Also, don't make them feel guilty about taking drugs. This may be the only way depressed individuals can deal with the acute manifestations of depression. However, drug therapy should be temporary and never a permanent crutch.

We need to bear in mind that depression is not a form of mental weakness but a genuine emotional imbalance or disorder. One cannot get over it by willpower, or by heeding the advice of friends and family. No one fully understands what causes such deep, unremitting despair. No one has the cure.

Coping with depression is one of the tasks involved in grief work. However, it is a task that cannot be accomplished alone. It will take the dedicated support and understanding of others.

Having a child taken by death will plunge even the heartiest individual into a state of loneliness, hopelessness, and depression. The physical and psychic pain occasioned by the emptiness of loss can be healed only by a spirit dedicated to survival and by the love and support of another person. Grief-stricken and depressed parents need *others* as well as *each other* during the course of their bereavement. Human support is essential as parents work through their grief. Such support is given not to help parents to avoid the matter but to help them to talk, to remember, and to cry. As Ross Mitchell has said, "there is work to be done" at this time, "not an illness to treat," and only other human beings can help complete this work.[26]

Friends and other family members can often make the difference between success and failure in one's coping ability. Failure to cope may mean the assignment of the individual to a life characterized by a deep-seated sense of loss and loneliness, with remnants of the cloth of shadow grief draped about the shoulders of the bereaved. Without help and support from others these individuals will be forced to wear this tattered dress for the remainder of their lives, with their feelings bottled up inside, unable to find suitable outlets.

By coupling the willingness and dedication of the bereaved parent with the free help and support of others, the task of completing the grief work and achieving some resolution of the grief can indeed be accomplished.

In the next chapter I will introduce the reader to an array of community self-help support groups that are presently available to parents suffering the death of a child. These support groups are known by various names and serve the positive function of assisting families—mothers, fathers, and siblings—in their journey through the bereavement process.

11

Support Groups Do Help

Don't know what I would have done without them. . . . I was in the pits of depression for weeks. . . . Thought seriously of suicide. . . . They literally saved my life.

You can only pretend so long. . . . You act as if you can deal with it when you really can't. . . . They were there when I needed them. . . . They made me face the reality of it.

It's a wonderful experience to be around those you know can truly understand how you feel because they feel the same.

It seemed as though no one could really understand what was happening to me until I became involved with the group. . . . They know because they've been through it!

As I have pointed out so many times before, the death of a child, unlike the death of an older member, can bring a family to the edge of absolute despair. Parents, particularly, often experience a terrible sense that others—even those close to the family—do not really understand the wretched agony they feel in the face of this loss. Parents seem to sink into the mire of their own grief. They often characterize themselves as "drowning" or as being "swept along" in the emotional storm that follows, unable to find any anchorage. They reach out to others only to have those toward whom they reach turn away.

One mother expressed the sentiments of many parents in the study group. She said:

After Jimmy died, we [the family] felt like we were standing up to our knees in quicksand. As we struggled to free ourselves, we sank deeper and deeper. It became apparent to us that we needed someone to throw us a line—to reach out to us. We needed someone to tell us that we wouldn't sink out of sight, that we could rely on them—our friends, our family—to give us what we so desperately needed. . . . However, wherever we looked, no one was available, no one seemed to care!

Although we know that the main source of support for individuals in the aftermath of child death must come from within the person, this internal strength is initially weak and takes time to realize and to develop. In the immediate aftermath of child loss there is always confusion, disorganization, anger, resentment, and despair that take their toll in terms of even the strongest individual's ability to respond rationally and effectively. Oftentimes there is a great gap between the person's ability to develop the internal resources necessary to deal with the death and the swift emotional impact the loss generates. The result is that the person is left floating in a limbo of grief so severe that the person's capacity for survival—let alone efficient living—is impaired.

It is at this point that the self-help community support group can often make its most startling impact. Although there are many such groups, designed to minister to individuals suffering from a variety of conditions, the groups that are the subject of this chapter consist of parents, and sometimes other close relatives, from the local community who have undergone the tragedy of child death and who come together, voluntarily and without compensation, to do what they can for others recently bereaved.

Listening to families and individual parents express their admiration and gratitude for what they received from such support groups tells us that nothing quite compares to the kind of help derived from those who have themselves undergone the same experience and who have apparently "survived" the ordeal. What is more important, however, is not what the members do for each other but what they do for themselves. It seems that "the very act of helping helps the helper."[1] This is in fact the key to the apparent success of any support group. Self-help groups therefore appear to be an ideal support mechanism for parents in the immediate aftermath of child death, and are strongly recommended.

Leonard Borman characterized self-help groups in this way:

> Their membership consists of those who share a common experience, situation, heritage, symptom, or experience. They are largely self-regulating, emphasizing peer solidarity rather than hierarchical governance. As such, they prefer controls built upon consensus rather than coercion. They tend to disregard in their own organization the usual institutional distinctions between consumers, professionals, and Boards of Directors, combining and exchanging such

functions among each other. They advocate self-reliance and require equally intense commitment and responsibility to other members, actual or potential. They often provide an identifiable code of precepts, beliefs, and practices that includes rules for conducting group meetings, entrance requirements for new members, and techniques for dealing with "backsliders." They minimize referrals to professionals or agencies since, in most cases, no appropriate help exists. Where it does, they tend to cooperate with professionals. They generally offer a face-to-face or phone-to-phone fellowship network usually available and accessible without charge. Groups tend to be self-supporting, occur mostly outside the aegis of institutions or agencies, and thrive largely on donations from members and friends rather than government or foundation grants or fees from the public.[2]

Unfortunately, self-help groups do not reach many people. Not every community has such groups organized. Therefore only a small proportion of those people who could benefit from the kind of help offered can actually take advantage of them. Even in communities where such groups do exist, they may remain unknown to the majority. Such groups do not usually advertise their services. They become known through word-of-mouth, through professional referrals, sometimes through announcements in church bulletins or on agency billboards.[3] These informal techniques of "spreading the word" often reach only a few who could benefit.

In addition it should be noted that some families are structured in such a way as to be unable to reach out beyond their boundaries to others in the community who are there to offer help. This inability on the part of some families was noted in Chapter 6 in the discussion of how different family *types* have different degrees of resources available to meet crisis situations. It was noted that some families are "resource poor" in the sense that they do not possess the necessary array of personal and internal resources that will allow them to deal effectively with the devastation imposed by child loss. Because of the isolation experienced and the tendency to withdraw from social contact, they do not characteristically seek help beyond the boundaries of their own units. Even though a self-help group may be conveniently located, many of these families would be unable to take advantage of it.

Also there is another characteristic that we should perhaps be aware of. Self-help groups tend to be *segregated* in the sense that they do not bring together different classes and different races. Most parent self-help groups were started by people from the middle of the socioeconomic bracket, perhaps because of the more liberal attitudes, cohesive neighborhoods, homogeneous lifestyles, and greater cognitive abilities of these community members. In fact the kind of mutual, highly personal support that is characteristic of these organizations tends to appeal more to the middle of the socioeconomic stratum than to either extreme.

Incidentally, the segregated nature of these groups is becoming of concern to some of the more highly structured self-help organizations. Some are beginning to recognize and address the issue of segregation. For example, Kinder-Mourn, Inc., a self-help organization located in Charlotte, North Carolina, is now beginning to reach out beyond the bounds of its typically middle-class membership to the minority groups in the area, not so much in an effort to integrate its membership but to extend its services to all members of the community who can benefit.

Actually, from another point of view there can be an advantage to homogeneous membership in that similarity in background and lifestyles can contribute to the group's ability to deal more effectively with intimate issues. This was probably one reason for the self-help groups' initial success. They consisted of people from similar socioeconomic and racial groups, who had a common sense of identity in addition to the loss experience. This in effect gave the membership a starting point in their mutual-support function and increased their sense of acceptance and belonging.

Self-help groups should not be thought of as cure-alls for what ails you. They are *not* designed as "therapy" groups for the purpose of getting at the root causes of problems. However, their informality and warmth seem to compensate for their lack of a "professional" attitude toward the "clinical" aspects of the problem. By doing whatever they can do for others in a warm, friendly sort of way, individual members derive great personal benefit from the experience. This is what makes these groups work—the mutual sharing of insights and information which reduces isolation and builds an esprit de corps among the members.

Sometimes professionals in the community become jealous of self-help groups, believing that the groups are usurping potential clients. However, professionals need to be made aware of the limitations of the professional services they offer in a community. They need to be made equally aware of the very important service self-help groups provide. Professionals should try to work in cooperation with them rather than considering them a threat to the power and pocketbook of the community professional.[4]

One thing professionals can do to support the work of self-help organizations is to *volunteer* their services as resource persons by simply being available to offer advice and assistance.

Self-help groups indeed offer a very different kind of help. It is help of an informal variety and of a highly personal nature, and is presented outside the usual bureaucratic structure surrounding professional services. There are some things individual members of self-help organizations can offer clients that professionals cannot. Professionals tend to treat the "patient" according to certain theoretical principles learned in their professional training. Self-help groups treat the individual as a next-door neighbor or as a personal friend, and respond with a sense of empathy and understanding that is rarely possible in the case of professional consultation.

Self-help support groups of the type discussed here are therefore informal, spontaneous, autonomous groups of parents who offer personal help and assistance to other bereaved parents, essentially giving them an alternative to the usual professional services offered in a community.

One way of coping with child death is to locate and join a self-help support group in the community. Or if none is available, to start one. I want to talk about some of the specific characteristics of two such groups that can be organized in any community which offer the kind of help and support families so desperately need during the critical first months after the loss.

One is called The Compassionate Friends, available to any parent who suffers the loss of a child from any cause. The other is called Parents of Murdered Children, available to parents whose losses are characterized by violence. A third group, called Kinder-Mourn, is the prototype of support activity as it is conceived in this book. Its uniqueness, its organizational structure, and the philosophy upon which it rests will be the subject of the last chapter of this book.

The Compassionate Friends

The Compassionate Friends was the first self-help group to be established in the United States offering friendship and understanding to bereaved parents. The purpose of the group is

> to promote and aid parents in the positive resolution of the grief experienced upon the death of their child, and to foster the physical and emotional health of bereaved parents and siblings. . . .
>
> The aims of a chapter are:
>
> - To offer support and friendship to any sorrowing parent, regardless of race, creed, or financial status.
> - To listen with understanding and provide "telephone friends" who may be called.
> - To provide sharing groups that meet monthly.
> - To give cognitive information about the grieving process through programs and library.
> - To provide acquaintance with bereaved parents whose sorrow has softened and who have found fresh hope and strength for living.[5]

The Compassionate Friends is open to parents who have experienced the death of a child, although other recently bereaved individuals also are permitted to attend the monthly meetings. There is little formal organization to the chapter groups. There are no formally designated officers or leaders in the bureaucratic sense. No dues or fees are assessed. Parents can come as long as they feel there is a need, which is an individual thing with each parent. Some come once or twice; others come over a long period of time; still others continue with the group, offering support to the newly bereaved.

As for the specific method or approach used in the meetings:

> Sometimes a conversation, a book, or a professional presentation may assist healing and give a new insight and understanding about a particular question or concern. In trying to help bereaved parents cope with their loss, Compassionate Friends does not focus morbidly on death and thus only rekindle unhappy feelings. . . .[6]

The group, however, does recognize that "pain is a part of loving. We have loved, therefore we grieve. We are willing to share someone's sorrow."

We call such groups "self-help" because at every meeting there are parents who have worked through their own grief, usually within the group, with the help of others. There are parents who have *survived* the onslaught of this most devastating experience and "who can empathize with a bereaved family and truly be with them." The Compassionate Friends states that the group is not a "therapy group, nor are chapter meetings 'therapy' sessions." Yet there is also *healing,* which

> is slowly and gently promoted as parents gain insight and understanding, have an opportunity to ventilate their feelings in an accepting atmosphere, and as they are able to reach out to the newly bereaved.
>
> While we share our sorrow and our struggle for adjustment to our loss, there is also talk of meaningful activities each of us has found to give new hope and direction to our lives. But underneath it all is a real concern for one another, a concern that does not shy away from reality and memories that are painful. It affirms life in the deepest sense by saying that there is a meaningful life beyond the pain, by recognizing that grief is an expression of love. Parents who felt they were coping effectively with their loss, as well as parents who felt loneliness and despair in their grief, have found Compassionate Friends helpful to them. While there are no instant solutions, no easy answers, and no timetable for recovery, there is a sense of direction to be found through knowledge and understanding of the grief experience. Bereaved parents can find healing and hope for the future.[7]

Listen to what Judy Osgood, a bereaved parent, says about her first encounter with Compassionate Friends:

> We went to our first meeting of The Compassionate Friends not knowing quite what to expect. We discovered a group of sensitive, caring people who understand how we felt because they'd all experienced the pain we were enduring. They didn't ask "How are you?" and expect us to answer with a platitude like "Fine, thank you," or "I'm doing okay." Instead, they told us about the children they had lost and gently asked questions about our situation such as "How long since your child died?" and "Could you tell us what happened, or is that still too painful to verbalize?"
>
> We quickly learned from this group that there was no need for small talk about the weather or the price of gas. No one cared how much money anyone else made or what they did for a living. Death made us all equals and everyone was there for the same purpose. We were hurting because our children were no longer with us, and our discussions centered on them and our grief.

To an outsider that sounds morbid, but it isn't. Whenever a loved one dies there is an intense need to discuss what happened, to review the circumstances and talk about significant events in the person's life. Professionals call that process "obsessional review" and say it is an important part of the healing process. The illness or accident that led to the death and the death itself must be discussed over and over until the survivors can come to grips with the "what ifs" in their minds, and accept that what has happened cannot be changed. The death can't be erased.[8]

Perhaps I should note that the financing of The Compassionate Friends depends entirely on voluntary contributions to cover the costs of operation at both the local and national levels. In addition, it has no religious affiliation and supports no religious creed of any sort.

The Compassionate Friends was founded in Coventry, England, in 1969, and grew rapidly throughout the United Kingdom. The first United States chapter was organized in Miami, Florida, in 1972. In 1978 it was incorporated as a nonprofit corporation. In less than 10 years it has grown into a national organization with chapters in practically every state.

For the addresses of local Compassionate Friends groups, or for information on how to organize one in your own community, write:

> The Compassionate Friends
> National Headquarters
> P.O. Box 1347
> Oak Brook, IL 60521
> (Tel. 312/323-5010)

Parents of Murdered Children, Inc.

This organization was referred to in Chapter 5. The national headquarters is in Cincinnati, Ohio, but there are presently dozens of chapters in the major metropolitan areas around the country.

Parents of Murdered Children was founded by Charlotte and Bob Hullinger in 1978, three months after the brutal murder of their daughter, Lisa, by her former boyfriend. Charlotte began a search for meaning and understanding immediately after her daughter's death. She was looking for some way to make sense of what had happened. A murder had been committed; the killer apprehended. This combination of events brought her face to face with a criminal justice system that appeared weighted in favor of the perpetrator of the crime. Her daughter's killer ultimately went free, a situation that so embittered her that she began to search out other bereaved parents whose children had been murdered to find out whether this case was unique. She found, to her astonishment, that others had had similar experiences. The feelings of comradeship that grew between these parents led to a bond that solidified them into a support group offering friendship and understanding to others in the community whose children had been brutally killed and their own lives brutalized by an insensitive criminal justice system.

In their mutual expressions of grief, these parents discovered that by listening and crying together, by understanding how each other felt, their grief was lessened.

A brochure titled "Parents of Murdered Children," available through the national headquarters, contains the following information:

> Parents of Murdered Children offers help to families cruelly bereaved. No one should have to endure the horror of a child's murder. But if you have endured it, or are enduring it; if you are still troubled about any aspect of your child's murder, we may be able to help each other. . . .[9]

Parents of Murdered Children provides continuous emotional support to parents by phone, by mail, in person on a one-to-one basis, in group meetings, and through literature. The purpose of the group is to serve as a link connecting any parent with others in the community who have survived their child's homicide. The national organization is available to help any interested parent locate or form a chapter of Parents of Murdered Children in his or her home community.

> We will communicate with any professional in the field of law enforcement, mental health, social work, community services, law, criminal justice, medicine, education, religion, and mortuary science, who is interested in learning more about survivors of homicide and their problems. . . .[10]

In the brochure, a college dean who was in attendance at a meeting tells what happens:

> The group starts each meeting with their stories which are a listing of the traditional acts of murder that we thought we have become

accustomed to ignoring. Again, this is a group of strong emotions, of people crumbling as they tell their stories, and of people laughing, sharing joys, and photos of the living and the deceased.

It is not an easy group to sit in or to try and help. There are many parents who want only revenge, who are bitter beyond Job's bitterness, who have tasted an experience which has sapped their belief in everything strong, good, and decent.

Yet they continue to continue. The process of discussion branches out to take in new members, who offer help to clergy, the criminal justice system, and others in the methods of humane and loving response. [11]

Also in the brochure, a newspaper reporter sitting in on a meeting in Wisconsin discusses his observations:

These mothers and fathers talked about their feelings of anger, hopelessness, bitterness, and their seemingly endless grief. No one told them "Forget about it" or "You should be over that by now." [12]

And finally, as one member of the group said:

We all have the same basic feelings and questions. We all have a great need to talk, and to go over and over the facts, and to ask "Did you feel this?" and to have someone say "I know how you feel" and they really do know. [13]

Like The Compassionate Friends, Parents of Murdered Children, has no religious creed or affiliation, and depends entirely on private donations to cover operating expenses.

Anyone is invited to write or call the national headquarters to receive information about the grieving process, information about the criminal justice system, more information about POMC, or the POMC newsletter. The address is:

> Parents of Murdered Children, Inc.
> 1739 Bella Vista
> Cincinnati, OH 45237
> (Tel. 513/242-8025)

There are a number of unanswered questions about self-help groups, probably because the ones I am discussing are so new to our experience. Elizabeth Ogg says on this point:

It would be useful to find out what kind of group contributes most to stability of membership, as well as benefits to members—one with a tight structure and imposed belief . . . or one with looser, more open-ended procedures. . . . What type of leadership is most effective: spontaneous, indigenous, rotating, or professionally sponsored? Could changes be made in the self-help approach that would extend its reach?[14]

Possible answers to some of these questions have already been considered by one group whose organization and purpose are somewhat different from other self-help groups. The group is called Kinder-Mourn and is located in Charlotte, North Carolina.

The Kinder-Mourn organization, as the prototype of support activity dealing exclusively with child death, is the subject of the last chapter.

12

The Kinder-Mourn Experiment

by Lucy D. Christopher

In 1978 Kinder-Mourn, Inc., was established and organized in Charlotte, North Carolina. Its fundamental purpose: to provide a safe harbor for parents whose lives have been wrecked and whose family intactness has been ruptured by the death of a child. Kinder-Mourn exists to meet the support needs of each of these survivors whose basic belief and value systems have been overturned, whose sense of identity has been flooded with overwhelming feelings of anxiety, sadness, guilt, helplessness, anger, and despair, whose wounds are so deep that the likelihood of healing seems hopeless, and whose hopes for resolution are dim without strong and enduring support.

Kinder-Mourn's program of direct support for bereaved families is sixfold: parent-support groups; individual counseling for families; monthly meetings for former parent-group members, quarterly workshops for entire families; semi-annual group socials; and a holiday memorial service each December.

Indirectly, Kinder-Mourn broadens its services for families by offering educational and support services to the community at large. Institutions, professionals, agencies, and individuals have access to educational workshops, in-service training, or staff assistance and consultation upon request.

Still unique today, the organization has grown from a small pilot program with a volunteer staff of two into a recognized community support agency. Each year five male and female facilitators meet on a weekly, monthly, quarterly, or annual basis with approximately 92 families in the Charlotte area who are trying to restore some sense of balance to their lives. In spite of the growth of the organization,

Kinder-Mourn leaders value the highly personal nature of the support offered to individuals and families.

Kinder-Mourn is not unlike The Compassionate Friends; however, its free-standing structure permits implementation of new ideas and programs with only the approval of its accessible *local* board of directors.

This final chapter will focus on Kinder-Mourn's development and on its uniqueness. The information can serve as a resource for future groups as well as suggest alternatives for other established groups.

Historical View: Organization and Structure

Like most support groups for persons facing a specific life crisis, Kinder-Mourn was initiated by an individual who had struggled with the death of a child. The founder had earlier been a co-leader of a volunteer group for parents of deceased infants. Because of the value of group support, she decided to organize a structure for broader impact and for continuity. Out of this commitment, the Kinder-Mourn agency was created.

For the first six months of the group's operation the founder and another bereaved parent agreed to work as the volunteer organizational staff; thereafter, to be salaried when the board of directors had begun adequate fundraising activities.

Prior to opening the Kinder-Mourn office in September 1978, the volunteer director had met with approximately 25 community leaders and heads of institutions, such as hospitals, churches, funeral homes, and county agencies. There were essentially five purposes for these meetings: (1) to share plans; (2) to begin educating the public about the effects of childhood death; (3) to determine community acceptance both as to attitudes and to referral sources; (4) to access funding possibilities; and (5) to determine that a new agency would not duplicate existing services.

At the time there were only two similar groups in existence in North Carolina: a small volunteer group in Greensboro; and in Charlotte, a loosely structured group for parents of older deceased children. This group met monthly without leadership, and its convener agreed in October 1978 to be incorporated by Kinder-Mourn once it was established. There were no Compassionate Friends groups in either North Carolina or South Carolina, nor were there groups for parents who had suffered losses through sudden infant death syndrome or for parents of suicides or murdered children.

By November 1978 the name Kinder-Mourn was chosen, the organization was incorporated, and 19 citizens in the Charlotte area had agreed to serve on the board of directors. A parent support group had already been meeting for two months prior to Kinder-Mourn's formal organization.

The name Kinder-Mourn explains the mission of this nonprofit social service and educational agency. *Kinder* is the German word for child. No matter what the age of the child, if his or her death precedes the parents', that child remains forever in the hearts of the parents a *kinder*. For the organization, *mourn* represents the natural, necessary expression of grief.

On November 30, 1978, the initial board of directors held its first formal meeting. The organization received federal tax-exempt status in March 1979.

At the first meeting the board adopted by-laws and began formal procedures for hiring the volunteer staff. In addition, members organized themselves into four standing committees: executive, finance, program, and education. Each committee was to meet bimonthly, with full board meetings during the alternating six months.

The members of the board of directors were chosen to represent various institutional, professional, minority, religious, and geographical segments of the community, including five bereaved parents. All members were expected to make a commitment to lead Kinder-Mourn in its first years of operation.

In order to add credibility to the new agency's public image, the board and staff asked for, and received, letters of endorsement and intention-of-referral from 10 strategic community organizations.

It should be noted that the decision to become a professional agency dictated that the board of directors assume responsibility for funding. This proved to be a monumental task. However, Kinder-Mourn views staff salaries as a sound investment for ensuring the growth and credibility of a valuable service. Those salaries also represent the organization's largest single budget item.

In Charlotte, as in any metropolitan community, successful fundraisers are generally corporate and business leaders. In retrospect, this fact was overlooked when Kinder-Mourn began. This error in judgment was a major factor contributing to the agency's long financial struggle. The suspicion lingers that the founding staff and the initial board were highly idealistic people who had to learn the hard way.

Thus funding must be given a high priority by those initiators of organizations who are committed to providing sound support for families after a child's death. Those for whom fundraising is an unpleasant task must be convinced of its necessity, of the importance of support, and of the repercussions to families when support is not available.

Present Organizational Structure

The executive director is the staff person directly responsible to the board of directors for all aspects of the program, including supervision and evaluation of other staff. Today the staff consists of an administrative assistant and six consultants: four group facilitators, a Certified Public Accountant, and a program evaluator. The latter two consultants provide accountability to the public and to financial investors.

The board approved the staff's early recommendation to organize as a free-standing group. This decision was made *after* communication with the Illinois headquarters of The Compassionate Friends concerning possible affiliation with that organization.

Some of the differences between Kinder-Mourn and The Compassionate Friends, which led to the decision to remain independent, are that Kinder-Mourn (1) requires more frequent meetings for parents; (2) requires group leaders; (3) limits both the number of group members and the length of meeting time; (4) expects a commitment from parents for regular attendance; and (5) charges a fee from participants. The separate educational thrust of the agency also sets Kinder-Mourn apart from other nationally established groups.

BASIC VALUE UPON WHICH KINDER-MOURN RESTS

It is important to clarify an underlying value to which Kinder-Mourn's founders were committed and which over and over again has dictated the direction of the organization. Kinder-Mourn's leaders have always valued the *highly personal nature* of the support being offered to individuals and families.

Even as the structure of a more professional agency has been sought by the founders, a high priority has always been to retain patterns of operating that set Kinder-Mourn apart from the traditional community agency stereotype. As critical as the funding situation has become on occasion, there has been a recurrent reluctance to be absorbed by more established community agencies. The temptation to affiliate is always present, as a way of solving critical financial problems. On at least three occasions the board has investigated mergers, even filed applications, only to withdraw as they realized that the personal, individual nature of Kinder-Mourn's services would be endangered by coming under the local United Way umbrella.

Kinder-Mourn exists to meet the unique and private needs of individuals at a time when they are often too devastated and vulnerable to seek help on their own. The staff has been willing to alter the usual agency expectation that parents themselves initiate contact. The director has agreements with many referral agencies in the community for the staff to telephone parents when notification has been received of the parents' request to be contacted.

Other examples of Kinder-Mourn's deviation from standard agency procedures are: (1) the staff will meet for the initial interview in the home when either a practical problem or emotional vulnerability makes the usual agency office interview difficult; (2) the staff will contact ministers, teachers, friends, physicians when they are known to the staff—anyone who can provide support and make a referral at this critical time; and (3) Kinder-Mourn will hold meetings in spaces that are furnished to suggest casual, intimate gatherings. One group even meets by candlelight.

Program Services for Parents and Families

There are six distinct program services which Kinder-Mourn provides directly to parents. These services begin for families as early as the day of the funeral and continue sometimes for years afterward, at Kinder-Mourn's annual memorial observance.

PARENT SUPPORT GROUPS

The support groups for parents are led by trained facilitators and meet weekly for one and a half hours in the evening. Parents who join are charged fees on a sliding scale. After attending four meetings, the parents are asked to commit to a strong and, if needed, long-term relationship with other current members.

The groups are limited to 12 parents—mostly couples, a few single parents. They meet in rooms, usually made available by churches, that are dimly lit and comfortable, and which have a home-like atmosphere.

Group Meetings. As noted, groups meet weekly in order to maintain continuity and to develop intimate relationships among members. The meetings are also time-limited. Parents can expect to experience painful feelings at the meetings; thus the time-limited structure helps reduce anxiety associated with the group experience. Readers may note how much attention is paid to *focus, direction,* and *structure.* Bereaved parents need all these elements reintroduced into their lives on a regular basis as they relearn normal patterns of living.

It was found that when groups met monthly or even on a twice-monthly basis, as the earliest groups did, precious time was spent getting reacquainted and catching up. Weekly gatherings eliminate this level of interaction as well as the need for most telephone calls between meetings.

The importance of intimacy is a primary value derived from the Kinder-Mourn groups, whose closeness is quite remarkable. Their common wounds knit the parents into a "community," where people of the most unlikely variety learn to care deeply for each other. One of the difficulties of grief is the sense of isolation encountered. Maintaining a capacity for affection sometimes means risking another loss. In the group, parents learn how to love again—a good sign that resolution of grief is achievable.

To be in a situation where affection and intimacy are experienced on a regular basis is a value almost without equal. Trust is developed in groups meeting often enough so that individuals feel free to share even their differences.

The Initial Interview. The director requests that parents meet for an initial interview prior to attending their first group session. At this meeting the director tells each parent what to expect from the group experience, lays out the goals of the Kinder-Mourn organization, and discusses the fee schedule and ascertains the amount each parent will pay. The parents relate information about their personal crisis and other related difficulties. They also tell the director what they hope to gain within the group.

Both parents are strongly urged to attend. The director emphasizes Kinder-Mourn's conviction that shared attendance is expected. One of the groups' purposes is to help prevent divorce; Kinder-Mourn believes that a growth experience for only one member of a couple can pose an even greater threat to their marriage. Fathers—or an occasionally reticent mother—are assured that attending just to please their spouses is a good enough reason for going to the first few meetings.

Also, the director emphasizes the importance of confidentiality and extracts a pledge from all parties to respect it.

Parents usually attend their first group meeting within a week of this initial interview.

When work conflicts with these appointments—or with the group meetings—parents are urged to tell their employers the purpose of their request to miss one to two hours of work. Experience has shown that employers are generally willing to cooperate in hopes that the employee-parent will receive help and return to a former level of competence. In fact employers actually make referrals to Kinder-Mourn, and twice have paid fees for parents.

Placement Within a Group. Kinder-Mourn's philosophy is that the cause of death is not a sound basis for mutuality; therefore, unlike other self-help support groups, cause of death is not used as a basis for group placement. Instead, the *age of the child* determines the parents' group assignment.

If, for example, each member's child had committed suicide, the temptation would be to remain paralyzed by the stigma and guilt common to suicide survivors. Conversely, sharing one's mourning with survivors of numerous kinds of deaths encourages individuals to deal also with their other grief reactions. For example, one parent observed that she had used her preoccupation with guilt in order to avoid the pain of how much she misses her daughter. It has been found that dealing exclusively with a target for anger (as in murder) or a stigma (as in chemical overdose) allows avoidance and postponement of pain.

This philosophy of combining survivors of all types of death has worked well ever since Kinder-Mourn's inception. It should also be noted that sometimes the *parent's age* (as when the child was the youngest, or a "late" child) will decide group placement. In this situation the parent's developmental stage in life is considered more important than the age of the dead child. Thus parents of a younger child could be members of a group with parents of older children. The director makes all group assignments.

Meeting with Group Facilitators. Prior to their first group meeting, parents meet for about 15 minutes with the group leaders. They are reminded about the confidential nature of the meetings. They are also told that they must not attend under the influence of drugs of any kind. This is actually an informal time for introductions, intended primarily as a way of easing the new couple or parent into the group.

The Role of Facilitators During Meetings. There are two facilitators in each group—always a man and a woman—to ensure a balanced leadership style.

For significant reasons, facilitators are viewed as important, if not essential, to the group process. Parents are relieved of leadership responsibilities and left free to focus on their grief. When necessary, for instance, facilitators assist parents in relating to the group, usually refusing to answer requests for advice. Instead they direct the questions to other members so that the response is a group answer. When a parent risks describing sensitive feelings or thoughts or behaviors, a facilitator may wonder aloud "Has anyone else been aware of a similar feeling or thought or action?"

One of the roles of the facilitator is to help focus the discussion, either at the beginning of the meeting or when a common interest has emerged during the check-in time. "Check-in" is the first 15 minutes of unstructured responses to "How is everyone?" or "How was the Mother's Day weekend?" or ". . . Christmas?" or after any event that might have proven difficult for parents. A facilitator might observe: "Sounds like most of you are feeling a lot of anger and frustration over how to express it." Any such objective comment from a leader or a parent might encourage a direction for that particular evening's discussion.

Sometimes one or two parents may not share the common interest that is emerging for that evening's focus. In these instances, after others have talked the leader may invite the silent parent to share whatever feeling or situation is keeping his or her attention distracted.

When parents seem isolated or distracted, most often they are deeply involved in a specific personal focus or even threatened by the discussion process. Their different needs are honored in the group if they wish to share. It is not uncommon that members are in need of an individual focus within group time.

Parents sometimes tend to turn meetings into gripe sessions, perhaps over their lack of support from friends and family. Rather than allowing the meeting to dissipate, leaders use role-play to help parents gain skills in coping with distressing people and situations. At times the group, including the facilitators, will affirm the parents' need to protect themselves for a time by avoiding stressful situations such as weddings, parties, or funerals.

The use of other exercises assists members in expanding their awareness of their unique reactions to their children's deaths. Often parents' thoughts become dominated by certain situations, places, or memories that evoke intense feelings. Such reactions may be of extreme revulsion or intense attraction. The scene of their child's death, the burial site, the son's or daughter's room, the child's favorite food, their photographs—all are examples of those memories likely to carry intense associations for family survivors. Generally people feel strongly, one way or the other, about these situations. Whereas one member may be comforted by trips to the cemetery or by looking at photographs, another parent—even that person's spouse—may avoid these reminders.

Facilitators actually elicit these associations from each member, offer reassurance of the normality of such reactions, and point out that the intensity *will* subside as one moves toward resolution of his or her grief. In fact this lessening is one indicator that a member has moved into a more integrated psychological space in the grieving process.

On some evenings questions about unfinished business may be posed. Some parents need to talk about the manner in which their child died, particularly in cases of suicide or murder. Leaders ask focusing questions such as "What message would I want most to hear from my child?" or "What do I still wish I had a chance to say or do in relation to my child?" Focusing on where one is "stuck" or even on what is unresolved makes parents conscious of some aspects of their remaining grief work.

In addition, facilitators continuously help members translate expressed thoughts and behavior into feelings. Whereas many people speak with ease of their ideas and actions, they often fail to be aware of associated emotions. It is in part the leaders' task to help clarify associated feelings and then to encourage members to claim them, regardless of how ignoble those emotions may be.

Focusing is a constant activity of leaders. When the group wanders from the agreed-upon meeting discussion, the facilitator usually points out the loss of direction. Members may then consciously choose to alter the focus. Also, at the close of group time leaders may assist members in summarizing the content of what took place that evening or of the group process that developed.

An atmosphere of safety is enhanced by the presence of leaders in the groups. As a parent begins to move beyond preoccupation with the child's death, the parent is often confronted with anxiety over his or her own identity. Often as the anniversary of the death nears there is an obsession with "this time last year" and a realization of the uncertainty of "this time next year." A child's death almost ensures an identity crisis. That crisis, however, is also an opportunity that can thrust an individual into a new stage of personal development. Facilitators respond to this anxiety by offering value-clarification exercises and other means of reflecting on the future.

It should be noted that these parent-survivors have the most difficult work of their lives ahead of them. To move through their mourning and to regain a sense of wanting to live again, they must express their sorrow and deal with—and accept—the powerful, often-conflicting feelings they are experiencing. The danger is that the parent may fall into a pattern of denying or repressing grief. Thus expressing feelings or confronting denial on a weekly basis will surely facilitate one's journey through the ravages of a child's death.

Husbands and wives have often revealed in meetings what they are afraid to risk at home. A facilitator, as well as other parents, can support a spouse, even protect him or her from the harshness of the other's pain and anger. One partner is relieved of the need to "be strong" for the other. Members are urged not to use anything said during the meetings against each other—especially their mates—outside the group meeting itself. For example, one spouse may become upset and angry that the other has shared some private matter without conferring beforehand. Facilitators request that these feelings be discussed as soon as the discomfort is noticed—in the group situation—and not between meetings. Otherwise, they insist that members save these issues for the next meeting.

At least one other element of security for parents is derived from the presence and attitudes of the facilitators. Because the leaders trust the mourning process—after years of working with bereaved parents—and because they are not frightened by the parents' pain, the parents also are inclined to trust.

In summary, Kinder-Mourn values group facilitation as part of its services in order that groups achieve objectivity, focus, clarity, guidance, and protection.

The Matter of Commitment. After four or five group meetings, in informal discussion with the group leaders, parents are asked to indicate their future intentions. Do they wish to continue as part of the group, or is there still a question of their commitment? Commitments last for whatever time is deemed appropriate or needed by the members themselves. Leaders do request that termination be *announced at a group meeting*, rather than permitting the parents merely to stop attending. To group members, "good-byes" represent another kind of loss, and need to be communicated in a personal manner.

All group members receive lists of names, addresses, phone numbers, and dates of the deceased children's birth and death anniversaries in order that they may be supportive of each other on those painful occasions. These lists are also useful for setting up group socials. Nevertheless, one of the goals of Kinder-Mourn is that members grow beyond their needs for each other. Facilitators encourage parents to use *other* support possibilities instead of one another between meetings in order to discourage dependency. Kinder-Mourn is not a permanent support facility, but a way-station between the agony of the past and the light of the future.

Indicators of Resolution. Facilitators look for numerous indicators that parents might be ready to terminate their group membership. Some examples of these indicators are found in parents who: (1) have established strong bonds with other group members or reestablished intimacy with their spouse; in short, those who are once more willing to risk affection and commitment in relationships; (2) have recalled happier memories of their child as easily as those surrounding their child's death; (3) have remembered the not-so-positive side of their dead son or daughter as well as *only* how special the child was; (4) have assumed active group participation and leadership roles; and (5) have become more involved with the remainder of their *own* lives than with a preoccupation with the past.

Parents generally attend Kinder-Mourn groups for one to one and a half years. A few leave after four to six months.

INDIVIDUAL COUNSELING

Parents and family members—including grandparents—may meet after the initial interview for individual counseling with the director, whose professional training and experience are in family therapy. The duration of these weekly sessions may be from a few meetings to several months. The purpose is to deal with unique problems that cannot be solved in the group meetings. However, the goal of individual counseling is to help the family to the point where the parents can join with other parents in the support group. The group process is the backbone of the Kinder-Mourn philosophy; therefore individual counseling is usually undertaken on a temporary basis.

However, complicated family dynamics sometimes dictate that intervention at the personal level is more important than the group experience. On rare occasions the counselor-director has determined difficulties of a pathological nature and has made appropriate referrals elsewhere.

FAMILY WORKSHOPS

Four times each year Kinder-Mourn offers workshops for entire families. These day-long meetings are held on weekends and include families not otherwise connected to Kinder-Mourn. Not only surviving brothers and sisters, but extended-family members such as grandparents, attend with parents of deceased children.

The value for workshop participants is the opportunity for family members to gain greater understanding of each other's grief and how to better care for each other during a highly stressful time. A parent, for example, may discover what his surviving children have felt or needed as he listens to the children talk with surviving siblings from other families.

Two group facilitators lead these workshops.

GROUP SOCIALS

At least twice a year socials are enjoyed by an entire group in one member's home, or occasionally a combination of groups will have a party. These get-togethers are organized and sponsored by the group members themselves. Facilitators also attend with their spouses, if married.

Socials are jovial occasions with hardly ever a mention of the children who died. An uninvolved observer might think that the conversations at these parties are superficial. However, one comment made after a party denies such a judgment: a facilitator said, "That was the most *special* party I've *ever* attended, anywhere!" When people have shared the greatest heartaches of their lives on such a deep level, the sharing of lighter moments almost overflows with joy.

THE DECEMBER MEMORIAL

In addition, a special holiday memorial with candlelighting and a responsive reading is held annually between Hanukkah and Christmas. Entire families attend and former members return, even from out of town. The intention is to remember the deceased children in a way that frees the surviving family to observe the holidays with less sense of having been disloyal to their children's memories.

SHARE CARE

Share Care is attended by those former parent-group members who want further contact and occasional support from other bereaved parents, but who no longer feel the need to meet on a weekly basis. This group meets monthly with the director as facilitator. There is no fee.

Because attendance has been erratic (from 3 to 40 persons), a smaller group of 15 self-selected parents is now notified of monthly support meetings. The larger group will be invited to quarterly gatherings which have an agenda planned and sometimes an outside speaker (perhaps a clergyperson or a physician).

Members of Share Care assist the Kinder-Mourn staff with community projects, outreach efforts, and preparation of bulk mailings. Also, they have initiated their own newsletter that is now distributed on a regular basis.

KINDER-MOURN'S FEE SCHEDULE

Kinder-Mourn's fee schedule might be of interest to other groups. The agency's philosophy of investing in a professional staff and group facilitators has already been discussed. The practical realities of Kinder-Mourn's financial commitments demand that services yield income to help meet budget needs.

Generally, group fees generate resources for meeting the facilitators' consultant fees of $30.00 per meeting. The fees charged presently range from $3.00 to $23.00 per family per meeting. The schedule is based on salaries of families, ranging from $9,999 to $50,000 and up. This schedule is adjusted downward by the director according to the number of family dependents, excessive medical expenses, current unemployment, and other difficulties. Adjustments are continued for a period agreed upon, and then reevaluated. "Scholarships" are provided when necessary; however, fees as low as 25¢ are negotiated in order that the parent sense more keenly the value of grief work as an investment.

In addition, fees are charged to satisfy Kinder-Mourn's financial benefactors. Private and corporate contributors clearly indicate that the agency must be at least partially self-supporting in order to be defined as a sound investment. "Why," they want to know, "would you give away something of value?"

Program Services for the Public

In its first year of operation the staff and board referred to their educational thrust as "indirect support." By creating awareness among the general public, Kinder-Mourn was able to broaden the support offered directly to bereaved families. The "public" is defined here as those individuals and institutions outside Kinder-Mourn itself to which bereaved families normally turn for support.

Community education is offered to individuals and groups at three levels: community professionals, friends and relatives, and community groups.

Individuals at all three levels often fail in their support efforts either by what they offer in the service of "helping" or by what is withheld. Usually they have little information regarding the needs of a family and unrealistic expectations after child death.

WORKSHOPS FOR PROFESSIONALS

Professional workshops sponsored by Kinder-Mourn are designed to bridge the information gap. Therapists, clergy, social workers, educators, personnel staff from industry and institutions, funeral home representatives, and medical professionals attend day-long seminars. These workshops, offered once or twice a year, are structured to provide awareness about issues and needs of the bereaved. At the same time participants can learn some of the basic skills for encouraging the grieving process through cognitive and experiential methods.

At these workshops the community professionals are also encouraged to consult with the director, via telephone, on problems as they arise with their various constituencies. In fact Kinder-Mourn now maintains a cross-referral system with more than 100 community agencies, professional associations, and health, religious, and educational institutions in the area. This cross-referral system has developed as a result of the staff and board commitment to education since the agency's inception.

The staff is also requested to visit with parents at three hospitals and to offer consultation to medical staff members.

FRIENDS AND RELATIVES

Kinder-Mourn also sees itself as a supporter of friends and relatives who are searching for ways to maintain some kind of meaningful relationship with bereaved families, but who nevertheless feel inadequate about what to do or how to respond. It offers telephone and office consultation on an individual basis to any friend or relative who seeks it.

Mistaken Assumptions and Expectations. Friends and relatives often operate under a false assumption. After a family has grieved for a time—usually a period of four to six months—an assessment is made that this length of time is long enough. Premature assumptions are generally made by those close to the bereaved because the grieving individual may seem to be coping well. In fact these observers seldom see *outward* signs of active grieving.

During the early months, survivors of a child's death may *appear* to be coping well only because they are still in a state of shock, disbelief, and denial. Sometime between four and six months the denial wears thin and the finality of loss becomes an overwhelming reality. Unfortunately, comforters have a tendency to withdraw support at the point where they are probably most needed.

A More Accurate View. The Kinder-Mourn staff helps friends and relatives to deal with the *frustration* over not being able to help and with the *fear* that underlies their helplessness. The staff will listen until the friend or relative is able to speak, at least indirectly, of his sense of being threatened by continued contact with the bereaved family. A child's death forces each person involved to realize the possibility of their own child's death, or the reality of each one's personal mortality.

Friends and relatives are encouraged to gain more realistic expectations of themselves as well as the bereaved family members. "Don't try to cheer them up and don't expect them to be normal in three months" is common advice. The staff suggests that possibly the most humane and comforting support is a wordless and warm hug, or to say "It's awful!"

The Kinder-Mourn staff seeks to help the public understand that those parents who mourn a dead child will never be the same again, that no matter how well an adjustment is made the bereaved are affected in a deep and lasting way.

COMMUNITY GROUPS

Presentations, upon request, to church and club groups in the area, as well as in-service training for other community agencies, give Kinder-Mourn the opportunity to talk publicly about its programs, the services it offers, and its goals.

Other methods for updating the public and referral sources are a quarterly newsletter, public-service announcements in all media, mailed announcements of workshops, and television and newspaper interviews. Kinder-Mourn has also placed almost 600 books in hospital, funeral home, and church lending-libraries for use by bereaved parents. Each book is accompanied by a Kinder-Mourn brochure.

More recently, Kinder-Mourn has completed a slide presentation which reveals the journey known only to bereaved parents. This documentary is the work of a local musician-photographer. The soundtrack for this documentary is made up exclusively of interviews with group parents and facilitators. Kinder-Mourn actively seeks opportunities to use this audio-visual resource for increasing community awareness and understanding, and for gaining both referral and financial support.

It might be added that Kinder-Mourn's comprehensive approach to working with bereaved families is spreading. In the first three years requests were received for information and assistance in organizing similar efforts from across the country. In addition to cities in North Carolina, requests have come from Alabama, California, Illinois, Massachusetts, Nebraska, South Carolina, Tennessee, and Virginia.

Staff Support

The Kinder-Mourn staff recognizes the likelihood of stress inherent in working in the midst of pain. A common question staff members hear from the public is "Don't you find this work depressing?" The answer to that question is "No!" On a conscious level, group facilitators are more aware of being *inspired* by the parents' struggles to survive and to live again. In a mysterious way, the leaders receive an inkling of hope from being fellow journeyers with bereaved parents. There is no doubt among those leaders who stand with these fathers and mothers that they are in the presence of profound possibilities for human development and growth.

Monthly Staff Support. However, there *is* some level of stress involved in bereavement work, and the staff addresses that strain in monthly meetings of the director, the associate director, and the facilitators. These meetings consist of sharing stories of human beings who are learning not to give up on life, of solving problems that may have arisen during the meetings, or of helping each other to deal with personal feelings associated with involvement in such intense grief. Current group facilitators have led Kinder-Mourn parents for three to six years with no sign of declining capacities.

Goals for Additional Staff Support. As its financial situation stabilizes, Kinder-Mourn hopes to increase provisions for nurturing its staff. Some ideas have already been suggested, such as fringe benefits (health insurance for the director and assistant), one paid absence a year (for facilitators), and inclusion in the budget of workshop tuition at educational facilities for the purpose of enriching the staff.

Future Goals

Though its founder is a bereaved parent, Kinder-Mourn is now at the stage of development where a priority is for the staff to become increasingly more professional and objective in nature. This is not to be regarded as a departure from the personal nature of the support presently offered but rather represents a commitment to broaden, refine, and strengthen program services and methods of delivery.

Kinder-Mourn was conceived and developed in an experimental fashion. Having now gained community recognition, the agency begins its seventh year committed to broadening its exposure and strengthening its credibility.

Kinder-Mourn recently hired its third executive director, a professional clinical social worker who has high personal esteem among her peers and long-established ties in the community. For two and a half years previously she served as a group facilitator.

In December 1982 Kinder-Mourn received an anonymous grant of $75,000, an amount adequate to meet budget needs for three years when matched with agency income. The board of directors was asked by the donor to match that amount with its own fundraising efforts. This gift represents a source of security. The staff and board now have the opportunity to make *objective* choices regarding program services instead of always having to meet only the most basic, immediate needs in the least expensive way.

Extended Outreach. It is time to reach more parents. In 1980 Kinder-Mourn noted that only *one-seventh* of the local bereaved parent population (whose children had died between birth and age 30) were being reached. It is time to build bridges to more black families and to the increasing numbers of ethnic groups in the area.

The staff and board have recently changed the orientation or thrust of the services offered. The focus will now be on the *entire family system*, rather than primarily on the parents as in the past. Within the next year Kinder-Mourn will begin developing its own model to include children—siblings—in the parent groups, at least on a bimonthly basis. Already the new director is encouraging the entire family to attend the initial interview.

New Program for Grieving Children. A natural development for Kinder-Mourn has been the realization of the need for development of a program for grieving children, both after the death of a brother or sister *and* after the death of a parent.

Initial attempts to address this need have been in the form of quarterly workshops for parents and children. What has been learned is how extremely protective parents are in trying to preserve their children's innocence and in shielding them from pain.

In the throes of their own grief, parents give off overt and covert messages that it is extremely important for the surviving children not to suffer also. Children thus respond by keeping their own feelings inside and labeling them as "wrong" or "bad." The stage is set for emotional problems, which sometimes do not surface until the children themselves are parents. These difficulties *can* be prevented or minimized.

Kinder-Mourn is in the process of creating a new program to address the needs of these children, through parent education and through follow-up support groups specifically for children.

Expanded Public Support and Education. Kinder-Mourn is ready to teach physicians how to "prescribe" the agency's support services, just as they now do for medication. The support offered by Kinder-Mourn is as much medication for sorrow as is any drug. Workshops and professional meeting presentations will be designed to convince the medical community of the importance of their referrals.

Kinder-Mourn will seek to reassure clergy in the area that the agency wants to *assist* in the religious mission, not to abscond with it. A pilot program is planned at one local church where one parent will gather others who have suffered the death of a child. Together they will recognize the birth and death anniversaries of all deceased children in this religious community. The intent is that people whose grief has isolated them from their lifelong beliefs may be helped to reestablish their link with a sense of transcendence.

The new director is committed to working more closely with The Compassionate Friends and with other related local agencies, in order to continue improving and expanding Kinder Mourn's services.

Workshops and community presentations will focus on dispelling taboos and myths about death. The agency hopes to develop educational programs that will help people prepare for fuller lives with lessons learned from those who have struggled with one of life's greatest tragedies.

After all, is there anyone forced to learn life's values on a deeper level than a family who buries the last person they expected to die?

Notes

PREFACE

1. Susan F. Woolsey, Doris S. Thornton, and Stanford B. Friedman, "Sudden Death," in *The Child and Death*, edited by Ollie Jane Z. Sahler (St. Louis: C. V. Mosby Co., 1978), pp. 102–3.

2. *The Compassionate Friends Newsletter*, St. Louis Chapter, 2 (June 1981): 11.

CHAPTER 1

1. Arlene Skolnick, *The Intimate Environment* (Boston: Little, Brown and Co., 1978), p. 275.

2. J. Ross Eshleman, *The Family: An Introduction* (Boston: Allyn and Bacon, 1978), p. 511.

3. Ibid., p. 527.

4. Ibid., p. 511.

5. Skolnick, *The Intimate Environment*, p. 304.

6. Ibid., p. 331.

7. Jo-Eileen Gyulay, *The Dying Child* (New York: McGraw-Hill, 1978), p. xi.

8. Ibid., p. x.

9. Charles A. Garfield, "A Child Dies," in *Stress and Survival*, edited by Charles A. Garfield (St. Louis: C. V. Mosby Co., 1979), p. 316.

10. Sheila Fox, "The Death of a Child," *Nursing Times* 68 (October 1972): 1322–23.

11. Ibid., p. 1323.

12. Teresa Crout, "Caring for the Mother of a Stillborn Baby," *Thanatos* 5 (Fall 1980): 4–8.

13. Ibid., p. 4.

14. Ibid.

15. Fran C. Northrup, "The Dying Child," *American Journal of Nursing* 74 (June 1974): 1066–68.

16. Erich Lindemann, "Symptomatology and Management of Acute Grief," *American Journal of Psychiatry* 101 (September 1944): 141–48.

17. C. M. Binger et al., "Childhood Leukemia: Emotional Impact on Patient and Family," *New England Journal of Medicine* 280 (1969): 414–18.

18. Larry G. Peppers and Ronald J. Knapp, *Motherhood and Mourning: Perinatal Death* (New York: Praeger Special Studies, 1980), pp. 47–50.

19. Lewis S. Feuer, *The Conflict of Generations* (New York: Basic Books, 1978), p. 68.

20. Harriet Sarnoff Schiff, *The Bereaved Parent* (New York: Penguin Books, 1978), p. 23.

21. Peppers and Knapp, *Motherhood and Mourning*.

CHAPTER 3

1. C. Murray Parkes, "Unexpected and Untimely Bereavement: A Statistical Study of Young Boston Widows and Widowers," in *Bereavement: Its Psychosocial Aspects*, edited by Bernard Schoenberg et al. (New York: Columbia University Press, 1975), pp. 130–31.

2. S. B. Friedman et al., "Behavioral Observations of Parents Anticipating the Death of a Child," *Pediatrics* 32 (October 1963): 614.

3. Ibid.

4. Ibid.

5. Joyce Guimond, "We Knew Our Child Was Dying," *American Journal of Nursing* 74 (February 1974): 249.

6. Friedman et al., "Behavioral Observations of Parents," pp. 617–18.

7. June S. Lowenberg, "The Coping Behavior of Fatally Ill Adolescents and Their Parents," *Nursing Forum* 9 (1970): 269–87.

8. Friedman et al., "Behavioral Observations of Parents," p. 616.

9. Lowenberg, "Coping Behavior," pp. 270–71.

10. Ibid., p. 273.

11. Hal Lipton, "The Dying Child and the Family: The Skills of the Social Worker," in *The Child and Death*, edited by Ollie Jane Z. Sahler (St. Louis: C. V. Mosby Co., 1978), p. 59.

CHAPTER 4

1. Susan F. Woolsey, Doris S. Thornton, and Stanford B. Friedman, "Sudden Death," in *The Child and Death*, edited by Ollie Jane Z. Sahler (St. Louis: C. V. Mosby Co., 1978), pp. 102–3.

2. Personal papers of Judith.

3. *The Compassionate Friends Newsletter*, St. Louis Chapter, 2 (July 1981): 9.

4. Ibid., 3 (October/November 1982): 7–8.

CHAPTER 5

1. From a brochure titled "Parents of Murdered Children" (published by the parent organization, Cincinnati, Ohio).

2. From a speech before the First World Congress of Victimology, Washington, D.C., August 1981.

3. From "Parents of Murdered Children."

4. *Minneapolis Tribune*, October 17, 1982.

5. Speech before the First World Congress of Victimology, Washington, D.C., August 1981.

6. *Minneapolis Tribune*, October 17, 1982.

7. Judy Tatlebaum, *The Courage to Grieve: Creative Living, Recovery and Growth* (New York: Lippincott and Crowell, 1980).

CHAPTER 6

1. Reuben Hill, *Families Under Stress*, (New York: Harper and Row, 1949), pp. 3–5.

2. Reuben Hill, from *Families Under Stress* as quoted in "Generic Features of Families Under Stress," in *Crisis Intervention: Selected Readings*, edited by Howard J. Parad (New York: Family Service Association, 1965), p. 34.

3. Ibid.

4. Quoted in Hill, *Families Under Stress*, pp. 5–10.

5. Phyllis Caroff and Rose Dobrof, "The Helping Process with Bereaved Families," in *Bereavement: Its Psychosocial Aspects*, edited by Bernard Schoenberg et al. (New York: Columbia University Press, 1975), pp. 237–38.

6. Hill, *Families Under Stress*, p. 9.

7. Hill, quoted in "Generic Features of Families Under Stress," p. 35.

8. Hill, *Families Under Stress*, p. 9.

9. Hamilton I. McCubbin et al., "Family Stress and Coping: A Decade Review," *Journal of Marriage and the Family* 42 (November 1980): 861–62.

10. Quoted ibid., p. 861.

11. Robert C. Angell, *The Family Encounters the Depression* (New York: Scribners, 1936).

12. Hill, *Families Under Stress*, pp. 17–18.

13. Ibid.

14. McCubbin et al., "Family Stress and Coping," pp. 862–64.

15. Ibid., p. 864.

16. Ibid., p. 865.

17. Ibid.

18. Hamilton I. McCubbin, "Integrating Coping Behavior in Family Stress Theory," *Journal of Marriage and the Family* 41 (May 1979), p. 241.

19. Ibid, pp. 241–42.

20. Hill, "Generic Features of Families Under Stress," pp. 35–36.

21. Donald A. Hansen and Reuben Hill, "Families Under Stress," in *Handbook of Marriage and the Family*, edited by Harold T. Christensen (Chicago: Rand McNally & Co., 1964), p. 805.

22. Ibid., p. 804.

23. Ibid., pp. 804–5.

24. Rita R. Vollman et al., "The Reactions of Family Systems to Sudden and Unexpected Death," in *Caring Relationships: The Dying and the Bereaved*, edited by

Richard A. Kalish (New York: Perspectives on Death and Dying Series 2; Baywood Publishing Co., 1980), p. 99.

25. Ibid.

26. Hill, *Families Under Stress*, pp. 44–45.

27. Ibid.

28. E. E. LeMaster, *Parents in Modern America* (Homewood, Ill.: The Dorsey Press, 1974), p. 23.

29. Ibid., pp. 23–24.

CHAPTER 7

1. C. M. Parkes, *Bereavement* (New York: International Universities Press, 1972), pp. 5–6.

2. David Peretz, "Development, Object-Relationships, and Loss," in *Loss and Grief: Psychological Management in Medical Practice*, edited by Bernard Schoenberg et al. (New York: Columbia University Press, 1970), p. 13.

3. Robert E. Kavanaugh, *Facing Death* (Baltimore: Penguin Books, 1974).

4. Elisabeth Kübler-Ross, *On Death and Dying* (New York: Macmillan, 1969).

5. Ibid.

6. Kavanaugh, *Facing Death*, p. 108.

7. Ibid., p. 109.

8. Erich Lindemann, "Symptomatology and Management of Acute Grief," *American Journal of Psychiatry* 101 (September 1944): 141–48.

9. Larry G. Peppers and Ronald J. Knapp, *Motherhood and Mourning: Perinatal Death* (New York: Praeger Special Studies, 1980), pp. 47–50.

CHAPTER 8

1. Charles A. Garfield, "A Child Dies," in *Stress and Survival*, edited by Charles A. Garfield (St. Louis: C. V. Mosby Co., 1979), p. 317.

2. Robert Woodson, "Hospice Care in Terminal Illness," in *Stress and Survival*, edited by Charles A. Garfield (St. Louis: C. V. Mosby Co., 1979), p. 330.

3. Stephen W. Munson, "Family Structure and the Family's General Adaptation to Loss: Helping Families Deal with the Death of a Child," in *The Child and Death*, edited by Ollie Jane Z. Sahler (St. Louis: C. V. Mosby Co., 1978), pp. 35–36.

4. Copyright 1980, The Compassionate Friends, Inc., Fox Valley Chapter, 406 W. Galena, Aurora, IL 60506.

CHAPTER 9

1. Eric Lindemann, "Symptomatology and Management of Acute Grief," *American Journal of Psychiatry* 101 (September 1944): 141–48.

2. Elisabeth Kübler-Ross, *On Death and Dying* (New York: Macmillan, 1969).

3. Margaret Gerner, *The Compassionate Friends Newsletter*, St. Louis Chapter, 2 (October 1981): 8–9.

CHAPTER 10

1. "Depression: Our Common Curse," *Saturday Evening Post*, December 1975, p. 55.

2. Ibid.

3. David Peretz, "Reactions to Loss," in *Loss and Grief: Psychological Management in Medical Practice*, edited by Bernard Schoenberg et al. (New York: Columbia University Press, 1970), p. 28.

4. James A. Brussel and Theodore Irwin, *Understanding and Overcoming Depression* (New York: Hawthorn Books, 1973), p. 26.

5. George W. Brown and Tirril Harris, *Social Origins of Depression* (New York: The Free Press, 1978), pp. 22–23.

6. Ibid., p. 24.

7. Ibid., p. 44.

8. Ibid., pp. 44–45.

9. Dan Kaercher, "Depression," *Better Homes and Gardens*, April 1982, p. 24.

10. "Coping with Life's Strains," *U.S. News and World Report*, May 1, 1978, p. 82.

11. Peretz, "Reactions to Loss," p. 29.

12. "Depression: Our Common Curse," p. 54.

13. Tim LaHaye, *How to Win over Depression* (Grand Rapids, Mich.: Zondervan Publishing Co., 1974), pp. 28–31.

14. Brown and Harris, *Social Origins of Depression*, p. 238.

15. Ibid.

16. Ibid.

17. Ibid., p. 25.

18. Ross Mitchell, *Depression* (Baltimore: Penguin Books, 1975), pp. 79–80.

19. Brussel and Irwin, *Understanding and Overcoming Depression*, p. 27.

20. Mitchell, *Depression*, pp. 18–19.

21. Mr. Lancaster discussed some of these suggestions at a meeting of The Compassionate Friends in Greenville, S.C., in the spring of 1982. These suggestions were taken from *Good Housekeeping*, March 1977, pp. 28*ff.*

22. "Coping with Life's Strains," p. 86.

23. "Depression: When the Blues Become Serious," *Changing Times*, March 1979, p. 39.

24. Ibid.

25. "Coping with Life's Strains," p. 86.

26. Mitchell, *Depression*, p. 34.

CHAPTER 11

1. Elizabeth Ogg, *Partners in Coping: Groups for Self and Mutual Help* (New York: Public Affairs Committee, 1978), p. 4.

2. Leonard Borman, as quoted in M. Lieberman, L. Borman et al., *Self-Help Groups for Coping with Crisis* (San Francisco: Jossey-Bass, 1979), p. 5.

3. Ogg, *Partners in Coping*, p. 25.

4. Ibid., p. 27.

5. From a brochure titled "When a Child Dies. . . ." The Compassionate Friends, 1978.

6. Ibid.

7. Ibid.

8. Judy Osgood, "Together We Can Make It," *Ladies Circle Magazine*, New York, 1982.

9. From a brochure titled "Parents of Murdered Children."

10. Ibid.

11. Ibid.

12. Ibid.

13. Ibid.

14. Ogg, *Partners in Coping*, p. 27.

Bibliography

Angell, Robert C. *The Family Encounters the Depression.* New York: Scribners, 1936.

Binger, C. M., et al. "Childhood Leukemia: Emotional Impact on Patient and Family." *New England Journal of Medicine* 280 (1969): 414–18.

Brown, George W., and Harris, Tirril. *Social Origins of Depression.* New York: The Free Press, 1978.

Brussel, James A., and Irwin, Theodore. *Understanding and Overcoming Depression.* New York: Hawthorn Books, 1973.

Caroff, Phyllis, and Dobrof, Rose. "The Helping Process with Bereaved Families." In *Bereavement: Its Psychosocial Aspects,* edited by Bernard Schoenberg et al., pp. 232–42. New York: Columbia University Press, 1975.

Crout, Teresa. "Caring for the Mother of a Stillborn Baby." *Thanatos* 5 (Fall 1980): 4–8.

The Compassionate Friends Newsletter, St. Louis Chapter. 2 (June 1981); 2 (July 1981); 2 (October 1981); 3 (October/November 1982).

"Coping with Life's Strains." *U.S. News and World Report,* May 1, 1972, pp. 80–82.

"Depression: Our Common Curse." *Saturday Evening Post,* December 1975, pp. 54–55.

"Depression: When the Blues Become Serious." *Changing Times,* March 1979, pp. 37–39.

Eshleman, J. Ross. *The Family: An Introduction.* Boston: Allyn and Bacon, 1978.

Feuer, Lewis S. *The Conflict of Generations.* New York: Basic Books, 1978.

Fox, Sheila. "The Death of a Child." *Nursing Times* 68 (October 1972): 1322–23.

Friedman, S. B., et al. "Behavioral Observations of Parents Anticipating the Death of a Child." *Pediatrics* 32 (October 1963): 610–25.

Garfield, Charles A. "A Child Dies." In *Stress and Survival,* edited by Charles A. Garfield, pp. 314–17. St. Louis: C. V. Mosby Co., 1979.

Good Housekeeping, March 1977, pp. 28*ff.*

Guimond, Joyce. "We Knew Our Child Was Dying." *American Journal of Nursing* 74 (February 1974): 248–49.

Gyulay, Jo-Eileen. *The Dying Child.* New York: McGraw-Hill, 1978.

Hansen, Donald A., and Hill, Reuben. "Families Under Stress." In *Handbook of Marriage and the Family,* edited by Harold T. Christensen, pp. 782–819. Chicago: Rand McNally & Co., 1964.

Hill, Reuben. *Families Under Stress.* New York: Harper & Bros., 1949.

———. "Generic Features of Families Under Stress." In *Crisis Intervention: Selected Readings,* edited by Howard J. Parad, pp. 32–52. New York: Family Service Association, 1965.

Hullinger, Charlotte. Speech before the First World Congress of Victimology. Washington, D.C., August 1981.

Kaercher, Dan. "Depression." *Better Homes and Gardens,* April 1982, pp. 23–24.

Kavanaugh, Robert E. *Facing Death.* Baltimore: Penguin Books, 1974.

Kübler-Ross, Elisabeth. *On Death and Dying.* New York: Macmillan, 1969.

LaHaye, Tim. *How to Win over Depression.* Grand Rapids, Mich.: Zondervan Publishing Co., 1974.

LeMaster, E. E. *Parents in Modern America.* Homewood, Ill.: The Dorsey Press, 1974.

Lieberman, M.; Borman, L. et al. *Self-Help Groups for Coping with Crisis.* San Francisco: Jossey-Bass, 1979.

Lindemann, Eric. "Symptomatology and Management of Acute Grief." *American Journal of Psychiatry* 101 (September 1944): 141–48.

Lipton, Hal. "The Dying Child and the Family: The Skills of the Social Worker." In *The Child and Death,* edited by Ollie Jane Z. Sahler, pp. 52–71. St. Louis: C. V. Mosby Co., 1978.

Lowenberg, June S. "The Coping Behavior of Fatally Ill Adolescents and Their Parents." *Nursing Forum* 9 (1970): 269–87.

McCubbin, Hamilton I. "Integrating Coping Behavior in Family Stress Theory." *Journal of Marriage and the Family* 41 (May 1979): 237–44.

McCubbin, Hamilton I. et al., "Family Stress and Coping: Decade Review." *Journal of Marriage and the Family* 42 (November 1980): 855–71.

Minneapolis Tribune, Oct. 17, 1982.

Mitchell, Ross. *Depression.* Baltimore: Penguin Books, 1975.

Munson, Stephen W. "Family Structure and the Family's General Adaptation to Loss: Helping Families Deal with the Death of a Child." In *The Child and Death,* edited by Ollie Jane Z. Sahler, pp. 29–42. St. Louis: C. V. Mosby Co., 1978.

Northrup, Fran C. "The Dying Child." *American Journal of Nursing* 74 (June 1974): 1066–68.

Ogg, Elizabeth. *Partners in Coping: Groups for Self and Mutual Help.* New York: Public Affairs Committee, 1978.

Osgood, Judy. "Together We Can Make It." *Ladies Circle Magazine* (1982).

"Parents of Murdered Children." Brochure published by the parent organization, Cincinnati, Ohio.

Parkes, C. M. *Bereavement.* New York: International Universities Press, 1972.

———. "Unexpected and Untimely Bereavement: A Statistical Study of Young Boston Widows and Widowers." In *Bereavement: Its Psychosocial Aspects,* edited by Bernard Schoenberg et al., pp. 119–38. New York: Columbia University Press, 1975.

Peppers, Larry G., and Knapp, Ronald J. *Motherhood and Mourning: Perinatal Death.* New York: Praeger Special Studies, 1980.

Peretz, David. "Development, Object-Relationships, and Loss." In *Loss and Grief: Psychosocial Management in Medical Practice,* edited by Bernard Schoenberg et al., pp. 3–19. New York: Columbia University Press, 1970.

———. "Reactions to Loss." In *Loss and Grief: Psychosocial Management in Medical Practice,* edited by Bernard Schoenberg et al., pp. 20–35. New York: Columbia University Press, 1970.

Schiff, Harriet Sarnoff. *The Bereaved Parent.* New York: Penguin Books, 1978.

Skolnick, Arlene. *The Intimate Environment.* Boston: Little, Brown and Co., 1978.

Tatlebaum, Judy. *The Courage to Grieve: Creative Living, Recovery and Growth.* New York: Lippincott and Crowell, 1980.

Vollman, Rita R. et al. "The Reactions of Family Systems to Sudden and Unexpected Death." In *Caring Relationships: The Dying and the Bereaved,* edited by Richard A. Kalish, pp. 97–102. Perspectives on Death and Dying Series 2. New York: Baywood Publishing Co., 1980.

"When a Child Dies." Brochure published by The Compassionate Friends, 1978.

Woodson, Robert. "Hospice Care in Terminal Illness." In *Stress and Survival,* edited by Charles A. Garfield, pp. 325–39. St. Louis: C. V. Mosby Co., 1979.

Woolsey, Susan F.; Thornton, Doris S.; and Friedman, Stanford B. "Sudden Death." In *The Child and Death,* edited by Ollie Jane Z. Sahler, pp. 100–112. St. Louis: C. V. Mosby Co., 1978.

Index